UNDER CONSTRUCTION

SUNY Series in the Sociology of Work
Judith Blau, Editor

UNDER CONSTRUCTION

*Work and Alienation
in the Building Trades*

Marc L. Silver

State University of New York Press

Published by
State University of New York Press, Albany

©1986 State University of New York

For information, address State University of New York
Press, State University Plaza, Albany, N.Y., 12246

Library of Congress Cataloging in Publication Data

Silver, Marc L., 1950-
    Under construction.

    (SUNY series in the sociology of work)
    Bibliography: p. 229
    Includes index.
    1. Building trades—Social aspects—United States.
2. Construction industry—Social aspects—United
States. 3. Construction workers—United States.
4. Industrial sociology—United States. 5. alienation
(Social psychology) 6. Trade-unions—Building trades—
United States.   I. Title.   II. Series.
HD6956.V92U67   1986   331.7'624'0973   85-30447
ISBN 0-88706-308-X
ISBN 0-88706-309-8 (pbk.)

To my father, who taught me the trade and the value of labor. To Adrian, not yet here when this project began, but who already knows the fascination.

CONTENTS _____

PREFACE _____

From my first introduction to the academic literature in the areas of industrial, organizational, and occupational sociology, I was struck by the extent to which a generally positive and sanguine assessment of productive relations in the construction industry contradicted my own personal knowledge. Supported by what seemed to me fairly superficial and formalistic analogies to the medieval guild and modern professional occupational structures, the notions of "occupational control," "professionalized workforce," and "craft administration" were pervasive and dominant in that body of literature. Around that same time, Anti-Vietnam War and New Left politial activism literally was coming to blows with the hard-hat labor aristocracy. The political conservatism of many building tradesmen served as grist for the mill of those rejecting Old Left class analysis. Here too I found my personal assessments at odds with the political analyses I encountered. This book has its origins in my basic discomfort with those widely accepted views of craft occupations and the organization of the labor process in construction.

For my own part, I grew up in a family in which both parents and relatives worked in construction-related jobs. I was no stranger to the construction site, serving as a helper/apprentice during summer vacations and school holidays from the age of fourteen, and later making my way as a journeyman wallpaper hanger. The construction world that I saw—in which extended unemployment was a dreaded but inevitable yearly occurence; in which union politics was frequently a matter of who worked and who did not; in which the relationship between workers' wages and contractors' profits seemed very much a zero-sum equation—did not find expression in the academic and political analyses encountered.

It was not that I disagreed with many of the specific observations made about construction work. Building tradespeople do have a degree of freedom on the job not present in many factory settings. The trade union is a source of protection. Political conservatism, as well as racist and sexist orientations, is all too easily found among tradesmen. My problem was with how those observations were interwoven into the larger analyses.

The task I thus set for myself was to attempt to explain the daily lives of building tradespeople within the context of the working out of the capitalist relationships. I felt that attending specifically to the organization of the labor process at the construction site and to the position of craft workers in the dynamic between contractor and union organizations would provide insights necessary to a better understanding of construction work. My efforts in this led me to question the extent of craft autonomy the strength of capital's (even small entrepreneurial capital's) imperative to dominate the labor process, and to examine the organizational mechanisms that systematically link them. Similarly, I sought to explain how the alienation of capitalist labor markets and relations in the labor process foster both progressive (class conscious) and reactionary (class accommodationist, coexploitative, racist, sexist) orientations among building tradesmen.

In carrying out this project I have been helped by numerous people. My thanks to Eugene Litwak, Alan Barton, and Joseph Schwartz of Columbia University for providing much needed guidance, encouragement, and criticism in developing the initial research methodology and then with the laborious process of analyzing and reporting the results of the study. Financial support for the original research came from the United States Department of Labor Grant (no. 91367902). The people of Columbia University's Center for the Social Sciences were always helpful and accommodating.

To Joe Conforti, John McDermott, and John Wildeman go thanks for taking my ideas seriously enough to disagree, and for being friends enough to always remain supportive. Judith Blau deserves my deepest appreciation for her patience and careful reading of multiple drafts of the entire manuscript. Her invaluable input has made the finished product slightly different and much better than it otherwise would have been. Thanks also to my trade union brothers and sisters who shared their insights and experiences with me.

Special thanks to Leon Silver and Evelyn Silver for many things, but also for their direct knowledge of the realities of local markets, unions, and small contracting operations that helped solve numerous problems in carrying out the research and understanding what I had found. Finally, to Vickie, no expression of gratitude does justice to the contributions and sacrifices.

1

INTRODUCTION
Contracting, Craft, and Control

Conflicting and contradictory images to this day color both popular and academic perceptions of work and organizational relationships in the construction industry. On the one hand, people see craft skills and unions to be sources of disproportionate power for building tradespeople in their relations with employers, builders, buyers, and other workers. Such power has presumably resulted in economic affluence and extensive control over the labor process. Partly as a reaction to that image, the unemployed demonstrate for construction jobs and entry to apprenticeship training programs, while the building trade unions are blamed for inflationary trends in housing construction costs. In a similar manner, major labor legislation accords industrial relations in the construction industry different status from that of other industries.

On the other hand, few people would eagerly take up careers in an industry where opportunities for employment are as uncertain and as periodic, or the work itself as arduous as it is in construction. Endemic unemployment, physically demanding work, a hazardous setting, and antagonistic labor relations all belie the unqualified power of craft workers to set the pattern of work and employment in their industry. Thus, it would appear that despite a bourgeoning body of literature in the areas of organizational studies, occupations, and work relations the construction industry remains poorly understood.

1

Labor aristocrat or beleaguered worker? Obviously, both images cannot be correct. Yet, each does appear to contain a glimmer of truth. In other words, while each one offers specific empirical observations that are in themselves accurate, neither one provides an adequate theoretical basis for conceptualizing the labor process in its totality.

How then to arrive at a better understanding of work and organization in the building and construction industry? The answer to that question must begin with an examination of the development of the conceptual orientations that have given rise to the discrepant images of construction. They stem from an overly static sociological analysis on the one side, and a too fluid historical view on the other. In contrast to both, what is offered then is a synthesizing political economy perspective. The latter thus forms the basis for the empirical analyses pursued in subsequent chapters.

Sociological Perspectives on Craft Work and Organization

Organizational and occupational sociology still tends to treat craft production in the industry as an anomaly in the overall dynamic of capitalist organization. As such, it has helped to perpetuate the idealized image of the industry's labor process as an example of craft administration. Deterministic models of technology and organizational rationality support the notion that product and labor market characteristics have given rise to nonbureaucratically structured and essentially worker-controlled organizations.[1]

According to the general view, organizations are shaped primarily by the need to adapt their work and authority structures to the nature of the tasks at hand, available technologies at their disposal, and their ecological circumstance. For example, small-batch unit production, the least sophisticated technology, is labor intensive and generally requires skilled workers and relatively loose supervision. The second type of technology, mass production, is more capital intensive and depends on closer supervision of a less skilled workforce performing routinized and repetitive tasks. The most advanced technology, process production, is an automated technique in which workers' skills and knowledge are devoted to machine tending rather than the actual transformation of raw materials. Since a particular method of production may be effective only under certain conditions, technology—an important determinant of work and authority structures—is itself conditioned by an organization's tasks and environment. A causal flow model (see figure 1) places technology between task/environmental factors and organizational work/authority structures.

TASK/ENVIRONMENT→TECHNOLOGY→WORK/AUTHORITY

Figure 1.

Without going into great detail at this point, craft production is applied effectively in situations in which new tasks present problems to be analyzed independently, in which there are many exceptions to general procedures, or in which there is unpredictable fluctuations in product demand. It is only where tasks are relatively well understood, where there are few exceptions to standardized procedures and where conditions are relatively stable that the more capital intensive and structurally inflexible mass and process technologies can be effective.

According to that logic, because of fluctuating demand from external sources, single unit construction, and localized markets today's building industry is characterized by craft production. It has not followed the dominant path to mass and process technologies taken by other sectors of the economy because of its inherent variabilities and uncertainties. To the extent that the labor process in construction is a link to a more primitive technology it is often treated by industrial sociology as an antiquated deviate case to the overall analysis. A surviving instance of a vestigial mode of production, it is often considered more of historical and anthropological—rather than of sociological—interest.

This perspective also includes an important occupational element. Extreme variabilities in production and market give the crafts a great deal of control over the production process. Single unit construction and site-specific production require that workers have to solve production problems as they arise. That has led to a nonbureaucratic form of work organization in which craftspeople self-administer many aspects of production: what sociologist Arthur Stinchcombe (1959) termed "craft administration." According to Stinchcombe, there are five basic elements of the work process about which administrative decisions are made: location of the work activity, coordination of the movements of tools and supplies, the actual activities the worker undertakes in performing his assigned task, production, and inspection criteria for particular operations. The distinction between bureaucratic and craft forms of production resides in the fact that in mass production work practices are decided and planned in advance by management while in craft administration "all these characteristics of the work process *are governed by the worker* in accordance with the empirical lore that make up craft principles" (p. 170, my emphasis).

Collectively possessing the right to establish general production-level and job-site rules for the allocation of work and the determination of work practices for members of the craft also mean that they hold power in relation to their employers. Consider the construction contractor who estimates production costs, bids for a contract, orders and delivers supplies and equipment to the site, and is responsible for assembling a workforce. When it comes to actually carrying out the job, however, he is forced to rely on the skills and knowledge of the people he has hired. His dependence on others compels him to trust, consult, and cooperate with his craft employees. The degree of cooperative interaction that presumably takes place between construction contractor and craft employee leads to the notion that craftspeople are not, strictly speaking, workers. Rather, craft administration merges worker and management. Some have argued on that basis that the crafts are more closely allied to professional occupations than to the other manual or so-called blue collar occupations (Freidson 1982; Edwards 1979; Hall 1975).[2]

The occupational element supplies the second reason for the prolonged use of craft production in the building industry. The crafts have been able to use their control of the production process in order to resist employers' attempts to modify building technology in any way that would undermine the sources of their power. Thus, they have successfully retarded developments that would have increased the effectiveness and efficiency of building production. That can be represented schematically with a slight modification of figure 1.

TASK/ENVIRONMENT→TECHNOLOGY→WORK/AUTHORITY→

Figure 2.

In other words, the kinds of work and authority relationships established by a given technology feedback to influence further technological developments. In the case of the building industry that feedback effect supposedly has contributed to its technological backwardness.

Harry Braverman, in his seminal *Labor and Monopoly Capital*, offers perhaps the best indication of the widespread acceptance of craft administration in the building industry. Braverman's thesis is that work under capitalism has undergone the steady process of simplification, bureaucratization, and degradation such that the worker, systematically, robbed of a craft heritage, is given little or nothing to take its place" (1974,6). However, he associates the process almost totally with the development of mass production technology and bureaucratization of office and shop organization. Thus the construction industry, "which because of the nature of its processes is still largely in the era of hand craftsmanship supplemented by powered hand tools . . . makes continual and determined efforts to climb out of this disadvantageous position." Capital's attempt to alter the building process is largely to try to move it into the factory:

> The trend of dwelling construction is best exemplified by the rapidly growing "mobile home" segment of the industry. The "mobile home" is a *mass-produced factory product*; of the three parties involved—the workers, the manufacturers, and the residents—only the middle one has any advantage to show from the transaction' (p. 209, my emphasis).

Presumably, the organization of production in the building industry resists the logic of capitalist efficiency because of a technological imperative that exists apart from the logic of capitalism itself. The labor process must be moved into the factory in order to achieve capitalist efficiency. As long as it remains outside the bureaucratized organizational setting, it retains the elements of craft administration and control. Thus in some respects, Braverman accepts the technological determinism of mainstream sociology, albeit with a radically different evaluation.[3]

Others, similarly critical of capitalist relations, have also paid little attention to craft relationships in the building industry. For example, both Richard Edwards (1979) and Dan Clawson (1980) define the transformation of the labor process under capitalism in technological and bureaucratic terms. Clawson considers much of the change in work during the twentieth century to be the result of capital's largely successful attempts to destroy craft administration in the factory. Edwards, on the other hand, associates craft work with advantaged labor market position and occupational characteristics similar to professional workers. His labor process/market sector analysis views craft occupations as benefitting at the expense of less advantageously situated workers. While Edwards and Clawson do much to further the understanding of the overall dynamics of capitalist relations, they are far less helpful in regard to the persistence of craft relations. In the work of market segmentation theorists such as Richard Edwards, and bureaucratization theorists such as Braverman and Clawson, craft administration is an exceptional case to the general dynamic of capitalist organization.

Part of the reason for the longevity of such perspectives is that the very concept of craft administration is a disincentive to research. Social scientists and political activists concerned with the quality of working life have concentrated the bulk of their attention on factory settings, assembly lines, and, of late, clerical and other white collar occupations where the quality of working life presumably is much more problematic. Those who have undertaken case studies of building work have done so within a craft administration framework: accepting it as the premise for exploring the interpersonal relations that define craft culture.[4]

In short, the a priori image of craft administration has provoked little sympathy for workers in the building trades. Construction workers confronting antiwar demonstrators during the 1960s and 1970s while industrial workers were fighting against the imperatives of capitalist efficiency (for example, the Lordstown strike) and against conservative or corrupt leadership in their own organizations (for example, Teamsters for a Democratic Union) bolstered this attitude. The contrast in the 1980s between the emergent signs of progressive leadership and rank-and-file militancy in the industrial unions and the almost total acquiescence in the building trades has cemented it. Economic affluence and craft administration of the labor process have offered very comfortable, although not necessarily accurate, explanations for political conservativism and apathy. It is ironic that both management-oriented organizational sociology and worker-oriented Marxism have come to the same conclusion on this issue.

Historical Perspectives

The popularity of the craft-administration thesis notwithstanding, it does not fit very well with the historical development of the industry's labor relations. One of the most significant factors influencing relations in the American building industry was the failure of the guild tradition to cross the Atlantic. The European model of the craft guild never became fully entrenched in the United States, although it did appear during colonial and postrevolutionary periods. In the absence of a self-perpetuating hierarchical structure that blended skill, employment status, and authority within the craft occupations, industrial relations moved fairly rapidly toward a differentiation between employing contractors and wage-earning journeymen.[5] In fact, the first strike in the building industry took place as early as 1791 in Philadelphia when journeymen carpenters turned out in reaction to low wages and a long workday. After losing their bid for a twelve-hour day, the carpenters attempted unsuccessfully to organize a cooperative to compete with master carpenter contractors (Haber 1930,270).[6]

Building trades unions spread fairly rapidly during the first half of the nineteenth century. Craft workers in the carpentry, mason, painting, stonecutting, and plastering trades formed unions to press for better wages and working conditions; but also to pursue social and political interests. Most of the early unions were organized on a local basis. Generally, they maintained jurisdiction over work in a single city with little if any communication or cooperation between unions in other cities. Their fortunes waxed and waned with the swings of the economy and could not contend with the economic crises that periodically ravaged the nation. The period between 1837 and 1850 was particularly difficult for the building trades. Unemployment was widespread and many of the small unions variously fell into disarray, inactivity, or were totally destroyed. It was not until after the Civil War, with its stimuli to industrial expansion and development of national rail and communication systems, that union organization took place on a broader scale and with a more lasting basis.

Although earlier attempts were made at forming a national trade union, it was not until the 1880s that enduring national organizations came to the industry. The conditions after the Civil War prompted the need for national organization. First, improvements in rail transportation meant a more mobile labor force. Building craft workers unable to find jobs in one city could, and often did, move on to another city. Second, construction contractors began to operate on a broader geographical basis. Companies no longer confined themselves to small localities, but expanded their operations to proximal cities. By 1885, a few construction contractors were operating on a national scale. Third, there was the growth in the practice of providing union members with various kinds of insurance (for example, strike pay, sickness insurance, death benefits). The success of those plans depended on a large membership and competent administration.

It became increasingly difficult for small, insulated local unions to be successful in this new context. In the face of direct wage competition from out-of-town journeymen, they could control neither labor supply nor working conditions. The power of the strike was similarly hampered by the employers' newly acquired ability to import skilled workers from neighboring towns. Finally, it was no longer possible for the small local craft union to match the bargaining and public relations power of the regional and national contractors. By the turn of the century, national unions had been established in most of the major trades—including bricklayers, carpenters and joiners, painters, steamfitters, plumbers, sheetmetal workers, electrical workers, iron workers, and operating engineers.

In order to understand the pattern labor relations in the building industry took, it is necessary to focus on three other developments: 1. the pattern of cooperative relationships among building contractors; 2. the conflictual relationships between worker and contractor organizations; and 3. the types of issues that were the source of antagonism between those two groups. While they are interrelated, each offers an insight regarding the basis of the craft form of capitalist production.

First, lest this description of craft unionization give the impression that employers were left unprotected and defenseless against the collective power of labor, it should be emphasized that employers' associations were initiated during the same period of unionization. In some areas, employers formed their association before workers tried to unionize.

The first instance of cooperative organization in the United States was a price-fixing association among Philadelphia master carpenters in 1724; a fact that may help explain why the 1791 strike by Philadelphia journeymen carpenters was the first recorded in the building industry. According to labor historian William Haber, employers' trade associations gradually developed from their local origins:

> Very early in the history of local organization of building-trades employers, the most common form taken was an organization of employers in one craft. Then these individual craft associations formed a national trade association of subcontractors. Before 1910, there was a national trade association for almost every important craft in the industry. Some of these have a long history (1930, pp. 451–52).

Contractor associations consolidating employers from different trades were also fairly common, especially in the major cities. For example, the Contractors' Council of Chicago and the Building Trades Employers' Association of New York were both organized at about the same time as the formation of workers' Building Trades Councils in the two cities. Both employers' associations were more than up to the task of dealing effectively with the unions' umbrella organizations, as events in these cities indicate.[7]

National contractors' associations were also prevalent by 1900. They were sparked by the need for national organizations as contractors moved beyond local markets. The National Association of Builders, established in 1887, is a case in point. For thirteen years it provided educational, financial, and organizational support to its membership. By 1892 it had a membership of 3,500 firms. In its guiding policy that the "freedom to work under private contract must be fully recognized as freedom to worship" (cited in Haber, 448) the association anticipated by some eighty years the increasingly successful antiunion open shop program of the Association of Building Contractors (the ABC). By the time of its demise NAB claimed success for turning around the tenor of labor relations in the country's building industry.

The tendency for building contractors in market competition with one another to also find mutual benefit through cooperation is in marked contrast to the continual conflict that has characterized relations between contractors and craft workers. By and large, building tradespeople were prompted to organize and join unions as a means of securing improvements in their conditions of work and employment. In the early stages this took the form of struggles for higher wages and a shorter workday. The traditional practice was for the building trades to work from sun-to-sun. That of course meant extremely long days during summer and shorter days during winter. Localized movements by journeymen to establish standardized twelve-hour and then ten-hour days occurred throughout the nineteenth century. The attempts often were restricted to a single trade and in a single locality. There were instances, however, of cooperative actions between trades and of movements spreading from one city to another.

The issue of control at the site of production was probably

the most salient point of antagonism between contractors and craft workers. Control over the allocation of foremen, rest breaks, safety requirements, the use of apprentices and employment of unskilled workers, fabrication of materials, and direction of the pace of work all were important issues. They were so important largely because of their impact on the power craft workers held in relation to their employers. Any reduction in the skills and knowledge required of the tradesman, resulting either from a change in the composition of the workforce or alteration of the division of labor, represented, on the one hand, a reduction in a craft worker's power based on his direct control over important facets of the labor process. On the other hand, it automatically meant an increase in power for the contractor who was then in a position to determine a greater portion of that process.

The overarching concern on both sides was the extent of craft control of the building work. Contractors' goal was the erosion of collective occupational power in production and the institution of a system that placed administration in the hands of their managerial personnel. The crafts naturally sought to protect themselves from such attempts.

A good example of the significance of the control issue is the success of Chicago contractors in 1900 to institute six *cardinal principles* of labor relations: 1. no restriction on the use of machinery; 2. no restriction on the use of manufactured (prefabricated) material; 3. no restriction on the quantity of work done by individual workers during the day; 4. no interference with workers during the workday by outside agents (that is, union representatives); 5. no restriction on the employment of apprentices; and 6. prohibition of sympathetic strikes (Haber, 375). Similar actions against craft power in production were taken by contractors in New York and San Francisco, among other cities. In San Francisco, institution of the so-called American Plan had by 1921 destroyed the productive and political strength of the Building Trades Council. In New York, contractors and building trades unions agreed, after more than two decades of intermittent conflict, to a set of principles nearly identical to that imposed on Chicago building tradespeople twenty years earlier.

The results of those early conflicts have been fairly enduring. Daniel Mills, reassessing the Chicago situation in 1972, argued that none of the cardinal principles had been abandoned by the contractors' association. Consider too the following passage from a recent, and not atypical, agreement between the Associated General Contractors of Massachusetts, the Building Trades Employers Association, and the Building and Construction Trades Council of Boston:

> The determination of the size of the workforce, the allocation of work to employees, establishment of quality standards and judgment of workmanship required, and the maintenance of discipline shall be the responsibility of the employing general or specialty contractor (cited in Mills 1972, p. 30).

The past decade in particular has been characterized by greater erosion of craft influence in the production process. Nonunion, open shop contractors, once an insignificant factor in the industry,now handle about 50 percent of the dollar volume of building and construction activity. Two conclusions from a recent study of union and nonunion contractors are instructive in this regard (Bourdon and Levitt 1980). On the one hand, Bourdon and Levitt report that union rules concerning the use of technology, work practices, hiring, and training "are neither as inefficient nor as inflexible as they have been portrayed" (54). On the other hand, they report that union and nonunion firms differ in that the latter have instituted a division of labor that simplifies work and cuts across craft jurisdictions and, consequently, have established work practices that use unskilled and semiskilled low-wage workers.

Since the building industry has not escaped the conflict over the crucial issue of control that has characterized other industries, it is also worth pointing out the form in which that conflict has manifested itself. The means used to carry out the struggle reveals as much about the nature of craft production as does the presence of the conflict itself. The strike and lock-out were frequently used tactics, of course, but sabotage and violence were not uncommon. With the stakes as high as they were—nothing short of control over the production process—it is not surprising. The extremity of the struggle is illustrated quite clearly by William Haber's appraisal of the Chicago lock-out of 1900. The issue of productive control, embodied in the contractors' cardinal principles, was intertwined with the existence of the workers' Building Trades Council. Destruction of the council was the essential key to ending craft control. At the same time, the solidification of contractor control would prevent the council or any similar confederation from reestablishing the same degree of power in the future. After a seven month lock-out marked by violence, intimidation, and the steadfast refusal by contractors to arbitrate any issue, the unions broke ranks and the council voted to disband:

> The unions were thoroughly defeated and discouraged; their closed-shop monopoly was broken, their funds exhausted and their membership depleted. *The employers had a free hand in administering labor policies* in the Chicago building industry (Haber 1930,377, my emphasis).

The discrepancy between the theory of organizations and the history of labor relations, at least in the case of the building industry, is fairly obvious. The former has conceptualized an association between endemic features of the industry's economic and social environments and its persistent reliance on craft administration of production. The latter records a continual class struggle that questions whether craft administration can be referred to as a viable form of capitalist work organization under any market, political, or social circumstances. Intense and prolonged conflict does not coincide with theoretical perspectives that posit naturalistic organizational adaptations to task contingencies and market uncertainties.

There are a few reasons for the empirical and theoretical discrepancies. One of them is the specialized nature of the social sciences.[8] In the present case, it has led to mistaken interpretations of the organization and control of craft work. The craft administration concept developed within the sociologies of work, organizations, and occupations partly because many of the issues being addressed by sociologists had been abstracted and removed from the realities of industrial relations. Information from labor historians and industrial relations theorists was not of obvious enough relevance to sociological theorists with a penchant for static and ideal-type models of work and organization. That, in turn, created an environment in which a theoretical model could survive unsupported by direct empirical work within the discipline.

On the other side of the academic divide, labor historians, economists, and industrial relations specialists have not found organizational theory central enough to their interests to present a challenge to such conceptions. Their work has been focused more on the outcomes of the relationship between employer and worker organizations such as strikes, wage rates, disruptions of production, and political influence. They have been less interested in the organization of work and the nature of work-related organizations, per se. What developed were two relatively independent lines of thinking with too little communication between them.

The second major source of discrepancy has been the ideological component of organizational theory. According to organizational sociologist Jeffery Pfeffer (1981), managerial bias in the organizational literature is based on the fact that, for the most part, it has served the legitimation and socialization needs of the managerial community of educators, students, and practitioners. That ideological bias takes the form of an inordinate emphasis on functional rationality and efficiency. As Pfeffer says:

> In this sense, organization theory and economic theory frequently find themselves fulfilling similar roles in explaining the status quo in terms which both justify and legitimate it. The theory of perfect competition of markets argues that when market processes are allowed to operate unimpeded by the intervention of politicians or monopolists, the best allocation results are obtained. . . . In similar fashion, the literature of organizational behavior has been dominated by a parallel form of functionalism. The strategic contingencies theories of organizational design . . . argued that there existed some optimal organizational design, given the organization's technology, size or environmental uncertainty (p. 13).

The ideologically based emphasis on an implicit functionalism, rationality, and efficiency has led organizational theorists to attend to topics which are compatible with the underpinnings of a managerial orientation and to ignore topics which detract from them. That has meant an almost exclusive focus on how organizations adapt to their environments and on identifying the most important influences, while ignoring issues of power and politics within and between organizations. Moreover, the latter issues are often studied only to understand how they intrude on the natural relationship between organizational form and technology and environment. They are not often analyzed as having significant impact on organizational design in themselves.

But if one effect of ideological bias has been selective attention, another is the tendency to uncritically incorporate those conceptions which fit comfortably within its framework. Craft administration is a case in point. The presumed presence of an organizational form characterized by nonbureaucratic structure and occupational control in the building industry reputed for its variable product demand, seasonal production activity, and skilled workforce, has been an idea so obviously correct as to make empirical verification unnecessary. At the same time, the fact of craft administration in the building industry is often cited as proof that capitalist work organizations operate on the basis of rational adjustment to task and market factors beyond the control of the enterprise. It is this tautological cycle that has in some respects contributed to the longevity of the craft administration model.

Ideological predispositions have also shaped the analysis of Marxists and others critical of capitalist approaches to production. Here too the effect has been to minimize the amount of direct attention paid to the building industry. One reason that those on the left have not been overly concerned with construction work is the prevalence of most-oppressed notions of class action. From this vantage, working class consciousness and revolutionary potential are treated as linear functions of the degrees of alienation and exploitation. Workers are most likely to develop a class conscious posture where and when conditions of alienation and exploitation are sufficiently severe. The presence of obvious economic and noneconomic inequalities within the working class thus has led to greater focus on those

industries and occupations where conditions are relatively
poorest. The situation for craft workers, clearly superior to that
of semiskilled and unskilled workers, has never been considered
to be alienating or exploitative enough to support the development of class consciousness.

A second reason is the attempt to explain the absence of a
viable socialist working class movement in the United States.
Ironically, that attempt has been made in the form of blaming
the working class, or at least segments of it, for its historical
failure. Some have argued, and not without empirical support,
that historically the crafts have benefitted at the expense of
other workers. Craft unions over the years have shown
themselves quite willing to compromise the situation of less
skilled workers in order to protect or advance their own interests. That, coupled with the conservative politics of the trade
unions of the American Federation of Labor—their conciliatory
orientation toward collective bargaining, their refusal to
organize on an industrial basis, and readiness to control an-
ticapitalist and communist tendencies within their own
ranks—has stifled any real empirical interest in craft production
as an enduring form of capitalist organization. The logic of a
labor aristocracy acting as a class traitor has been one way to
save class theories of capitalism in the face of American excep-
tionalism.

Thus ideological tendencies of bourgeoise organizational
theory and Marxist class theory have yielded the same
disinterest in contemporary forms of craft production. For one
of them, craft administration is too comfortable an idea to be
concerned with empirical confirmation. For the other, the
presumed advantages of craft production offer little incentive to
do research for those interested in the sources of class struggle
at the point of production. Both have tended to treat the
building industry as an isolated deviant case that, for specifiable
reasons, has resisted the imperatives of technology and class
relations. The result for both of them is basic misconceptions
about craft work.

What is needed in order to understand craft production in
the building industry is a conceptual base that permits a connection to be made between the distinctive features of organization

in the industry with the broader dynamics of a capitalist political economy. By analyzing craft production as it occurs within the broader class structure, it is possible to be somewhat protected from the tendency to consider it *sui generis*. As has already been seen, attempting to analyze a particular occupation or organizational form without an explicit reference to its structural context leads to artifically fragmented and reified perspectives. It is also important to contextualize the analysis as long as our interest is in the human consequences of how production is organized. It is necessary to avoid such reifying tendencies if an understanding of how it is that people both reproduce and reshape the societies they live in is to be achieved.

The Political Economy of Craft Production

The relationship between profit and competition are the most significant aspects of the capitalist organization of production. Together they condition the problematics of maintaining control of an alienated workforce while promoting efficient operation. The profit relationship establishes an inherent antagonism between worker and employer which can be seen in the nature of the employment contract. Workers entering the employment relationship agree to provide a given number of hours of their daily life in exchange for a given income. In general, workers do not agree to provide a given amount of labor, merely their capacity for laboring; they sell their availability for productive activity, not the activity itself. The amount of work performed is, to begin with, a potential but unrealized commodity. It is the employer's burden to convert labor power (potential work) into actual labor (activities that contribute to production). From the employer's side of the relationship, it is only through the realization of labor power that he realizes a profit. At the same time, the most rational stance from the position of the worker is to limit inputs in terms of actual work activity while seeking the highest income possible.

That conflict, rooted in capitalist production, determines the general form of its work organizations. Very simply, capitalism is more than a formal set of arrangements in which one class owns the means of production and dominates the spheres of exchange and distribution, while the other must work for wages. It is a system in which the dominant class must continually defend its position in an inherently antagonistic relationship that partially defines profitable operation. That means it is a system in which control over the production process is an ever-present consideration.

Coercion and direct personal control have in the past provided solutions to the problem (Edwards 1979; Clawson 1980; McDermott 1981). However, except for the limiting cases of the small entrepreneurial organizaton and periods of extreme economic crisis, they are too cumbersome, expensive and ineffective to rely on as a principal means of defending class interests at the point of production. Growth in the size of industrial organizations has led to a greater reliance on normative and ideological means of control.

Some of the most important mechanisms of class domination/legitimation are contained in the machinery and social organization of production itself. On the one hand, it is in production relationships that the structures of subjective and intellectual domination can be most effective. It is for this reason that Marx associated control over material production with control of mental production. The means of production are, in fact, a means of producing subjective, psychological, and intellectual orientations as well as material goods. Thus the capacity to generate and sustain an ideology that legitimates class domination depends on how production relationships are organized. This is part of what Marx was referring to in the frequently cited passage from *The German Ideology*:

> The class which has the means of material production at its disposal has control at the same time over the means of mental production, so that thereby, generally speaking, the ideas of those who lack the means of mental production are subject to it. (p. 64).

To understand the logic and dynamics of production, one must look to the means of mental production as much as to the means of material production. The ideas of the dominant class do not hold sway on the basis of their persuasiveness or ir-refutable logic. They do so because they are produced in the sense that they permeate the channels of communication and the avenues of social intercourse in the labor process. In other words, the ruling ideology is transmitted through, indeed is a part of, social organization itself.

On the other hand, it is in production that the inherent an-tagonisms and contradictory material interests are most likely to come to the fore. It is a tendency that has continued to emerge at particular periods in American history. Relationships occur-ring at the point of production being among the most critical facets of social reproduction have made workplace control pivotal to the class struggle.[9]

Capitalist organizational forms thus have to be able to restrict the creative participation of workers while simultaneously enhancing the creative roles of owners and managers. Both technical organization—the methods and techniques characteristic of the production process—and social organization—the structured arrangement of communication and interaction defining relationships of authority and subor-dination—function to meet the imperatives of legitimated domination and control. Generally speaking, there are fewer control problems when workers play little or no intellectual role in the production process. Further, the more the restriction on the creative participation appears as a necessary and inherent feature of the functional requirements of a rational organiza-tional system of production (and not as the result of conscious attempts by management to impose its will) the broader and more flexible are the parameters for maintaining a sense of legitimacy. It is in that manner that technology and social organization are two sides of the same coin. They mutually rein-force one another, but more importantly, they both pertain to the overarching logics of control and legitimation.[10]

At the same time, capitalism's competitive element makes it extremely difficult, if not impossible, to structure organizations solely on the basis of enhancing managerial control. As developments in organizational theory and practice throughout the nineteenth and twentieth centuries have borne out, organizational systems often contend with market and environmental contingencies that require greater flexibility than permitted by a single organizational model that maximizes control over the labor process (such as, Scientific Management). Alternative organizational arrangements are usually necessary to achieve that flexibility. Market competition between firms creates an inherent pressure toward efficiency, both in the sense of minimizing the loss of material in the production process by reducing physical waste, and in the sense of minimizing the ratio of production costs to revenues by reducing labor and administrative overheads.

According to the multimodel and contingency theorists, managerial planners and administrators must ensure that their firms have the capacity to deal effectively with a multitude of factors as cost efficiently as possible. Production thus tends to be organized according to the specific features of a firm's relevant labor and product markets. Highly bureaucratized structures and routinized work are relatively efficient when market conditions are stable, production can be planned in advance, and where the skills and knowledge needed by workers is merely of a technical nature. Less rigid structure for production are needed when markets are unstable, production is adaptive rather than planned, and workers are highly skilled. Similarly, strategies concerning corporate expansion, diversification and vertical integration may have serious implications for how a firm's production tasks and general operations are structured. According to Alfred Chandler (1963), the increasing complexity of the diversified corporate structure may limit the utility of centralized bureaucratic control.[11]

What many organizational theorists ignore, however, is that the imperatives of efficiency occur along with those pertaining to legitimated domination. On the one hand, not all market and environmental contexts permit the application of routinized technologies, rigidified and hierarchical authority relationships, centralized managerial planning, and closely supervised work: all of which enhance domination and control. In many circumstances, more flexible technologies, relative autonomy for those making production-level decisions, and loosely linked, collegially structured relationships may be more appropriate. On the other hand, the imperatives of control do not disappear under such conditions. To the contrary, they are likely to become even more acute if organizational structures do not emphasize direct supervision of workers performing routine and regimented tasks.

Thus, class-dominated work organizations are characterized by neither efficiency nor control imperatives alone, but by their reciprocity. If the structure of the labor process is partially determined by cost-efficiency criteria, it is so determined within the boundaries established by the need to ensure legitimated control. Because variable and uncertain market conditions require prompt and repeated responsiveness from the organization, the problems of control may actually increase under such circumstances. Managers dealing with volatile markets may turn to informal communications, face-to-face interactions with workers and trustful interpersonal relations, but, such practices do not mean the reduction of managerial control. There still must be assurances that specific directives and general strategies are carried out quickly, smoothly and in such a way as to maximize the firm's adaptability. In short, conditions requiring greater technological and structural flexibility also require more flexible means of exercising control. Owners and their managers do not abdicate control over workers' activities when markets are variable and uncertain: they alter the manner in which they exercise it.

The various ways in which that has been attempted conform to much of what is termed "craft administration." One is to shift to an emphasis on ideological and normative forms of control. Normative control establishes a bond between successful organizational operations and the beliefs, orientations, and personal interests of workers. This is often achieved through persuasive and suggestive manipulaiton of symbolic rewards such as prestige and occupational identification. According to Stinchombe (1959), this takes the form of socialization to the lore of craft principles. Alternatively, such normative control can be built into the structure of the enterprise such that workers are able to see and anticipate direct rewards from compliance with organizational practices.[12] The nonbureaucratic structures associated with craft administration permit craft workers to see the direct association between organizational success and their own economic security. When the workers accept the goals of the firm as legitimate and, more importantly, identify personal interests with the survival of the enterprise, rigid and direct control are not necessary. The normatively controlled worker thus requires minimal direct supervision, can assume self-managerial responsibilities, and even take on the quasi-managerial functions of informally supervising other workers.

A second means of control is to shift to indirect surveillance and evaluation. Such practices are most effective when conditions do not permit the constant monitoring of work, but when the results themselves are easily assessable. For example, if wages are linked to productivity by a piece rate, workers can be relied on to be somewhat self-monitoring since personal interest and organizational compliance are the same. Indirect control is also possible when the inherent nature of the product makes the quality of workers' efforts readily apparent. As long as the consequences of workers' performance are highly visible the activities themselves do not have to be. Two situations commonly associated with craft work conform to this condition. When stages of production are interdependently linked in a sequential manner (for example, Thompson's [1967] long-linked technology), outcomes of a single position in the process are highly visible because poor workmanship prevents completion of subsequent tasks. In construction, for example, it would be difficult to erect vertical walls and square corners if the framework and studs to which the drywall boards are nailed are not themselves properly plumbed and leveled. Alternatively, close supervision may not be necessary when the outcomes remain visibly or functionally apparent in the finished product. The finishing touches may not always be the most crucial facets of production, but they often are the most noticeable.

Craft production can thus be viewed as being different from other capitalist organizational forms in quantitative, but not qualitative, terms. If the conditions facing craft workers make it difficult at times to assess their activities directly, thus giving them some measure of release from constant supervision and evaluation, it is not to say that they experience no pressures at all to perform at levels deemed adequate by management.

Similarly, if the administrative costs of bureaucratic control mean that craft workers experience some measure of on-the-job discretion, freedom from supervision, and protection from the constant scrutiny of foremen, it does indicate the total absence of accountability. To the contrary, structures of managerial control are likely to be present, and in such forms as to be congruent with the industrial market conditions bearing on the situation. This holds for comparisons between craft and noncraft circumstances as well as for comparisons among craft occupations. Simply put, the dynamics of craft production reflect pressures common to all capitalist economic enterprises; namely, to achieve a level of output sufficient for the extraction of profit from the cumulative efforts of the workforce while maintaining control of the production process.

To the extent that craft production reflects the continual dialectic between legitimated domination and efficiently profitable operation, it is misleading to consider it a unique situation within capitalism. Forms of production do differ from each other, but the manner in which they do so is most likely to be patterned by the larger system they comprise—not in isolation from it. As such, workers experience the systemic imperatives of profit and competition as direct constraints on their actions, ideas, and social choices, on the one hand, and as pressures to perform in accordance with the wishes of management, on the other. Generally speaking, people who participate in production systems in which labor is used for the selective interests and profit of others are alienated *in* and *from* social relations; although not necessarily to equal degrees.

At the same time, because people work at different tasks and in different kinds of organizations they do not experience exactly the same degrees and kinds of constraint, infringement, and alienation. To the extent that occupations and organizations are distinguishable with respect to their technology, tasks, and forms of control, they also differ with regard to the impact they have on workers. In this sense, we can speak of organizations and occupations as mediating the consequences of the system as a whole. The latter establishes the broad parameters of the quality of working life, but does not determine a uniformity across all positions in the system. The severity and extent of personal consequences of participation in the labor process varies with the specific conditions workers experience. The alienation of craft workers results from the mediated systemic imperatives of capital. Consequently, rather than assume that the personal consequences for those in craft occupations are uniform and positive, they should be considered to be potentially as variable and problematic as in other forms of capitalist production. In other words, the relationships between the conditions and consequences of work for so-called blue collar aristocrats are empirical questions worthy of our attention.

Craft Production in the Building and Construction Industry

Although it is commonly acknowledged that market activity in the industry is largely dependent on extraindustrial conditions, the implications for industrial practices and working conditions generally have not been recognized. The primary influences on construction activity are actually twofold: demand from other industrial sectors and federal monetary policy. Commercial construction is particularly sensitive to the growth and contraction cycles of other sectors. An expanding economy requires the modification of old buildings and the construction of new ones as companies attempt to keep up with current product demand while anticipating future trends. Periods of contraction or recession mean a decline in demand for new facilities as business strategies become more cautious. For these reasons, commercial construction activity is considered to be relatively price inelastic. Demand is not greatly affected by modest or even substantial shifts in the costs of construction. That means greater opportunity for favorable wage agreements for construction workers during periods of strong demand. But it also means that there is little that can be done within the industry to stimulate demand during slack periods.

Residential construction is similarly sensitive to the general state of the economy. People's ability to purchase new homes depends on the level of employment, wages, and, of course, mortgage interest rates. Clearly, when many people are out of work or fearful of losing their jobs or struggling against inflation, little can be done to stimulate demand for new homes. The cost of borrowing money is an especially strong determinant of residential building activity. It is estimated that a one percent increase in the interest rate translates into a 13 percent increase in construction costs (Mills 1972). Similarly, high interest rates also depress buyer demand for homes, as recent events have indicated. It is precisely for these reasons that building activity, as evidenced by housing starts, is monitored by economists as an extremely sensitive market follower.

When considered in the proper light, it should be no surprise that the industry's sensitivity to external factors affects its internal work practices and labor relations. For one thing, contractors place special value on their ability to hire and fire workers on a job-by-job basis as a principal method of dealing with unstable market conditions. They emphasize the need to adjust work rules to fit project-specific circumstances for the same or similar reasons. In contrast, such conditions limit the power of building trades unions to set patterns of employment in the industry and work rules on the job. An unstable product market and the demands of contractors seeking flexibility in their operations may force trade unions to adopt defensive or adaptive orientations; while employment uncertainties may limit the degree to which workers can exercise power on the construction site.

The industry's well-developed subcontracting system both reflects and conditions its production relations. The system comprises two facets: a formal contracting structure existing between organizations, and an informal contracting structure within organizations. The first is the widely recognized subcontracting practice of distributing responsibility for specific craft-related functions among numerous employers.[13] Actual practices vary from area to area, but in general a builder or general contractor divides the total building project into smaller components for which specialty (that is, trade specific) subcontractors assume responsibility. For example, a subcontractor may do the plumbing, painting, roofing, or electrical wiring on a project. On very large construction projects it is not unusual for subcontractors to do only a part of the total job for that specialty.

As a result of taking responsibility for a single aspect of the production process, subcontractors usually hire and supervise craft workers from one or two building trades. That simplifies the internal operation of the specialty contractor's firm, while leaving the task of coordinating the activities of the various subcontractor organizations to the general contractor or builder. The building site thus can be viewed as a temporarily structured, interorganizational network, lasting only as long as the production process, and changing its composition as subcontractors start and finish their parts of the project.

Three major factors have made subcontracting the common practice. First, market variability and uncertainty make it economical for builders and general contractors to shift some of the production liability to specialty contractors. Subcontracting is a principal method of diffusing risks on a project that, by its very nature, is a short-lived venture. Externalizing responsibility reduces the financial investment in any single project. That, in turn, permits simultaneous involvement in more than one project and greater financial flexibility.

Second, it is rather cumbersome for the general contractor to hire, supervise, and supply equipment and material for all aspects of construction. The typical building project may require the presence of workers from fifteen to twenty-two different trades. Since the relative contributions of the trades are far from equal, doing so would entail inordinate administrative costs and complexities. Most of the trades represent only a small proportion of total labor time. Only two trades, carpenters and laborers, account for about 41 percent of labor time. Thus, it is not coincidental that these are the two occupations most often hired directly by general contractors. In this, the interfirm subcontracting structure is an adaptation to market and labor characteristics in the building industry (Eccles 1981). At the same time, the formal structure establishes the organizational parameters for the ways in which control and efficiency pressures are manifest within each contracting firm.

In fact, those pressures constitute the third reason for subcontracting. Subcontracting institutionalizes the historical process by which work has been redivided and specialized within traditional craft jurisdictions. The development of contracting reflects the dialectical relationship between employers seeking more effective methods of control that also enhance profitability, and craftspeople performing similar tasks seeking greater collective strength in dealing with common employers. That dynamic continually narrows the range of activities craftworkers perform on the job. On the one hand, subcontractors begin to estimate costs and productivity on the basis of the output of a workforce specializing in that delimited facet of the craft. That level, of course, becomes the standard the employers' foremen seek to enforce on the job.

On the other hand, craftspeople find it increasingly difficult to satisfy their employers' productivity standards and also maintain their general craft skills. It becomes ever more necessary to focus only on a specific range of activities. Such redivision of labor within craft jurisdictions leads, in turn, to a divergence and fragmentation of interests among members of the same general trade. Specialized craftspeople find that their economic and on-the-job problems are often not the same, and even that they often work for different subcontractors.

The relationship between redivided labor and subcontracting in the painting craft is a good illustration of this development. Traditionally, painting has included all those activities involved in the finishing preparation of interior and exterior walls (for example, scraping and sanding), application of a primary preparatory coat, and then the finishing coat of paint or wallpaper. The painter also had the skills and knowledge to do woodstaining and finishing, graining (giving a painted surface the appearance of a bare-wood finish), and metal leafing (applying a very thin layer of metal, usually gold or silver, to ceiling or wall ornamental designs). Some of the painting skills, such as wood graining and metal leafing have fallen into disuse and all but disappeared as the techniques have become obsolete. The others have undergone the process of redivision and specialization.

The division between paperhangers and painters, for instance, took place fairly early on in the United States. By the beginning of the twentieth century, paperhangers had already made two short-lived attempts at national organization. The Paperhangers Union of America was formed in 1882 and lasted six years. In 1895, the National Paperhangers Protective and Beneficial Association was organized. It met with variable success until 1902, when it merged with the International Brotherhood of Painters and Decorators. Today there are a small number of paperhangers' local unions within the international, but most locals have mixed memberships of painters and paperhangers.

Both paperhanging and painting skills have undergone further redivision in the twentieth century. Durability and ease of installation have made vinyl wallcoverings so popular for commercial buildings and offices that is is often the only type of wallcovering included in a painting subcontractor's contract. The contractor's interest in achieving the highest levels of productivity possible lead them to hire those paperhangers who are especially fast when handling the heavy duty vinyl material. That, in turn, has encouraged some paperhangers to specialize in vinyl installation in order to establish and maintain sufficient speed with that kind of work. Since it is generally recognized that work with vinyl materials requires much less skill than work with other materials (such as fabrics and metallics), specialization has been associated with deskilling.

Similarly, painting skills have been redivided in such ways as to lower the general level of craft skills and knowledge in the trade. Contractors' use of spraying machines in commercial work whenever possible in order to increase productivity has undermined craft skills. Many young painters do not get the range of experiences with different types of paint materials and brush techniques necessary to be a fully skilled painter because the spray machine and roller are so popular with contractors. Moreover, some contractors have sought to specialize within the painting craft by contracting only for such preparatory work as taping. When gypsum wallboards, also known as sheetrock or drywall, are used in a building, it is necessary to smooth over the joints between the four by eight sheets of wallboard with a combination of paper tape and adhesive compound. The practice of subcontracting only that step of the production process has led some painters to specialize in taping to the exclusion of other painting and paperhanging skills. Once established, the specialization is institutionalized partly by the subcontracting structure and partly by training new workers only in that skill.

Bob Reckman (1979), in a very insightful analysis of the carpentry craft and trade, makes similar observations. According to Reckman:

> Speculative building requires the contract/subcontract system, and this, in turn, encourages specialization. Specialization, finally, has two effects. It works against quality by limiting responsibility to small, specific tasks. More importantly, the specialized small subcontractor or worker becomes only a part of what the carpenter used to be. The total carpentry of on-site residential building is at least as complex as ever. To do it all would require a carpenter who could easily hold his head up historically. The system of financial organization and social relations, however, works to ensure that few carpenters do, in fact, do it all. They do this part or that, thereby perhaps earning more in the short run, but ironically locking themselves into relatively narrow, powerless, repetitive jobs (pp. 101–102).

Subcontracting also means that craftspeople work in relatively small organizations. According to government figures, the average size of specialty contracting firms is 3.3 employees. Eighty-four point seven percent of building firms hire no more than four employees, while 92.4 percent hire less than ten. The predominance of the small firm has direct bearing on the degree of bureaucratization of the organizations in the industry and how control over production typically is exercised. Other things being equal, fewer formal positions of authority and fewer written rules and procedures mean that control is manifest directly through interpersonal contacts between craftspeople and contractors or foremen. Chapter two will focus on the impact of organizational characteristics such as size and bureaucratization on the conditions of work at the construction site.

An informal contracting system within building firms complements the formal subcontracting structure. It differs slightly from interfirm contracting in that it depends on unwritten agreements and direct personal relationships. It follows, however, from the same basic logic by which management seeks to economize on its liabilities and direct responsibilities while maintaining control over the labor process.

In some respects it is similar to the inside contracting or coexploitation that existed in the pre-twentieth century factory system. Essentially, inside contracting was a system in which jobs were subcontracted at a fixed price or piece rate to employees who then hired and supervised other workers. Inside contracting is notable here for two reasons. First, it was a form of indirect exploitation and control. Inside contractors both direct labor on behalf of management and share the profit from the labor of their fellow workers. According to sociologist Dan Clawson (1980), it added significantly to the complexity of capitalist class relations:

> Contractors were in a supremely contradictory situation within class relations: on the one hand, they managed workers and made a profit on each piece produced; on the other hand, they often did production work, were generally regarded by capitalists as more-or-less workers, and they bargained antagonistically over contract prices in much the way that pieceworkers do. Contractors were capitalists in relation to their employees and workers in relation to their employers (p. 90).

Second, it established a nonbureaucratic way of organizing work. According to Clawson, there were few written rules, no written files and records, and no formally established levels of authority. Most important, work relations depended more on personal interaction than on bureaucratic depersonalization and legal/rational decision making. Contractors hired workers they knew personally or who were referred by personal acquaintances. Supervision also tended to be direct and personal; contractors at times working alongside their employees. In some settings, particularly in the steel industry, contracting had a more collective and nonhierarchical characteristic as groups of workers could contract a job and make collective decisions about allocating duties and responsibilities within the group (Montgomery 1979; Stone 1974). Basically, then, the inside contracting system enabled capital to avoid much of the expense of bureaucratic control over production by placing managerial responsibilities on the shoulders of a minority of specially selected members of the workforce.

The informal contracting system in the building industry results from the same pressures that gave rise to formal interfirm subcontracting. Informal contracting within firms reduces the costs of control and reduces economic risk through non-bureaucratic mechanisms of control. There are two basic ways in which this is achieved. In the first type, foremen act as inside contractors in their employers' organizations. The interfirm subcontracting structure that, as previously discussed, has led to the proliferation of numerous small firms specializing in a single part of the overall production process has also placed a foreman in a pivotal position that is ideally suited to the role of inside contractor.

In class terms, the foreman is involved in a set of contradictory relationships in production. On the one hand, because of the constraint small size places on the hierarchical structure of contractors' firms, foremen are often the contractors' sole managerial agent on the construction site. As such, he takes responsibility for coordinating the delivery of supplies to the job site, the laying out of work, and the allocation of tasks to the workforce. Most significantly, he is frequently the person who directly carries out hiring and firing decisions. These duties, of course, give the foreman a good deal of control over production and power over the craftspeople under his supervision.

On the other hand, foremen are union members and wage workers rather than salaried managers. In general, they share with their fellow tradespeople the insecurity of project-specific employment. Although practices do vary between trades and from one firm to another (in the latter case depending on size), foremen are usually not kept on the payroll between jobs. Second, foremen frequently engage in production work. It is only on the large projects that one or more foremen perform only managerial tasks for the specialty contractor. Many jobs are of too small a scale to carry the administrative costs of a full-time, nonproducing manager. Foremen often divide their time on the job between production and managerial responsibilities.

A foreman can use his managerial position, however, in order to limit the economic insecurity he experiences as worker. He can do so by acting as an inside contractor. Contractors and foremen commonly arrange a profit-contingent bonus for the foreman who manages to fulfill a contract for less than the costs estimated in the original bid. In exchange for a share of the excess profit accumulated by the end of the job, the foreman will push his workforce to maintain uncommonly high levels of productivity. Foremen can also use methods that keep costs at a minimum. They can convince their workers to accept unsafe conditions on the job (for example, to work from structurally unsound or inadequate scaffolding) or to use production tools and techniques proscribed by the trade agreement.

The nonbureaucratic structure and small-scale production help the foreman carry out the role as inside contractor.[14] For one thing, since he often works along side those he supervises the foreman apparently suffers the same set of working conditions. If there is an effort to push out the work, the foreman is a part of that effort; if a scaffold is of questionable safety, the foreman shares in the danger. The cash bonus at job's end, however, is the unmentioned differential that may make it worthwhile for the foreman to make the extra effort or accept the additional danger. Small and unbureaucratic production also makes it possible for the foreman to make his appeals to fellow tradespeople on a personal basis. Small firms accentuate the perception of a close tie between the fate of a contractor and the fate of the tradespeople he hires. A foreman can thus appeal to fellow tradespeople because the boss is "really in trouble on this job and we have to pull him out of the hole." In fact, I even heard it explained by a foreman on one job how the contractor had submitted an extremely low bid against those from nonunion contractors so that "we" could have work. Similarly, the foreman can cry about the pressure he is under from the contractor. The foreman's request to "help me out on this one, guys" is followed inevitably by the assurance that he will make up for it on the next job.

The second type of inside contracting is commonly known as "lumping." Lumping essentially means that a specialty contractor agrees with a worker or group of workers to a single, fixed price for a job. Instead of receiving their normal hourly wages and fringe benefits as employees, tradespeople who lump a job accept payment as if they were nonemployee contractors. workers who lump a job generally do production work on it, but also hire others from the trade to help them. In addition to the managerial responsibilities they assume in lumping a job, they also assume the risk of encountering unforeseen delays in production that would require more time being spent on the construction site without any additional remuneration.

Contractors find lumping an attractive arrangement because it transforms a variable wage cost into a fixed contract cost, thereby protecting their profit margins against uncertainties in the production process. It also enables them to be involved in more than one project at a time without significantly increasing their administrative and managerial overhead since the burdens and risks are shifted to workers acting as inside contractors. Employers also benefit from lumping by being able to avoid paying fringe benefits and other mandated taxes and contributions on smaller projects.

Some craftspeople thus lump jobs because they are pressured by their employers. The uncertianties of project-specific employment make the employer-employee relationship a particularly dynamic affair. In this rather fluid context, a worker may be compelled to lump a given job in exchange for the promise of regular employment on future projects. Widespread unemployment in the industry makes it difficult for many tradespeople to jeopardize good relations with an employer by refusing such arrangements.

On the other hand, not all construction workers see lumping as an unavoidable evil. Some see it as an opportunity for the possibility of greater economic return than they would have realized if paid their hourly wage. These workers are gambling that the job proceeds smoothly without any major delays. Others see an advantage to receiving undeclared payment on which they hope to avoid paying taxes, or which includes additional sums that would in other circumstances have gone to make the employer's contribution to the insurance and welfare fund. Still others, however, see lumping as an opportunity to exploit the labor of fellow workers. They can accomplish this by hiring others at wages lower than union scale, or by paying cash at the union hourly rate—but without fringe benefits.[15]

Both formal and informal contracting have developed interdependently with other critical aspects of the industry's structure. Thus, while they shall be considered in greater detail in subsequent chapters, it is necessary to this introductory overview of the industry that three of the most significant be touched on briefly. One of them, the localized labor market, has facilitated contracting relations within firms. Local markets are particularly fertile soil for cultivating intimate and personalized social relationships. Such local social networks—among craft workers and between contractors and craftworkers—are crucial to informal contracting. Foremen, for example, must be able to develop confidential and trustworthy relationships with other tradespeople if they are to act as an inside contractor. Similarly, lumping arrangements are feasible only on the basis of close ties between employers and craftworkers. Both forms of inside contracting require the intimacy and direct interpersonal reciprocity characteristic of local markets.

Moreover, once it is established, informal contracting encourages, if not compels, workers to develop the close and intimate relationship with a few employers that are associated with local networks. Greater employment security, of course, is the primary economic benefit of local networks. However, the weakness of strong ties is their very closeness which makes it both hard for individual tradespeople to disassociate themselves from a microstructure that often works to their detriment, and difficult for union officials to institute alternative labor relations practices.

Through its impact on the division of labor, contracting also has had an indirect effect on the construction trade unions. As will be explored in greater depth later, one result of the historical redivision of labor linked to the subcontracting structure has been the Balkanization of the trades unions in the industry. Unionization according to occupation, in which the jurisdiction of a union is determined for the most part by productive function in the building process, has its own historical basis (for example, Salzman 1952). Excessive subdivisions within occupational groups and a body of labor law which gives those divisions legal standing have left the industry's unions fragmented, strategically isolated, and, as it often happens, in competition with one another. In general, Balkanized unions operating at the local market level offer their members adequate protection during periods of growth and peak activity. Specific trade jurisdiction and laws that make it impossible for local unions to legally coordinate their activities also make it nearly impossible for them to develop coherent and comprehensive local or regional programs. Many local trade unions are thus left too weak to provide adequate protection for their members during those economic periods when it is needed most.

Numerous factors bear on the question of how well a particular local union actually protects the interests of its members. As shall be seen, they include such factors as the centrality of the trade's production functions to the building process, occupational skill level, and the union's size. Their confluence has fostered a situation within the unionized sector of the industry that bears striking similarities to the distinctions made at the interindustry level between core and peripheral segmented labor markets. Some local unions, on the basis of favorable structural location in production, are able to obtain economic advantages that are often denied less advantageously located trades. In some instances such advantages come at the expense of the structurally weaker trades.

The final characteristic of the local building market that must be highlighted is the practice of making special arrangements—some legal, others only debatably so—that in one way or another contravene formal provisions of the union-management contract (the trade agreement). In some important respects their prevalence is a result of the combination of a local labor market, labor intensive production, contracting, and the relative weakness of local trade unions. Such special arrangements usually concern changes in work rules, hiring practices, wages and benefits, and methods of payment to workers. Contractors generally argue that such agreements that provide working conditions below those specified in the trade agreement are necessary in order to maintain flexibility of operations and to meet the competition of nonunion contractors. Arrangements are frequently enacted through the informal contracting system, although there are instances of formal arrangements directly between contractors and union officials.

The bottom line, of course, is that the craftworkers on the job are the ones who bear the burden of those special arrangements.

The rest of this book is devoted to a closer look at the impact of market and organizational conditions on the working lives of craftspeople who rely on work in the industry for their livelihood. My interest in each chapter is in understanding how construction tradespeople are affected by the conditions of work and employment they experience, but also how their active participation in the labor process serves to reproduce essential aspects of the industry's structure. Chapter two focuses on the construction site. It presents an analysis of the issue of control over the labor process at the point of production by examining the structure of work in relation to organizational and occupational conditions on the job. Chapter two also deals with the managerial position. As discussed briefly, the foreman plays a pivotal role in both formal and informal contracting. Here the question is how this strategic location in the labor process translates into economic and noneconomic advantages. Chapter three focuses on the trade union and collective bargaining. Specifically, I look at how workers' attachments to and participation in the local trade union combine with important characteristics of the unions themselves to determine conditions of work and employment. Then in chapter four the issue of alienation is explored as it pertains to the lives of building tradespeople. Salient aspects of production, as well as important aspects of the local labor market, are examined with respect to their influences on workers' alienation and discontent. The conclusion, chapter five, shifts the focus slightly from construction workers and their work organizations to the construction industry and the issues of ownership and control. Arguing that most conditions of work and employment are embedded in the structure and practice of labor relations and capitalist markets within the industry, it is further argued that they are not problems that are likely to disappear with minor adjustments, corrective policies or traditional governmental regulation. Instead, significant restructuring of both labor and product markets are necessary. In line with that reasoning a primitive sketch is offered of an alternative model of relations for the building industry that seeks to meet both workers' needs for a safe and humane workplace and society's need for socially useful construction.

The Research

The empirical analyses of the issues raised in the following chapters are based on research conducted over the course of one seven-month period from March to September 1979, and further investigations conducted between June 1983 and August 1985. Data were collected by a variety of techniques, including direct personal interviews, construction site participant-observation, and a mail survey conducted in 1979 that utilized a self-report questionnaire. The latter method serves as the primary data base for the statistical analyses pursued in subsequent chapters, with the others providing supplementary qualitative information.

The survey of building tradespeople encompassed respondent from nine building and construction occupations (glaziers, ironworkers, plumbers, painters, wallpaperhangers, roofers, electricians, laborers, and tilesetters-helpers) belonging to ten different locals. The occupations present in the sample are generally representative of the ranges of skill, work organization, conditions of work and employment, and union-contractor relations among the building trades generally. Individual respondents were selected through random sampling procedures from union rosters of active members. Fifty-five members of each union were mailed a questionnaire that queried about various aspects of their experiences on the job, as a union member, and as craft employee (See appendix C for sample questionnaires). Two follow-up mailings were sent to initial nonrespondents.

Multiple mailings resulted in responses from 273 crafts-people with an initial response rate of 49 percent. Deleting returns which were either completed incorrectly or with too many omissions left a usable sample of 260 total respondents (47 percent response rate) of which fourteen were union officials.

In addition, personal interviews were conducted with at

least one full-time official—a business agent or business manager—from each of the participating locals. Union officials provided information about labor relations practices, employment patterns, and local union organizational characteristics. Finally, I spent six months in 1979 doing participant-observation on construction sites. I spent time (a minimum of one day per week) with business agents from participating unions. I was also permitted to attend some official meetings among busines agents. As a participant-observer, I also joined various union activities, such as membership meetings and picketing actions. I returned to work in the area in 1983. I took the opportunity to reexamine some of my earlier conclusions and to bring my observations about union-contractor and worker-employer relations up to date.

Throughout the text, I have sought a balance between methodological and substantive discussions that does not over-burden the reader with technical descriptions of statistical procedures and variable construction. To correct for what might appear to some as a glossing over of matters of technical importance for the data analysis, I have included a more detailed description of the research methodology in appendix A. Appendix B is a glossary of the variables used in the analysis. Appendix C contains the questionnaires used in the research. The reader should refer to the appendices when the text does not make the definition or measurement of a variable sufficiently clear.

2

WORKING AT THE CONSTRUCTION SITE

Autonomy, Management, and Control

To the uninitiated, the construction site can seem to be a confusing beehive of activity, which, without any apparent guiding hand, eventually concludes with the finishing touches on a new physical structure. The casual passersby who briefly stop to observe what occurs on the other side of the fence that keeps them safely out of the "Hard Hat Area" may see numerous kinds of work going on at once in a noisy, dirty, and, by today's standards of hi-tech robotics and computerization, primitive atmosphere. They can easily come away with the impression that the process is an organized anarchy that gets the job done almost in spite of itself.

A few special characteristics of construction work encourage this perception while masking the actual situation. First of all, the construction site bears little resemblance to the more accessible sequential logic of the factory assembly line where functions are usually performed one after the other, or in distinct and separate facilities. In construction many production activities occur simultaneously rather than sequentially. Different tasks and operations are being taken care of not only at the same time, but also at different locations of the same site. Imagine, if you will, an urban skyscraper under construction. At the upper levels, structural ironworkers are connecting the basic steel skeleton. The middle floors are being closed in by bricklayers, glaziers, wire lathers, and stone masons. In the already closed in lower floors electricians, plumbers, steamfitters, painters, plasterers, carpenters, and many other trades are hard at work on interior components.

Second, in construction the site of production actually undergoes structural transformation as the production process progresses; giving the impression that the conditions of work are constantly changing. Again, the obvious comparison is with the factory setting. Factories are themselves relatively stable physical aspects of the work environment in which the manufactured product changes as it is assembled. In construction, however, where the object of production houses the producers, the stages of production seemingly correspond to unique physical conditions of work. There is an apparent flux in working conditions that contrasts with the stability of the factory.

Third, correspondence between object and site of production means that the location of production constantly changes. When one project is completed, workers move on to a different building. It is thus easy for outsiders to interpret the move from one completed building to a new construction site as corresponding to a move on to an entirely different set of conditions, labor on a product of totally different design, and therefore distinct new problems to solve and novel opportunities for creative activities in work.

As was argued in the preceding chapter, however, such superficial perceptions may conform to managerial and vulgar class theories of the labor process, but not necessarily to the on-the-job reality construction workers deal with daily. Because a builder or general contractor divides the total project into smaller components for which subcontractors assume responsibility, the latter hire and supervise craftspeople from only one or two trades. For workers, the subcontracting structure means that they perform the work corresponding to a single trade. The range of activities they engage in in the labor process are limited to the contractual agreements with general and subcontractors, as well as the arrangements between the trade unions themselves. This has led to fairly specific spheres of production activity for the different craft occupations. The subcontracting structure over the years has narrowed workers' productive responsibilities. It also has increased the likelihood that task conditions and occupational circumstances are recurrent rather than idiosyncratic from one project to the next. Superficial features of two buildings may be radically different. But the division of labor in the subcontracting system means that the conditions for workers in any given trade are fairly similar from one construction site to the next, and are characterized by less opportunities for autonomy than many authors have claimed.[1]

On the other hand, the situation is far from uniform. A variety of factors operate to determine the conditions existing in contractor organizations, across construction sites, between the building trades and between managerial foremen and non-managerial tradespeople. Some workers seem to meet with similar conditions from one job to the next, while others deal with different conditions (see table 2.1). A majority of tradespeople responding to the survey questionnaire, for example, report that conditions are identical or similar on different construction sites, while 21.6 percent report substantially different conditions. The issue, of course, is which aspects of the labor process determine these differences.

Table 2.1. The Variability of Job Site Conditions for Building Tradespeople (including foremen). Distribution of responses to the question, "How would you categorize the conditions of the job sites you go on?"

	Number	*Percent*
1. They are all the same	7	2.9
2. They are mostly the same	117	47.8
3. They are mostly different	68	27.8
4. They are all different	53	21.5
Totals	245	100%

Questions about work autonomy yielded similar patterns. Almost 60 percent report that they are instructed what tasks to perform, while 38 percent are also told how to accomplish their assigned tasks (table 2.2). On the other side, there are 40 percent of the sample who report at least some prerogative as to what they do and how they do it. While many craftworkers exercise self-direction in their work, significant numbers have little or no control over what they do and how they do it in the labor process.[2] Similarly, building tradespeople are not uniformly left unsupervised to do their work (table 2.3). Among those responding to the questionnaire, 27.5 percent report having their work

Table 2.2. Self-Direction for Building Tradespeople (including Foremen). Distribution of responses to the question, "Which of the following statements best describes your job", asked with respect to respondents' "General Experience" and "Most Recent Job."

	General Experience		Most Recent Job	
	Number	Percent	Number	Percent
1. I am told what to do and how to do it	15	6.1	18	7.6
2. I am told what to do and job conditions determine how I do it	76	30.9	72	30.4
3. I am told what to do and I decide how to do it	49	19.9	52	21.9
4. I have some freedom to decide what I do and how to do it	44	17.9	42	17.7
5. I am left alone as long as the job gets done	62	25.2	53	22.4
Totals	244	100	237	100

evaluated constantly or frequently during the workday. More than 82 percent report at least occasional checks on their performance.

Table 2.3. Frequency of Supervision Experienced by Building Tradespeople (including Foremen). Distribution of responses to the question, "How often is your performance evaluated during the job?"

	Number	Percent
1. Constantly during the day	26	10.8
2. Frequently during the day	40	16.8
3. 1–3 times per day	20	8.3
4. 2 or 3 times per week	43	17.9
5. Once per week or less	68	28.3
6. Never	42	17.5
Totals	239	100

How then to account for such a range of experiences? Personal experience tells me it is not reducible to simplified a priori constructs such as craft administration. Many researchers, having adopted the craft-administration framework, were thus blinded to the significance of first-line managerial positions in the construction labor process. Instead, it is necessary to look at the multiplicity of forces bearing on the organization of the labor process at the job site. Accordingly, the rest of the chapter describes the on-site work structure in terms of the combined impact of organizational and occupational factors impinging on the labor process at the construction site.

Organization and Craft as Determinants of Work Autonomy

The question of workers' autonomy in the labor process is

an issue central to both questions of managerial control and worker alientation and discontent. It thus figures prominently in most recent discussions of organizational performance and worker safety and health. Indications of broadly felt discontent and alienation among workers have spurred an interest in the quality of work, in which much of the focus has been on the relationships between the inherent complexity of work, the opportunities for self-direction in work, and the consultative versus authoritarian nature of managerial styles.[3]

However important workers' reactions to their conditions of labor are to issues of productivity, efficiency, and individual well-being, the imperatives of capitalist political economy also dictate that management must retain sufficient control over the labor process to guarantee the implementation of long-range strategies as well as the daily operational decisions about material resources and work activity. In the words of Braverman, "control is indeed the central concept of all management systems" (1974, 68). These two concerns—worker autonomy and management control—are inherently conflicting tendencies in the labor process of the capitalist enterprise. On the construction site, as in other work settings, workers directly experience the supervision, external direction, and managerial hierarchy that result from the working out of that conflict.

For purposes of empirical examination of on-site work structure work autonomy has been defined in terms of two basic components: supervision and self-direction. In brief, the less frequently workers are supervised by managerial personnel, the greater their autonomy. Similarly, the more self-direction they exercise (opportunities to use individual discretion about what they do and how to do it) the greater the autonomy. Using these two variables as indicators of autonomy, it is possible to examine the organizational and occupational conditions that either enhance or detract from workers' opportunities for autonomy on the job.

Two basic sets of factors generally determine the degree of workers' autonomy in the labor process: that bearing on the inherent task complexity of the craft and that related to the economic and political efficacy of a formalized control structure. Occupational complexity includes the substantive complexity of the worker's relationships to people, data, and things in fulfilling the requirements of the job. It also includes the task's demands on a person's mental or intellectual involvement (that is, the division of labor between tasks which require one to deal with written material as well as perform manual operations on the job, versus those which are predominantly or totally manual).[4] The construction trades which require workers to deal regularly or frequently with written material correspond to a greater importance of mental labor than those for which occasional or no contact with written material is the rule.

Other things being equal, construction jobs that are complex and demand mental as well as physical labor should enhance workers' autonomy. Detailed instructions and constant supervision are impractical when the job is complicated, involves numerous operations, and requires workers to refer fairly regularly to written material. According to organizational sociologists Gordon and Becker (1966), the benefits-to-cost ratio under such conditions make an extensive authority structure uneconomical.

In addition, there are two organizational variables that most likely have a direct impact on the feasibility of structured control on the construction site. The size of the workforce on the site and the length of time workers are present on the site affect the relative necessity of formalized structures of supervision and control. Larger workforces require more supervision. Peter Blau (1972) among others has pointed to the positive relationship between the actual size of the administrative component and the number of organizational members.[5] The scale of the organization determines the demands for coordination and control of production functions. It should be expected that the same relationship will pertain in construction. Subcontractors with more tradespeople on the job can be expected to institute formalized structures of control, as reflected by the number of officially designed authority positions, the frequency of supervision, and the reliance on management-specified directives. Similarly with the duration of stay on the job site. By definition, the utilization of people to supervise productive operations entails additional overhead. A supervisor or foreman does not contribute to the production process directly; he or she merely ensures that others contribute as fully as possible. It makes sense to assume this added cost only if the economic benefits compensate for the added cost. Construction differs from factory-based manufacturing where production occurs relatively constantly and at a single site. Both the size of the construction project and the peculiarities of the building being erected, however, have an influence on the length of time workers from different trades will be on a site.[6] When workers are to be on a site for only a short period, it makes little economic sense to institute formalized control structures; for there will not be enough time to recoup the additional expense. Formalized control is more likely when workers stay on the job for an extended period.

Quantitative results from the research offer a clearer perspective on these issues. These results are shown in tables 2.4 and 2.5, which contain the separate regression analyses of bureaucracy, supervision, and self-direction on the two organizational variables (on-site size and duration) and the two craft occupational variables (craft complexity and craft mentality).

Table 2.4. Regressions of Bureaucracy, Supervision, and-Self-Direction on Job-Site Production Factors.

Predictors	Bureau-cracy	Supervision	Self-Direction
Production Location			
On-Site Size (log)	.37***a	.22***	-.19***
Duration	.17***	.11	-.12*
Craft Complexity	-.12**	-.09	.00
Craft Mentality	-.05	-.09	.15**
$\bar{R}^2$	.21	.08	.06

*p<.10; **p<.05; ***p<.01
a. Table contains only standardized regression coefficients. Subsequent tables reporting regression results similarly show only standardized coefficients. For more detailed reporting of results see Silver (1981).

Bureaucratization of managerial authority (number of management positions) tends to vary positively with workforce size and on-site duration (column A). This probably reflects the difficulties of coordination and control. When there is a large contigent of workers, they are usually scattered around the site and likely doing somewhat different tasks, or similar tasks at different stages of completion. In order to ensure proper coordination of functions, smooth distribution of task assignments, and sufficient supervision there must be more officially designated management positions. That is accomplished by assigning one or more strawbosses with responsibility for their specific workgroup and a foreman who decides on the distribution and organization of work. When the number of tradespeople working for a contractor is sufficiently large, one of the foremen may be designated supervisor. The supervisor usually has no production responsibilities whatsoever, and devotes his time strictly to managing the labor process. The positive association between duration and bureaucracy is also in line with the management-control thesis according to which the overhead of a formal managerial hierarchy is efficient only in the longer run. Thus short jobs tend to limit the use of formal authority positions.

It is also significant, although very much in keeping with established organizational theory and research, that the complexity of building work has a negative effect on bureaucracy. Controlling for the influences of size and duration, the occupational complexity of craft work tends to reduce the number of positions (bureaucracy). Conversely, building contractors tend to appoint more on-site managers when tasks are routine and less complex.

It appears that the bureaucratic structure of the craft production organization reflects the impact of both the organizational logistics of control and the task components of the craft occupation. Craft, in the sense of the degree of skill, knowledge, and variability of work, does not solely determine the extent of managerial bureaucracy on the construction site. Nor is it the most significant factor. The problematics of control and coordination on the site associated with increased size and greater site duration are at least as important, and very likely more so.

The determinants of work autonomy shown in columns B

and C of table 2.4 follow a similar pattern. The frequency of evaluative supervision appears to be sensitive primarily to workforce size—those working in larger contingents reporting more frequent supervision. Self-direction is dependent on both organizational and occupational level variables. It is negatively related to size and duration. This signifies that those in smaller workforces and those who work on sites for only a brief time tend to have greater opportunities for making production decisions than those in larger workforces and those remaining on-site for extended periods. Self-direction also partially reflects the relative mental composition of manual work. Jobs that require reference to written material such as blueprints, codebooks, and instructions tend to be associated with greater opportunities to decide on the precise tasks to under take and how to go about accomplishing them. In other words, when the mental component of what are essentially manual jobs is relatively high, there is a greater likelihood that a worker will have to exercise discretion about procedures and techniques of production.

The impact of the organizational variables in this analysis suggests that it might be fruitful to extend the predictive model for work autonomy by adding bureaucracy as a predictor variable.[7] As shown in table 2.5, the addition of the bureaucracy variable yields some interesting relationships. First, size and site duration have no appreciable effects on workers' autonomy once the number of authority positions is accounted for. This indicates their influence on autonomy to be almost completely indirect through their combined impact on bureaucracy. In other words, the organizational factors, workforce size, and on-site duration, are principle determinants of bureaucratic structure which, in turn, is the primary determinant of workers' autonomy.

Second, the relationship between self-direction and craft mentality obtains, even when controlling for bureaucracy. Functions in the labor process that demand direct mental involvement in the form of frequent reference to written material and communications tends to allow for greater procedural and technical autonomy, regardless of size and bureaucratic structure. The division between mental and physical labor thus relates directly to involvement in production-level decision making.

Table 2.5. Regressions of Supervision and Self-Direction including Bureaucracy.

	Supervision	Self-Direction
Production Location		
On-Site Size (log)	.10	-.09
Duration	.05	-.07
Craft Complexity	-.07	-.03
Craft Mentality	-.08	.14**
Bureaucracy	.32***	-.28***
$\bar{R}^2$	.15	.12

*p<.10 **p<.05 ***p<.01

In sum, it is possible to define the structures of work most directly experienced by building tradespeople in terms of three sets of actors. Work autonomy—self-direction in work and freedom from constant managerial supervision of work—reflects the combined effects of bureaucratization of authority, task composition of the craft, and the logistics of organizational and workforce control. These findings are relevant to the extent that they bear on the issue of craft administration of construction work. Obviously, occupational factors commonly associated with craft work are linked to autonomy on the job. One would be in error, however, to place heavy emphasis on their role in shaping the structure of work. Craft-related factors do influence the nature of work, but apparently within the context established by the logistics concerns of contractors seeking to maintain control over the labor process.

Moreover, the importance of nonoccupational factors encourages a redirected search for explanations for how work is structured on the construction site. If the answers are not solely to be found in simplistic occupationally based theories, then one must look to precisely those areas which the craft-professional orientation overlooks. The formal and informal relations between building tradespeople and contractors is one such area. As noted in the first chapter, basic (mis)conceptions about craft work have led many theorists to take the presence of cooperative, consultative, and informal hierarchical relations for granted. The following section describes how formal and informal relationships associated with managerial positions on the construction site both play strategic roles in employers' organizations and greatly influence the work structure for production-level managers.

Managerial Location: Authority, Consultation, and Autonomy

The relationships between craft workers and contractors are an important aspect of life in the industry. Whether tradespeople experience congenial, informal, and consultative relations, or authoritarian, highly directive, and formalized patterns of contact with supervisors and owners has far-reaching impact on their lives on and off the job.

Actually, autonomy and consultation are two sides of the same coin. Whenever a worker is not completely autonomous, the question then is the quality of interactions with superordinates. This point has been appreciated by most organizational and work relations theorists, but especially those emphasizing process and intepersonal factors in production.[8] From theories "Y" and "Z" to theories of worker management and workers' control, it is recognized how important it is not only to increase the positive affectual and perceptual orientations among employees, but also to ensure patterns of meaningful exchange of information, advice, and expertise in which workers are active participants.[9]

Thirty years ago, sociologist Alvin Gouldner (1954a, 1954b) offered his classic analysis of the serious organizational consequences of how authority is wielded at the point of production. Since then, organizational research has consistently pointed to the linkages between delegation of authority, participative decision processes, and workers' satisfaction and productivity. Summing up the literature on task design and authority to that time, the HEW Task Force noted that, "high worker satisfaction is associated with considerate and thoughtful behavior among employers . . . [and] supervisory behavior that shares decision making with subordinates" (O'Toole et al. 1973, p. 94). During the past decade there has been a substantial amount of research, under the general rubrics of "worker participation" and "worker management" dealing with the consequences of alternative forms of organizational structure. Thus one question that will be addressed here is who benefits from such consultative relationships among building tradespeople.

A second, but interrelated issue, concerns the correlates of the managerial location itself. Max Weber ably delineated the importance of hierarchical position as a determinant of one's organizational experiences. Weber's distinction between management and labor, the initial point of his analysis of the division of labor, can serve as a useful grounding for an examination of management on the construction site:

> Human services for economic purposes may be distinguished as a) "managerial"; or b) oriented to the instruction of managerial agency ("labor") (1978, p. 114).

According to Weber, managerial and labor functions can "accumulate" to individuals such that people perform both kinds; or there can be a "combination of function" such that organizational participants perform specialized functions of either management or labor. The modern rational-bureaucratic form, of course, is characterized by specialization of managerial and labor functions. Based on rational and legal criteria such as technical expertise and formally specified spheres of authority and control, managerial incumbents experience different opportunities than nonmanagement functionaries:

> The organization of offices follows the principle of hierarchy; that is, each lower office is under the control and supervision of a higher one. There is a right of appeal and of statement of grievances from the lower to the higher (1978, p. 218).

Those higher in the organizational hierarchy experience greater powers of discretion and control over organizational processes. Moreover, to the extent that "bureaucratic administration means fundamentally domination through knowledge" there exist tendencies for those who occupy managerial offices to accumulate advantages of knowledge. Such advantages of knowledge can then be used to enhance one's range of organizational prerogatives, decision-making responsibility, supervisory control, and consultative relations with superordinates. The processes of accumulated advantage, initially noted by Weber, were further analyzed by Robert Michels (1962) and many contemporary social scientists examining the issues of organizational power.

Weber's insights have also been incorporated in the works of recent Marxist theorists. Erik Olin Wright (1976, 1980), for instance, includes organizational relationships as a central element of his definition of class location. He derives a "production relations" concept of class by focusing on the patterns of superordination-subordination attached to specific locations in the social system of production. In addition to the polar capitalist and proletarian classes he defines "contradictory class locations." The former are defined partially by consistent patterns of work autonomy and supervision; the latter by mixed patterns. For example, semiautonomous employees are those who are hired by capital but neither receive nor enact supervisory functions. His categorization of the bottom managers, foremen, and line supervisor class location comes closest to present concerns. Comprising 13 to 23 percent of the economically active populaton, Wright argues this group includes those who are not self-employed, do not hire employees, and do supervise the work of organizational subordinates (1980, 202). Wright's use of the term "contradictory" in his definition of class location is not gratuitous.

> They are contradictory in the precise sense that they are located simultaneously in two classes and thus share basic class interests with both of these classes (bourgeois and proletarian). Managers/supervisors have one foot in the bourgeoisie and one in the working class, and this means that their class interests are objectively torn between these two classes (1980, pp. 182–83).

Barbara Ehrenreich and John Ehrenreich (1979) take a slightly different orientation in their analysis of the Professional-Managerial Class (PMC). They argue that the unique position of the PMC, situated between capital and labor, prompts a unique configuration of class interests. The ambiguous rather than contradictory nature of the PMC's class location likely results in the eventual development and solidification of an independent class position. In this Ehrenreich and Ehrenreich are much more closely allied to the positions advanced by Djilas (1957) and Gouldner (1978). In any event, in terms of organizational processes and the broader considerations of class relations, managerial location in production is significant as both analytic and practical elements of the labor process.

As discussed in the first chapter, the predispositions of organizational and class theorists have inhibited research about the role of managerial positions in craft production generally and construction specifically. This study has tried to correct in some measure for this by focusing on two aspects of production relations: 1. the direct consultative interactions between craftspeople and contractors; particularly, explaining the degree of consultation as determined by other production factors; 2. the structures of on-site control and supervision; addressing the issue of the relationship between formal managerial position (foreman) and consultative employer relations on the one side, and patterns of autonomy in work (supervision and self direction) on the other.

Consultative relations as a structured feature of building construction can be divided into two types: administrative consultation and on-site consultation. Each involves substantively different aspects of the contractor's overall operation as well as distinct phases of the production process.

Administrative consultation refers to discussions between contractor and craftsperson about matters pertinent to *preproject* decisions. Prior to the start of a project, indeed prior to the obtaining of a contract, there are numerous decisions to be made in order to derive an estimate of costs. Submission of an official bid for a contract covering some portion of the building project is of primary importance, for obvious reasons. When the bidding process is truly competitive, which it often is not, an accurate estimate of costs is essential if the subcontractor is to win the contract on the basis of low bid and still extract a profit from the job. Underestimation of labor costs or failure to leave enough margin for unforeseen problems can be the difference between profit and loss on a job, especially on a small project where the scale of operation precludes large margins for error. Even in a noncompetitive bidding situation—that is, when a subcontractor gains a contract through recommendation or has an established relationship with a building or general contractor—cost factors are important. Such situations may create greater leeway for the subcontractor. Ultimately, however, the basis of the intercontractor relationship is economic and the major constraints are those associated with profitability. The favored contractor still must be accurate in his cost estimates and offer a price which reflects general market conditions if he expects to maintain the relationship.

The experienced craftworker can be of great service to the subcontractor in deriving an accurate estimate of costs prior to the start of a job. His knowledge of materials, ability to work off of blueprints and specification lists, and make assessments of volitional factors are essential aids to formulating a successful bid. The craftworker's on-site practical experience can be especially useful in the estimation of labor costs. The size of the workforce that will be required, the number of person-days of work the project will entail, and the anticipation of practical and technical problems potentially associated with the design of the building are in many ways the most variable and least certain but also the most important factors to be included in the calculations. The subcontractor often is not in a position to make impressionistic appraisals of these factors without some consultation with a person with direct, or at least more recent, experience with the actual production process.[10] This is most clearly the case when the specifications call for the use of a material new to the market. Architectural and decorative plans often specify materials not yet widely used or proven completely useable. Nonetheless, the subcontractor must base his bid on some guesstimate of the likely labor costs.

Two situations from the present study illustrate the role of administrative consultation. Both involve a finishing trade with which the researcher has had intimate contact. In one case, prior consultation about the workability of a new product led the subcontractor in a noncompetitive bidding situation to seek a cost-plus agreement.[11] This turned out to be decisive as it took a long time on the job for workers first to figure out satisfactory methods of handling the unwieldy material. It took longer still for them to gain enough manual experience with the material to develop the necessary dexterity and speed of production to establish and maintain a satisfactory level of productivity. By the end of the job, it was clear that all of the previous cost estimates which had been considered were far too low. Adoption of any one of them would have cost the subcontractor his profit.

In a second case, the subcontractor was skeptical about submitting any bid at all for a job because of his own lack of familiarity with a new product. Consultation with a trusted craftsman, however, convinced him to compete for the contract. The worker had dealt with the product before and was confident that there would be no major difficulties in fulfilling the specifications of the job. Furthermore, the craftsman was able to estimate a reasonable labor cost which allowed the subcontractor to win the contract. The job was completed as the tradesman had predicted, yielding the contractor a satisfactory profit. In both cases, preproject consultation with a craftsperson was an important element of the contractor's decision-making process.

These examples point to the way in which preproject administrative consultation is a part of the subcontractor's estimation and bidding activities. Employers do seek the advice of workers with direct on-site experiences in developing realistic projections of labor costs to include in contract bids. On the other hand, it would be a mistake to overestimate the degree of contractors' dependencies on craftworkers in this area. In an industrial sector marked by competitive bidding for control over relatively labor intensive processes, careful calculation and shrewd financial judgment are the hallmarks of the successful subcontractor. Ultimately, the subcontractor must rely on his own knowledge, judgmental skills, and business contacts in deriving bids which consistently win contracts while yielding satisfactory rates of return. These cases merely indicate that administrative consultation in this area does take place regularly and when it does can have significant ramifications for the sub-contractor.

In addition to cost estimation, administrative consultation occurs in three other areas of production operation. Subsequent to winning a contract and prior to its commencement, supplies and materials must be procured and shipped to the site. Workers must be recruited in numbers sufficient to begin work on the site, and, of course, with the proper qualifications in speed and workmanship to handle the job. A single contractor, however enterprising, cannot handle these tasks alone, especial-ly when there is more than one project underway at the same time. Obvious limitations on personal resources of time and at-tention require that some responsibility for logistics and worker recruitment be delegated to others. Consultation in regard to the latter can be especially useful to the employer since the best judge of a worker's value as a producer is another worker. There are many things an experienced worker can purposefully hide or demonstrate to an employer during an inspection tour of a job site. But working alongside one another every day on the job offers ample opportunity to evaluate the worth of fellow tradespeople. In the smaller specialty trades a subcontractor may become familiar with the working habits of many of the tradespeople he hires, but this is not possible for most employers because of workforce size or the variabilities in employment patterns.

A final area of administrative consultation involves the scheduling of contracted jobs. All subcontractors have to be looking ahead to future contracts. Few projects are large enough that a subcontractor either does not need to run more than one job at a single point in time, or does not have to bid on future jobs even when one or more projects are still in progress. In such situations, prior estimations of how long it is to take are major elements of scheduling process. The importance of scheduling can be even further accentuated for relatively small contractors with limited financial resources. A small employer can easily find himself overextended as labor costs multiply when he attempts to handle numerous jobs simultaneously. Cash-flow problems can lead to legal difficulties, as well as create tensions in relationships with trade union officials. Either one can have serious implications for an employer's chances for future success.[12] Therefore, advice from a good estimator of labor factors is essential to the operation.

The term "on-site consultation" is used here to refer to consulting which takes place after a project is underway and while a craftsperson is on the job. It is operationalized as the frequency of direct interpersonal interactions between the respondent and contractor during the workday. As a quantitative measure it forms a scale with "no interactions" and "constant interactions" at the polar extremes.

On-site consultation entails four main areas of regular discussion between contractor and craftworker. For the most part they concern technical problems arising in the course of the construction project handled by the contractor as well as supervisory matters pertaining to the surveillance and control of workers' activities on the job. Once a job has been started there are a wide range of practical, logistic, and supervisory functions which are delegated by the subcontractor. Material and supplies must be moved from main storage facilities on the site to the locations which are more easily accessible to workers at various points around the project site. The allocation of supplies further involves responsibilities for such things as keeping inventory and maintaining steady supply flow. The first is obviously important in order to prevent or limit pilfering and accidental loss of expensive equipment and raw material. Additionally, a careful inventory is necessary if restocking is to occur without costly delays in production. That, of course, requires proper planning and sufficient communication between the contractor's office and the project site.

Continual presence of some managerial agent is also important in order to handle technical problems which arise. Defects in materials, discrepancies, errors or inaccuracies in blueprints, or belated changes in architectural and decorative plans frequently occur. If losses in labor time and material are to be avoided, these technical problems must be handled promptly and with as little disruption to ongoing production as possible. Decisions about such matters can have extreme consequences for the progress of the project as a whole. A substantial delay for one trade can mean delays for other trades, as well. Unanticipated pauses in production may also create problems by forcing workers to do their tasks out of their normal sequence.

Production consultation does not only take place about material and supplies, but also about the work itself. Work assignments must be made and constantly adjusted as needs on the site change. Responsibility for the division and distribution of work is an important function and must fall to somebody with knowledge of the working skills and capabilities of the people on the job. Consultation about the performance of workers can, and often does, lead to firings and hirings as inferior and nonproductive workers are replaced.

Table 2.6. Managerial Function in the Construction Process: Administrative and On-site Production Consultation Between Contractor and Craft Employees.

Administrative Consultation

1. Estimation and Bidding: labor costs, product evaluation

2. Employment and Recruitment: assessment of labor-power needs and personnel selection

3. Supply and Material Logistics: intrasite and intersite movement of material; coordination of resupply and distribution of material

4. Scheduling: time estimations of site duration and site succession

On-Site Consultation

1. On-site Material and Supply Allocation: distribution of material to work locations at job site

2. Technical Problems: assessment and advisement about material and supply defects; decisions about production methods

3. Performance Supervision: general workforce control and management

4. Labor-Power Regulation: distribution of work assignments deployment to work locations; assessment of labor power needs and adjustment of workforce size

The functional aspects of the two consultative relationships are contrasted in table 2.6. While they touch on distinct areas of the contracting operation, they do not always fall to different people. In Weber's terms, administrative and on-site functions may accumulate to a single person in the contractor's organization.

The Determinants of Consultation

The opportunities for consultative relations with contractors are conditioned by the range of organizational and occupational variables discussed thus far. The most obvious a priori factor is the regularity with which a tradesperson holds a formal managerial position.[13] In addition to being party to preproject planning, the foreman is also responsible for handling on-site matters. Foremen, similar to first-line supervisors in factory production, have direct contact with the workforce and assume responsibility for technical problems as they arise in the course of construction.

Foremen, however, do not always have opportunities for regular administrative consultations. When the contractor's organization includes one or more full-time supervisors there usually is a division of managerial functions that reduces the foreman's role in administrative affairs, but sometimes enhances it at the production level.

It also happens that those not holding formal managerial position periodically experience consultative interactions with employers. One does not have to be a foreman to be consulted by an employer. All workers acquire a working knowledge of the production process through direct experiences on the job. Sociologist Ken Kusterer (1978) has demonstrated the significance of such practical expertise born of direct involvement in the production process. Workers gain an understanding of the raw materials they transform, a sensitivity to the limitations of the tools they use, and a commonsense appreciation of the interrelated facets of the production system. This holds, as Kusterer argues, even in the mass production factory associated with the greatest extent of routinized and deskilled labor. In most situations there are reasons why workers are consulted directly about technical decisions. Their strategic location in the production process avails them of expertise not accessible to those higher in the organizational structure.

In construction, as has been shown, both workforce size and job-site stability have a significant impact on organizational structure. This, in turn, influences the relationship between hierarchical position and consultation in two ways. First, a very small project with few workers on an employer's payroll will not require the appointment of an official foreman, nor a formal division between management and labor on the construction site. Rather, production-related consultation can occur directly with craftworkers singly or as a group. In many cases group consultations are the direct result of small size. Technical problems on a small project will likely affect the ability of all workers for a specialty contractor to continue their work because they are doing the same task at different locations on the site, or working as a team on a single operation. It is a natural consequence that they will mutually consult when the same problem affects their tasks. Such a pattern of direct worker-employer consultation reflect the realistic variabilities, in terms of organizational contingency and practical activity, that occur on the construction site and form one project to the next.

The statistical analysis of workers' survey questionnaire responses reveals the multiple determinants of consultative relationships with employers (tables 2.7 and 2.8). As expected, the strongest and most stable predictor of administrative and on-site consultatons is regularly holding an official foremanship. Contractors do indeed rely on their formally designated management personnel to plan upcoming projects and to maintain control on the job. This finding in itself is hardly startling; except for the fact that the reference here is to the construction industry where presumably craft administration minimizes the role of formal managerial positions.

In addition, the impact of organizational and occupational factors are worthy of note. When organizational conditions justify them, contractors engage in more frequent interactions directly with the craftspeople they hire. In the present case,

Table 2.7. Zero-Order and Multiple Partial Correlation Coefficients for Administrative Consultation and On-Site Consultation with Managerial Position and Task Factors.

	Administrative Consultation	On-Site Consultation
Craft Complexity		
r	.12*	.10
partial r (controlling foreman-ship)	.05	.05
Partial r (controlling foreman-ship, size, duration bureaucracy, supervision, and self-direction)	.05	.00
Craft Mentality		
r	.22**	.32***
partial r (controlling foreman-ship)	.03	.19**
partial r (controlling foreman-ship, size, duration, bureaucracy, supervision, and self-direction)	.05	.22***
Foremanship		
r	.50***	.39***
partial r (controlling complexity, mentality)	.46***	.30***
partial r (controlling complexity, mentality, size, duration, bureaucracy, supervision, and self-direction)	.39***	.28***

*p<.05 **p<.01 ***p<.001

Table 2.8. Regressions of Administrative Consultation and On-Site Consultation with Job-Site Production Factors and Foremanship.

	Administrative Consultation	On-Site Consultation
Production Location		
On-Site Size (log)	-.05	-.04
Duration	-.13**	-.17***
Bureaucracy	-.07	-.06
Craft Complexity	.04	.00
Craft Mentality	.04	.22***
Foremanship	.40***	.30***
$\bar{R}^2$	.29	.20

*p<.10 **p<.05 ***p<.01

shorter projects seem to encourage the practice of direct consultations about preproject and on-site concerns. Conversely, workers on longer jobs tend to have fewer direct contacts with their employers. Other things being equal, a longer presence on the construction site may reflect a degree of stability in working conditions and managerial exigencies such that shifts in labor power and material can be planned for in advance. Unanticipated problems (such as, defective material or externally imposed delays) have less impact because they occur in the context of a broader time span and are more easily absorbed into the production schedule. On the other hand, when a contractor expects a job to last only a brief time, unforeseen delays can have a greater impact on his overall operation. Delays can disrupt the start of another project, or place serious shortrun strains on this organizational resources. In general, there are narrower financial margins for absorbing costly inefficiencies on projects of shorter duration. Thus, contractors must keep a closer managerial eye on them.

Most interesting, however, are the associations between consultation and occupational composition uncovered by the statistical analyses. Once again, occupational *craft* characteristics are more tenuously tied to other productive relations than is usually thought to be the case. Substantive complexity of work shows no significant impact on either consultaton variable; while working with written material has mixed effects. The division of mental and manual labor does correlate with consultation. However, with respect to administrative consultation, the relationship appears to be spurious. The association between mental work and administrative consultation is determined by its relationship to managerial position. In other words, mental labor on the construction site is related to more frequent consultations with employers only to the extent that foremen fulfill tasks on the construction site that place greater demands on their mental as well as physical abilities.

On the other hand, more involvement with mental labor on the job significantly increases the opportunities for on-site consultations, even when controlling for managerial position. With such tasks at hand, it is likely that contractors do not rely on delayed or second-hand reports or indirect surveillance to keep abreast of progress on the construction site. Rather, they often employ more direct person-to-person interactions with craft employees. This tendency is in keeping with general organizational practices, as established by the work of numerous organizational researchers.

To summarize this discussion, the frequency with which a tradesperson holds a formal management position as a foreman is the most important, but not exclusive, determinant of patterned consultative interactions with employers. Performing intellectually involving work also increases the likelihood of on-site consultations. The latter finding of the analysis supports the position that craft-related factors are significant secondary consideration in the structuring of the labor process in the building industry. Similarly, the organizational and entrepreneurial importance of the duration of the project emphasizes the overarching salience of managerial imperatives of coordination and control of production.

Before moving on to the issue of work autonomy, it is

necessary to mention that the discussion has oversimplified the actual situation by proceeding as if there is a unidirection causal ordering that places managerial position prior to managerial consultation. It is reasonable to posit such an ordering only for a given point in time, or for a specific job situation. I would argue, though, that the relationship when analyzed as it translates from one project to the next is actually bidirectional. The opportunities for consultation (even if fortuitous) often lead to a subsequent appointment to a foremanship position. An exchange in which the craftsperson impresses an employer with his or her knowledge and expertise may result in the offer of an official position to manage future projects. Of course, once obtained, the official position can be a source of accumulated advantage to the extent that it makes the chances for further consultative interactions less problematic. Stated slightly differently, there is probably a reciprocal and interdependent influence between the formal (management position) and contentual (quality of exchange) facets of the managerial location in the labor process.

Managerial Location and Work Autonomy

It is necessary to return to the issue of work autonomy in order to discuss the broader importance of the managerial location on the construction site. There are two facets to this inquiry. The first is the impact of the managerial location on the structure of work on the site. Specifically, the question is whether being a foreman and engaging in consultative relations increases self-direction and freedom from supervision. The second issue is the extent to which managerial location variables intervene in the relationships between on-site work autonomy and occupational and organizational factors.

Daily work on a construction site affords one many opportunities to see how foremen have greater autonomy than the craftworkers they supervise. The very tasks that are their responsibility lend themselves to a greater degree of independent decision making than those strictly production tasks performed by nonmanagerial craftworkers. Even when actually engaged in production, their position as their contractors' sole managerial agents on the site frees them from constant supervisory evaluations.

Moreover, there are many unanticipated situations that come about on the job which further enhance the foreman's autonomy. When workers run into problems completing their tasks, they call their foreman to decide or help decide how best to proceed. It is the very rare building that is constructed without alterations to the original architectural plans. Thus, craftworkers may not be able to do their work exactly as initially planned. For example, water and heating pipes may have to be rerouted if the placement of structural columns or walls have been changed. Similarly, electricians may have to run their wires slightly differently or place electrical lighting fixtures, outlets, and switches in different locations if there have been prior alterations in the work done by carpenters. Such production snags are not necessarily major problems, but they do require foremen to intervene.

The industry's subcontracting structure also increases the autonomy of foremen. However efficient subcontracting is as a way of distributing financial responsibility for construction work and truncating bureaucracy for the builder, it also creates many problems of coordination between the various trades on the construction site. In a real sense this aspect of subcontracting is an example of how the capitalist market creates financial efficiencies (by distributing risk and responsibility among numerous subcontractors) for the entrepreneurial builder, but production inefficiencies (the costs of which are passed on to the consumer). It is fairly common that workers from one trade assigned to a particular task find that they cannot proceed because workers from a different trade (and employed by a different contractor) had not completed their work. Or, equally disruptive, tradespeople from two different contractors are sent to the same place on the site to do jobs that simply cannot be done at the same time. Foreman have on-site responsibility for resolving such problems of intertrade coordination. They are thus in a position to make relatively independent decisions about rescheduling work and reassigning tasks to their crews.

It is interesting to note as well that these job-site functions of foremen are not tied only to the higher-skilled trades. They are important for foremen at all skill levels—laborer, painter, ironworker, carpenter, electrician, and plumber alike. Unexpected changes in the production schedule or coordination problems for tradespeople occur. Thus contractors usually rely on their on-site managerial agent to solve them.

Such straightforward connections between managerial location and work autonomy are clearly evident in the regression analyses shown in table 2.9. According to the building tradespeople surveyed, regularly holding a foremanship tends to reduce the degree of supervision and increase self-direction.[14] Similarly, frequent administrative consultative relationship with contractors has the effect of decreasing supervision and increasing self-direction on the job.[15]

In this it would appear that both formal and contentual facets of the managerial location are closely associated with greater autonomy in work on the construction site. However, the regression analyses also reveal patterns not easily uncovered by qualitative observational techniques.

First of all, in contrast to the effect of administrative consultation, on-site consultation operates to increase supervision. Why should interactions in which contractors are asking for the advice and knowledgeable judgments from craftworkers be a source of added supervision? The answer probably is that on-site consultaton, by definition, increases the number of contacts with contractors (or other management personnel) during the course of a project. Even though the explicit pretext for the interaction is the contractor's desire for an informed opinion, the contact also contains an unavoidable evaluative fact. Richard Sennet (1980) elaborates the point that in the industrial context the mere presence of a superordinate signifies that implicit or informal evaluations are occurring. The superficial qualities of interpositional exchange do not in and of themselves alter the deeper significance of the relationship. The hierarchical element adheres and gives meaning to the social relationship.[16] The connection between consultation and supervision also suggests that shifts in managerial style that encourage such bidirectional exchanges do not necessarily correlate with alterations in basic power relationships. The effect is only to remove the elements

Table 2.9. Regressions of Work Autonomy (Supervision and Self Direction) with Production Factors and Managerial Location.

| | Work Autonomy | | | |
| | Supervision | | Self-Direction | |
	1[a]	2	3	4
Production Location				
On-site Size (log)	.10	.10	-.09	-.08
Duration	.05	.07	-.07	-.10
Bureaucracy	.32***	.23***	-.28***	-.14**
Craft Complexity	-.07	-.05	-.03	-.04
Craft Mentality	-.08	-.03	.14**	.02
Managerial Location				
Foremanship	—	-.15**	—	.28***
Administrative Consultation	—	-.17***	—	.14*
On-Site Consultation	—	.13*	—	-.04
$\bar{R}^2$	.15	.19	.12	.20

*p<.10 **p<.05 ***p<.01
[a]Columns 1 and 3 are reproduced from table 2.5 for comparison.

of control to a more subtle level (Strauss 1963; Silver 1981b).[17]

The extent to which the managerial variables have intervening impact on the relationships between organizational, occupational, and autonomy variables further evidences the central role of the on-site manager. Variables associated with the managerial location attenuate but do not eliminate the impact of bureaucracy. Thus, while foremen are generally supervised less often and exercise self-direction more often than their non-managerial counterparts, working in the more bureaucraticized organization (in which there are more managers) increases supervision and decreases self-direction for foremen as well as for the tradespeople in their crews.

Furthermore, managerial variables have even greater impact on the autonomy-occupation relationship. Comparing columns three and four of table 2.9 it is seen that the effect of craft mentality on self direction is eliminated by the inclusion of the managerial variables. The apparent conclusion is that the intellectual involvement attached to managerial positions, but not to productive activity, leads to greater self-direction on the construction site. In other words, frequently using written material on the job may result in greater self-direction, but it is foremen who usually (if not always) assume responsibility for those activities.[18]

Social Relations on the Construction Site

The final topic to be discussed in this chapter is the social relations among building tradespeople that develop on the job. Discussing the patterns of intertrade contacts that occur in the course of production, involves the questions of which trades work closely together and which trades tend to come into contact with many or few other trades. Interest here is not in the informal social interactions, friendships, and nonproduction social activities workers engage in during the workday. Those topics have been handled extensively by others (for example, Myers 1946; Haas 1974, 1977; Cherry 1974; Riemer 1979; Applebaum 1981). Nothing would be gained by yet another addition to the literature on play while on the job, girl watching, or workers' symbolic attachments to their trades.

The question of production-related contacts bears on various issues in the organization of craft work.[19] Through my years in the industry, I have been struck by the degree to which the organization of the labor process itself determines the opportunities for social relations among workers on the job. Notwithstanding the notion that construction work is a craft-directed operation in which workers are left on their own, one's role in production largely determines which other tradespeople one deals with on the job. For example, structural ironworkers and operating engineers work closely together. The heavy structural steel I-beams and reinforcing rods are hoisted to the proper elevation by operating engineers working their crane or derrick. The ironworkers then jockey and fasten the steel into place. The coordination and cooperation between those trades must be close and continuous if fatal accidents are to be avoided. On the other hand, neither one has much, if any, contact with trades working at later stages of production such as plasterers, drywallers, tile setters, or painters.

Nontemporal factors are important, as well. Wallpaper-hanging and painting obviously are closely related crafts. The work of those in these two trades are closely coordinated. But their work often brings them into contact with electricians, carpet installers, carpenters, and many other trades. What you do as well as when you do it establish the parameters of your social relations on the job.[20]

Such production-based interactions between trades can add to the complexity of work in ways that are not often recognized. For one thing, doing your job may require cooperating with others doing very different tasks. Handling the diverse demands of a well developed role-set is more stimulating, and at times more challenging, than working in relative isolation from other trades. Second, such intertrade coordination adds to the complexity of work by requiring tradespeople with broader role-sets to have at least a secondary working knowledge of some aspects of those other trades. Not wishing to overburden the reader with too many technically detailed examples, I will only state that from extensive experience such secondary knowledge of other building trades can make the difference for workers between being able to do their work easily and efficiently or having to continuously refigure plans, make repeated adjustments, and, ultimately, work harder than would otherwise have been necessary. Few things are as frustrating than a job made more difficult by the activities of other workers without enough knowledge to be considerate of the needs of your trade. Conversely, nothing makes work easier, not to mention more enjoyable, than working on projects where everyone seems to possess enough general knowledge such that cooperation and mutual sensitivity to the needs of workers in other trades are the rule. It also can be the difference between a building that is a hodgepodge of minor (and at times major) mistakes and corrections versus one that is sturdy, well-built, and as functional and attractive as initially intended.

The quantitative analysis presented in table 2.10 identifies the major determinants of social relationships on the job. As can readily be seen, explanatory power largely resides in the combined effects of occupational variables. Jobs that entail mental calculation and frequent reference to written material also engender regular contact with other tradespeople. In other words, the division of physical and mental labor influences the degree of contact the worker maintains with others doing different work.[21]

In direct contrast, the complexity of work, has an inverse relationship to intertrade relationships. People in the higher-skilled building trades tend to make fewer contacts outside their own trade while doing their job. Even though complex tasks demand greater intensity or intricacy of interactions on the job—requiring the worker to establish and maintain mutual and bidirectional interactions with employers and workers in the same trade—the effect simultaneously is to restrict the range of social contacts among other trades. Complex tasks, at least in the context of building work, bind the worker to a narrowly circumscribed network of associations tied to one's trade and employers.

This can be compared to the less skilled trades such as laborer and helper occupations. Their jobs apparently bring them into contact with a relatively larger sphere of other trades. The laborers at the construction site often fulfill many informal social functions precisely because of their unique position in the building process. The generality of the laborers' tasks and the fact that their work takes them to all parts of the site mean that they also come into contact with almost every other trade entering the site. In fact, because of the role of the laborer, workers from other trades often will seek them out when first coming on the job. Laborers are on the construction site from a project's beginning to its conclusion. They are in the best position to ac-

Table 2.10. Regression of the Number of Intertrade Contacts with Production Factors, Management Location Factors, and Work Autonomy Factors.

	Number of Intertrade Contacts
Production Location	
On-Site Size (log)	.12
Duration	.13
Bureaucracy	.05
Craft Complexity	-.26***
Craft Mentality	.29***
Managerial Location	
Foremanship	.04
Administrative Consultation	-.09
On-Site Consultation	-.01
Work Autonomy	
Supervision	-.01
Self Direction	-.09
$\bar{R}^2$	.12

***$p < .01$

cumulate important site-specific knowledge. Much of the laborers' site-specific knowledge would seem mundane and inconsequential to an outsider, but knowing the location of running water, supply shanties, and even the whereabouts of other workers is important information to the building tradesperson. Getting such information from a laborer can mean many steps and much time saved while getting acquainted with a new work site. In fact, such knowledge can be an important source of power for laborers on the job. In many respects their lack of craft power is compensated for by their social power. There is a direct analogy here to the sources of power Michel Crozier

(1964) found to be available to maintenance workers in his classic study of French bureaucracy (also, see Perrow's [1970] treatment of an industrial relations department in an American organization). The extensive role-set is a social advantage in the work organization partly because it supplies information and knowledge about organizational operations and the production process. But it also places incumbents in a good position to serve informal integrating functions in the labor process. For example, the laborer can, if he or she chooses, relay messages between workers at distant locations on the site in the course of his or her own work. A laborer can also do the tradesperson the favor of bringing a needed tool or material, or check on the status of an area of the site the tradesperson expects to work at in the near future.

As a final point, it is also interesting to note that managerial position does not have appreciable influence on social network formation on the job. It might have been expected that managerial position would increase the role-set. However, craft occupational variables emerge as the salient determinants of social relations in the labor process. As shall be seen in chapter four, they are also important influencers of social associations off the job.

Conclusion

Having used a combination of interpretative and quantitative data to describe the structure of work on the construction site, it is now possible to elaborate on three conclusions of the analysis. First, the foregoing discussion makes it clear that the label "craftsperson" or "tradesperson" is not a guarantee of work that is complex, inherently interesting, or relatively autonomous. In this respect, craftworkers in construction do not necessarily differ very much from their counterparts in other industries—a similarity possibly deriving from the imperatives of control and efficiency common to both industrial settings in the capitalist political economy. As major sources of constraint on the labor process such imperatives supersede socalled craft traditions in the determination of work practices.

The primacy of organizational considerations further suggests that the dual imperatives of efficient coordination of production and effective control of workers' labor often operate in contradiction. As I have described, production inefficiencies are often the result of contractors' need to control the labor process; a far cry from the idea that contractors are forced to rely on craft administration.

The issue of control also raises the question of the division of labor, especially that between physical and intellectual labor. Manual work that also affords frequent opportunities to do head work allows one to develop his or her range of mental and social capacities and to avoid the ennui of repetition. As social research in many industrial settings makes clear, it is not simply a matter of manual, blue-collar work. Studies of office and clerical occupations show that white-collar jobs can be routinized, repetitious, and debasing. It is the balance between the mental and manual functions that establishes a barrier against the drudgery of routine. On the construction site the need to refer to architectural plans, project schedule, bluepeints, and technical manuals ensures that periods of strictly physical operations are not onerously long.

Those construction jobs that are not compartmentalized into manual and mental tasks reflect work that is more interesting and more absorbing of the attention and energies of the worker. When these components are linked in the craft occupation, they enhance the individual's role in the labor process. Manual/mental interdependence means that manual operations can be performed only if the intellectual aspects are first addressed. Conversely, intellectual components are only significant to the extent that the worker has the physical dexterity and skill to complete the required tasks. Clearly, jobs that integrate mental and physical labor situate the worker more centrally in the labor process.

Finally, the fact that managerial variables loom so large in the foregoing analyses indicates that it is class over and above craft that is the determining factor in the labor process. Managerial class location emerges as the single most important set of factors influencing work experiences. Occupational factors associated with craft work are best understood as secondary elements of production relations. It is possible, therefore, to speak of a class of tradespeople located between craftworkers and contractors. In some respects, it seems to be a contradictory class, in Erik Wright's sense, that members have a foot in each of the polar classes. In other respects, it may possess more autonomous class characteristics. In order to gain a clearer perspective on this, it is necessary to extend the analysis beyond work structure per se to include employment and trade union practices.

3

TRADE UNIONS, CONTRACTORS, AND EMPLOYMENT

If the construction site remains very much the hidden abode, what can be said of the local unions of the building trades? The commonplace association of the building and construction unions with big labor at the national level leaves unanswered many questions about how local unions and district conçils operate in the local product and labor markets. Local union officials themselves contribute to the mystery by hiding their organizations' activities, both positive and negative, behind a veil of secrecy. Whether resolving collective bargaining disputes, organizing in the nonunion sector, or engaging in the broader political aspects of labor relations, the guiding principle is to maintain a low public profile. There thus exists an almost unbridgeable gap between the actual world of conflict, bargaining, and hand-shake agreements that take place in the offices of union officials and construction contractors and the abstracted images of unions that derive from social scientists' analyses of national wage patterns, strike rates, and the public statements of representatives from international unions and contractor associations.

Generally speaking, unions are "organizations designed to protect and enhance the social and economic welfare of their members" (Tannenbaum 1965). In theory, trade unions affect the worklives of their membership in two spheres. First, it is the decision-making mechanism through which workers first define

75

their collective interests and then express their collective will. In this sense, it forms an organizational context for individual participation in decisions and policies having direct impact on workers' livelihoods. Second, it is the organizational vehicle for protecting and advancing those interests against outside political and economic forces. From this vantage it is the interorganizational relations of the union, primarily those with employers' and other union organizations, that influence workers' lives. These spheres of activity are, or course, highly interrelated. But as numerous authors have pointed out, the reciprocities between union political democracy and union goal-effectiveness are complex and often contradictory (Aronowitz 1983; Von Beyme 1980; Montgomery 1979; Brecher 1972; Serrin 1971; Michels 1962; Lipset et al 1956). As in other industries, external political and economic pressures often encourage construction union officials to sidestep truly democratic processes; while the principles of democratic rank-and-file participation are not always compatible with the backroom deals of free-market entrepreneurs. Thus it is both the union's participatory practices (or lack of them) and the union's role as collective bargaining and labor relations agent that defines the nature of the construction craft union.

The internal characteristics of the various construction trade unions tend to be similar, although they do differ in size and in some formal structures.[1] The typical union is administered by an elected body of full-time officials and an executive board of elected officers. Paid officials, usually referred to as business managers, agents, representatives, or delegates, are responsible for the daily operation of the union; handling the distribution of work among members needing employment and managing contractual relations with employers about ongoing or upcoming projects. The executive board acts as the directive component, making policy about some of the local union's financial and collective bargaining decisions and making recommendations to the membership about others. In theory, the board establishes policy, while the role of the business manager and agents is to execute the board's and membership's wills. In practice, the two administrative branches are often intertwined in a single political entity. Paid officials and executive board officers usually run for office on a single ticket headed by the person running for the top position. Thus administrative control actually rests with that person, although oppositional elements do occasionally get elected to the board. In such cases the relationship between business manager and executive board can become antagonistic and serve as the arena for intense internal political conflict.

Rank-and-file participation occurs through monthly or semimonthly membership meetings. Members hear reports from various officers on financial and international union matters and from the agents about current projects in the local's jurisdiction. In addition, they hear the recommendations of the executive board on pending decisions and vote on matters brought before the body. The dynamics of the membership meetings will vary according to prevailing circumstances. Prior to and during contract negotiations attendance tends to be higher than at other times, and discussions from the floor will be longer and more intense. Election time, of course, is another period when attendance and active involvement of the rank-and-file increases. Throughout the year attendance at membership meetings tend to average between 10 percent and 30 percent of the active membership, with larger unions having somewhat higher rates of attendance ($r = .17$).

The local craft union is also part of an interunion network formally structured in a Building Trades Council (BTC). The relationship between the BTC and member unions differs between regions of the country (Mills 1972). In the region of this study, the BTC forms a loose confederation of local unions from the various building and construction trades and is administered by a single full-time officer. The BTC has no actual power over the affairs of individual member unions. Rather, it serves as a forum for regular discussion, an organizational mechanism for resolving interunion conflicts that arise from time to time, and as a liaison for the member unions with local government, economic, and political agencies.

In addition, agents meet in weekly organizing meetings within each geographical jurisdiction (the political boundaries between counties serve as convenient dividing lines, reflecting the importance of local politics to affairs in the industry).

Organizing meetings are smaller decentralized offshoots of the BTC and, like the BTC, have no real control over individual unions. Agents participate on a voluntary basis, although informal pressures serve to encourage them to attend and cooperate. The organizing meetings function as information sharing sessions about local conditions, ongoing projects, and interunion politics. Additionally, the meetings provide the opportunity for cooperation between the various craft unions in resolving problems on specific projects.

On the last point, it is important to point out the labor law restricts the extent to which unions of different trades can aid each other in conflicts with employers (Feldacker 1980; Mills 1972). Business agents are thus reticent to risk legal actions against their own local unions or against the BTC. Nonetheless, they find ways to cooperate informally while minimizing the risks of legal sanctions. The support of other trade unions can be a major factor influencing the success or failure of a single local's attempt to favorably resolve a dispute with a contractor.

Of course, the most important set of interorganizational relations for the craft union are those with employers and their trade associations. Local unions sign trade agreements (TA) with subcontractors for their trade. All ten unions studied deal with a contractors' association. The negotiated contract between the craft union and the trade's employer association establish the prevailing standards for the area. Independent contractors, those not belonging to an association, are signed to separate agreements which conform to the TA.

The trade agreement serves as the framework for conditions and wages, not as a categorical guarantee. The contract specifies what amounts to the upper limits for wages and on-the-job working conditions. Through mechanisms discussed more fully later in the chapter, actual conditions are often below what is formally prescribed in the TA. The degree to which they approximate formal standards is one result of the dynamic relationship between the craft union and employers.

The craft union ostensibly operates to defend the working conditions and job rights of craftspeople in their relations with employers. It is the principal agency for establishing wage and working conditions standards in the union's geographic and occupational jurisdictions. This, of course, is the usual collective bargaining functions previously mentioned.

Second, the trade union aids workers in handling conflicts with employers when questions about adherence to the provisions of the TA arise in particular job situations. Areas of dispute often concern wages and working conditions on specific construction sites. Problems in interpretation and application of the TA come up fairly regularly because there are so many different projects, most with different contractors and each with its own slightly different set of conditions. Usually problems on a job can be settled informally by mutual consent among the workers, employer, and union steward. Sometimes the involvement of the business agent serves to resolve the matter. At the final level, the typical contract specifies standardized procedures for the resolution of grievances. Most often this takes the form of a joint trade board, comprised of union and employer representatives, which hears the case under dispute and renders a ruling.

Third, the union serves as hiring and placement agency for members. Construction workers who fall out of work usually report their unemployment to their local union; thus making them eligible for reassignment. Local unions use various methods for determining priority for reassignment. Some consider seniority, those with more years of union membership having first choice from among new jobs. Others reassign members based on recency of last employment, the member unemployed the longest being first on the list. Both methods conform to what is typically termed "hiring hall" practices, that is, situations wherein the union has the sole right to allocate employment opportunities. The alternative method—and by far the most common—is the referral system. Under referral procedures the union maintains a listing of workers available for employment from which the employer has the right to select those craftspeople of his choosing.

In practice, what actually operates is a marriage of the two procedures. Employers formally retain hiring and firing prerogatives under the provisions of the trade agreement, but do not exercise them. Instead, they leave to the union the responsibility for fulfilling requests for workers. Employers often reserve the right to refuse particular workers, preferentially to select others, and to limit the number of workers on a site. The result is a referral system over which employers retain effective control, but with the formal appearances of a hiring hall.

The maintenance and expansion of employment opportunities for its members remains a continuously problematic goal for the local union leadership under this system. For instance, current labor laws restrict the methods trade unions can employ in efforts to secure employment for their members. According to Landrum Griffin Act of 1959, it is illegal for unions to utilize membership as a criterion for determining job placement. Hiring hall and referral practices technically pertain only to those criteria bearing on workers' skill qualifications. In theory, the union cannot refuse the referral of nonmembers if they possess the skills of the craft. Even in those states which permit closed-shop agreements, nonunion workers must be permitted to become members after seven days. If the union refuses membership such workers have the legal right to remain on the job regardless of union policy. It is relatively difficult under these circumstances for unions to monopolize labor supply through restrictive labor practices under anything other than ideal conditions.

Craft Union Power: Militancy and Production Location

The local union's ability to meet the needs of the membership (by minimizing unemployment, reducing the need to seek nonunion work, and protecting members' contractual rights on the job) is best understood in terms of the power relationships between unions and contractors.[2] Two sources of union power bear on its ability to perform for its members. One is the structural advantages specific to various locations in the production process. Power dependencies between workers and contractors tend to correspond to placement and role in production. Thus, some trades have more power vis-à-vis employers than others. The other source of power is the union organization itself. Workers' willingness to engage in collective action in defense of group interests stands as the foundation of workers' power in all systems of production.

There are a few aspects of building production that bear directly on union-contractor power relations: occupational composition; centrality in the production process; trade union size; and contractor size. Each influences the strength of the craft union's position when attempting to protect the interests of its members.

The substantive complexity of work establishes basic employment dependencies. Workers with more technical skill have the advantage of not being easily replaced by an employer. A contractor is more dependent on his employees when there are relatively few other workers in the labor market with the appropriate skills and knowledge. He or she is thus in a weaker position to push for concessions from craftworkers when there is little in the way of an alternative labor supply. Hence, substantively complex craft occupations are significant in giving "the working class more effective means of pressure . . . ; one does not replace an electronics technician overnight as one replaces a semi-skilled worker" (Mallet 1975,41; also see Stark 1979; Montgomery 1979; Jackson 1984). One can easily observe this basic protection in operation on the construction site. Workers in the skilled trades are usually quicker to object to conditions they find unsatisfactory and more demanding that the situation be altered to suit them. They also tend to be the one, when confronted by management, to threaten to walk off the job: "If you want me to leave, just say so. I don't need this job. There are plenty of others I can go to!" In contrast, a general contractor's supervisor once ordered two semiskilled workers off the job with the following remark: "Just get your tools together and go! There are a thousand guys I could get. And they would do it right!"

Centrality in the production process likewise reflects the relative power of the workforce. The greater the functional importance and the more centrally located in the process, the greater is the organizational dependence on those workers. In construction, the element of productive centrality corresponds fairly closely to the point at which a craft enters in the process. Other things being equal, those trades that come on the site earlier are those which play the roles most central to the overall project. Tasks pertaining to the laying of the foundation, constructing the frame, wiring, and piping are the ones most related to the structural integrity of the building. They obviously are the tasks on which the work of later trades are based. Temporal primacy on the construction site carries with it the additional advantage of reducing economic pressures since unanticipated delays and unforseen costs have not yet created budgetary cutbacks and greater productivity emphases. In general, the earlier a trade enters the construction process the greater its locationally based power in dealing with contractors.

Two final factors related to production power, union and employer size, have more ambiguous influences. The former is a source of power to the extent that it indicates control over labor supply. Union size is a further asset to the extent that it means more organizational resources available to union officials. On the other hand, the size of the membership also determines the amount and kinds of pressures on elected officials. A larger membership may make it more difficult for the union's administration to keep unemployment rates at a politically acceptable level. Large size may also mean less opportunity for officials to maintain interpersonal and affective ties to the rank-and-file; and therefore a tendency for the membership to use strictly objective criteria such as unemployment in evaluating the performance of the administration in office.

Similarly, contractor size, as reflected by the average number of workers usually hired for projects, can either enhance or reduce local union power. In one respect contractor size determines the dependence of the contractor on the union for supplying labor. In other respects, however, the larger contractor inherently offers direct relief to the union agent seeking to place his unemployed members on jobs. This means a relatively weak bargaining position for the union since larger employers can hold out the promise of numerous jobs in exchange for project agreement concessions.

The second source of craft union power, militancy, has been the historical cornerstone of workers' power in every industrial context. It is the capacity and demonstrated willingness to formally withhold labor; or refuse collectively to participate in the production process. In addition, the union officials' willingness to engage in various other actions based on their perception of the union-contractor relationship as being basically conflictual (as opposed to cooperative) indicates the trade union's militancy.[3]

The militant craft union has many resources at its disposal besides a formal strike to utilize in dealing with contractors. As noted earlier, the union seeks to protect the membership not only through collective bargaining and contract negotiations, of which the strike is now an institutionalized component (Aronowitz 1983; Serrin 1971) but also by monitoring ongoing projects for infractions of the TA and abridgements of members' rights. The regularity and intensity with which union officials closely scrutinize conditions on the sites in the area is one method of exercising its organizational power.

Many of the tactics employed by union officials are, however, illegal or quasilegal by current labor law standards. For the most part, they center around a willingness of business agents to risk unfavorable court rulings and to rely on informal channels of communication with contractors. The differences between union-employer interactions that fall within the standard collective bargaining structure and those which are either conspiratorial or acts of intimidation are not well defined. They often depend on prevailing circumstances and subjective interpretations. Similarly, the cooperative relations among the officials of the various building trade unions are often of questionable legal standing. The point at which information exchange and mutual consultation become collaboration in restraint of free trade, or indicate the presence of a secondary boycott is not at all clear. In many ways the conduct of labor relations in the construction industry conforms to a contest of intrigue and subterfuge. The borderline legal status of inter-union cooperation requires a great deal of trust among union officials. At the same time, successful application of work stoppages, slow-downs, informational common situs picketing, refusals to cross the picket lines of other trades, or other job-related actions depends on the accurate reading of the employer and the judgments of union agents about the chances for retaliation, legal or otherwise, from the contractor.

Locational power in production and union militancy are logically independent although they may converge empirically (table 3.1). All unions possess the same theoretical capacity for militant action. In contrast, power based on locational factors is not distributed evenly among trade unions. Their differential access to the sources of power has obvious consequences for power enactment in union-contractor relations. Locationally disadvantaged unions are forced to rely solely on their militancy, while those with locational sources of leverage have the option of utilizing structural sources of power rather than militant tactics. Locationally advantaged unions are likely to rely on locational power first and leave militant actions in reserve as measures of last resort since there are fewer risks and lower potential costs associated with locationally based power. Moreover, locational advantages can become structured features of nonantagonistic labor relations; allowing for greater cooperation and mutual benefit while leaving the costs to be borne by those in less advantaged locations.

What is here then is the suggestion of a parallel to sectoral analyses that distinguish between core and periphery or monopoly and competitive sectors (for example, Averitt 1968; O'Connor 1973; Edwards 1979; Baron and Bielby 1980). Within the construction industry it is possible to differentiate between core-type unions—those at central productive locations, representing a more skilled and larger membership and using more cooperative and less militant tactics in dealing with larger employers—and perhiphery-type unions—those with less skilled and smaller memberships at less central productive locations and using more militant tactics against smaller employers. In general, given an obvious political preference for locationally based power over the other, unions that rely on the former will not as often have to resort to militant actions. This suggests an accumulation of advantage for some craft unions. The confluence of structural sources of advantage minimizes the need to use more risky practices; a point emphasized by market segmentation theorists in reference to intersectoral comparisons.[4]

This basic power differential between unions has more than mere theoretical or statistical significance. It is a major practical factor in the activities of business agents trying to protect against the infringement of nonunion elements. According to many of the business agents that were engaged in extended

Table 3.1. Zero-Order Correlations Among Trade Union Variables and Production Variables

	1	2	3	4	5	6
Trade Union						
Militancy[a]	-					
Union Size (log)	-.50**	-				
Production Location						
Craft Complexity	-.48**	-.05	-			
Craft Centrality	-.64**	.77***	-.02	-		
Contractor Size (log)	.02	.24	-.21	.33	-	
Labor Supply	-.57	.49	-.04	.32	.15	-
X̄	-.03	6.02	-12.23	2.42	.14	9.28
SD	1.64	.77	2.72	1.18	.7	2.97

*p<.10   **p<.05   ***p<.01

[a] All variable scores are to be read in the positive direction (for example, more militancy, larger size, large labor supply).

discussions, attempts to organize a job are often hampered by an absence of cooperation from key trades. The subcontracting structure makes it possible for builders/general contractors (GC) to have unionized firms do some parts of a job and nonunion contractors do others. GCs try to protect their own interests by subcontracting only central production functions to union companies (for example, operating engineers, ironwork, electrical work). In so doing, they guarantee themselves adequate labor supply and top quality production for such essential functions as laying the foundation, erecting the steel skeleton, and wiring the structure for electricity; while planning to save on costs for other functions by contracting them out to nonunion firms.

This presents obvious problems for the unions trying to organize the nonunion segments of a project. Their best chances for success are tied to union workers on the job either refusing to cross an informational picket line or refusing to work alongside nonunion trades.[5] Unfortunately for them, the locationally advantaged unions are often not willing to risk the cooperative and mutually beneficial relationships they enjoy with their employers by taking such actions. Because these unions rely on their production location rather than militancy as their source of labor relations power, they are usually not in a position to have to worry about the other unions similarly refusing to cooperate with them. The less advantaged unions, however, relying as they do on militant job actions, are considerably weakened by this position. It is also the source of considerable hostility and antagonism between the officials of core and peripheral trade unions.

In addition to the above factors, the relative availability of labor within a craft (Labor Supply) also influences the competitive power relationship between craft union and contractor.[6] Other things being equal, the union is in a better bargaining position when the labor supply is low and in a poor position when it is high. Conversely, the contractor's bargaining position is enhanced when many workers are seeking employment and weakened when there are relatively few craftspeople out of work.

Labor supply outcomes of the union-contractor relationship have a duel effect on workers' employment opportunity structure. One function of the construction union is to serve as a repository for volitional resources not stored by the employer. This permits contractors to avoid the costs of maintaining a constant payroll during slack periods (Bourdon and Levitt 1980; Gordon and Becker 1966; Stinchcombe 1959). The start of a new project requires that there be craftspeople available for work precisely at that moment. Similarly, the completion of a project means simultaneous unemployment for workers. In other words, contractors favor a large pool of craftworkers from which they can draw necessary labor and to which they can return surplus labor. Large craft unions thus bear the dual burdens of a weaker bargaining position by virtue of a larger labor supply and the political liabilities associated with high unemployment for the membership as a whole.

Craftworker Employment: Unemployment, Nonunion Employment, TA Concessions

The ability of the building trades unions to serve their collective bargaining and protective functions should not be taken for granted, as it often is by the popular and business presses. Local trades unions differ as regards their labor relations environments, as well as their comparative resources for dealing with them. Unions also face many common problems that limit their activities and reduce their potential effectiveness.

The bottom line, of course, is that it is the craftworkers themselves who are most affected. Three conditions stand out as the most direct and important elements of workers' economic and social welfare: unemployment, nonunion employment, and trade agreement concessions. They are also among the most problematic aspects of labor relations in the local market. They stand therefore at the nexus joining workers' quality of work and employment as craftspeople, the trade unions' ability to achieve its formally established goals, and contractors' ability to extract profit from and maintain control over the labor process. One does not have to subscribe to a Marxist class theory to appreciate the inherent antagonisms between labor and capital about these three basic conditions of employment. For each, the interests are in direct and immediate opposition (table 3.2).

Table 3.2. Trade Union and Contractor Orientations Toward Employment Structure

	Trade Union	*Contractor*
Employment/ Unemployment	Low unemployment favors union power in labor relations; increases workers' economic security, enhances agents' political power.	Moderate to high unemployment increases contractor power in labor relations; eases control problems on job sites.
Nonunion Employment Sector	Contracted nonunion sector favors union power; expanded nonunion sector increases wage and conditions competition; reduces union cohesion.	Moderately expanded nonunion sector benefits employers in labor relations; permits double-breasted operations contracted nonunion sector limits labor alternatives for contractor.
Trade Agreement Concessions/ Compliance	Full compliance is direct benefit to workers; reduces political pressures on agents from members and agents from other crafts.	Limited compliance is direct addition to profitability; eases control problems on job sites/legitimation; weakens union cohesion.

Unemployment, used by contractors to help satisfy their economic and control imperatives, is, at the individual level, a direct threat to the income security of workers. At the organizational level, it weakens the political position and collective bargaining strength of the trade union officials. Both types of unemployment (unemployment and labor supply are used to distinguish between individual and organizational level variables) increase the ability of contractors to press for various kinds of concessions from individual workers and union officials. Similarly, nonunion work favors contractors' power; at least to a point. It provides a visible competitive factor to which the unionized contractor can refer when negotiating with unions and individual craftworkers. Third, patterns of TA noncompliance that yield substandard working conditions, the use of poorly designed equipment, unsafe or unhealthful techniques, and wage concessions translate into lower costs and greater profits for the contractor. In contrast, the interests of both individual workers and their unions are served best by the opposite set of conditions. Union power and individual welfare are improved by low unemployment, a small nonunion sector, and full compliance with the trade agreement.

Unemployment as a variable tapping one dimension of workers' opportunity structure is an easily understood and obviously important condition for individual craftspeople. The other two variables, however, demand some additional explanation before discussing an empirical analysis. The frequency with which union workers find it necessary to seek employment in the nonunion residential sector of the building industry (nonunion employment) reflects the problematic situation presented by nonunion contracting. As long as union work is not available to all union members at all times, there is the temptation to seek nonunion opportunities. According to the estimates of business agents interviewed, about 25 percent of the rank-and-file regularly work in nonunion settings when union employment opportunities are in short supply. This practice is highly sensitive to situational factors, however, as reflected by the range of responses between the representatives of the different locals. At one extreme an agent reports that none of his members switch to nonunion work. At the other, one official estimates that as much as 98 percent of the local's membership do nonunion work in the residential sector when they cannot get unionized employment. Because residential and commercial construction differ in both basic design and materials, occupational differences account for much of this variation. There are greater opportunities for residential sector work for painters, carpenters, electricians, and paperhangers than there are for ironworkers, operating engineers, or bricklayers.

Direct reports from rank-and-file confirm the perceptions of union officials (table 3.3). Overall, 43 percent of the craftspeople who returned questionnaires report doing nonunion residential work at least on an occasional basis. Almost 20 percent report regular patterns of nonunion work and 7.4 percent work in unorganized situations most or all of the times they cannot find union work. The finding that so many craftspeople interviewed have to rely on this type of employment for at least part of their income reflects negatively on the union's ability to control the labor market. Nonunion work pays lower wages, offers no fringe benefits, entails poorer working conditions, and little if any protection from the prerogatives of contractors (Bourdon and Levitt 1980).

It is in a similar manner that noncompliance with the trade agreement indicates that most local unions have problems in their collective bargaining relationships with contractors. Non-

Table 3.3. The Regularity of Residential, Nonunion Employment Among Union Tradespeople (including Foremen). Distribution of responses to the question; "How often do you work directly for homeowners?"

	Number	Percent
No jobs	138	56.8
Rare Jobs	57	23.5
Some Jobs	30	12.3
Most Jobs	15	6.2
Every Job	3	1.2
Missing	3	—
	246	100

compliance comes about in two ways. Project agreements are formal arrangements between contractors and unions that pertain to particular construction sites. Depending on the specific situation, they are sought by general or specialty contractors for exclusions from the TA. In theory, project agreements allow for a degree of flexibility required by variable conditions across different jobs which cannot be handled by the TA (Mills 1972). The project agreement amends the rules of employment as specified in the TA so that they provide both satisfactory conditions for craftworkers on the job and adjustments to general TA provisions needed by the contractor.

The most frequent argument made by contractors for the necessity of project agreements is their inability to compete with the increasing presence of nonunion contractors. They contend that as long as they must estimate costs on the basis of work practices and wages specified in union TAs, they cannot match the bids of their nonunion counterparts. The willingness of local unions to grant project agreements has made their prevalence a serious and growing threat to the protections won over the years through collective bargaining.[7] The practice of regularly granting permission for substandard wages and working conditions is symptomatic of basic weaknesses of local trade unions. In other words, craft unions demonstrate in practice a relative inability to uphold the formal provisions of their TAs negotiated through collective bargaining.

Second, the problem is compounded by the similar arrangements made directly between contractors and workers. Contractors seeking to improve profit margins or to minimize losses on various projects will approach workers directly without going through formal channels. Workers often find it necessary to accept substandard conditions as a means of getting a job. As will be discussed more fully, this can take the form of acting as inside contractors (lumping), agreeing to work under unsafe or unhealthful conditions, or accepting below-scale wages or fringe benefits.

The pervasiveness of the problems of TA compliance is reflected by data from the study (table 3.4). All of the local union agents interviewed on this issue acknowledge its presence. Agents from every local report having at least occa-

Table 3.4. The Regularity of Trade Agreement (TA) Concessions Experienced By Tradespeople (including Foremen).

(A)
"How often are you [Business Agent] able to enforce all the provisions of your Trade Agreement?"

	Number (members)	Percent
No jobs	0	0
Rare jobs	38	16.7
Some jobs	141	62.2
Most jobs	48	21.1
Every job	0	0
Missing	19	—
	246	100

(B)
"How often are you [member] pressured by your employers to ignore the rules of the Trade Agreement in order to stay on the job or be hired?"

	Number (members)	Percent
No jobs	90	36.9
Rare jobs	54	22.1
Some jobs	61	25.0
Most jobs	31	12.7
Every job	8	3.3
Missing	2	—
	246	100

sional instances where they are unable to enforce the full extent of the TA. Two representatives are unable to uphold their contracts on most sites. Five report such inabilities to occur moderately often and two are occasionally unable to enforce their TA. This pattern, shown in terms of the relative distribution of rank-and-file craftspeople, shows that most workers belong to unions moderately successful in enforcing the TA (62.2 percent). Approximately equal proportions of workers are members of unions with high and low success in upholding formal standards (21.1 percent and 16.8 percent).

Table 3.4 also shows the distribution of responses by members about how often they are personally pressured to ignore aspects of the TA in order to be hired or to stay on a job. Approximately 63 percent report occasional or more frequent instances of such pressures, while 16 percent report them to arise on most or every job site they work on. Obviously, the majority of building tradespeople interviewed do not take it for granted that they will work on sites where conditions actually reflect their union trade agreement.

Not nearly so obvious are how production and labor-market factors affect the workers' employment. Among them, only labor supply significantly affects unemployment (table 3.5, column 1). While it is neither surprising nor illuminating to find a positive association between aggregate and individual measures of unemployment, that skill level, production centrality, and union militancy have no direct consequences for how

Table 3.5. The Regressions of Individual Employment Variables on Trade Union Factors, Production Factors, and Labor Supply.

	Unemploy-ment	Nonunion Employment	TA Concessions
Trade Union			
Union Militancy	.01	.33**	.42**
Union Size (log)	-.02	-.81***	-.07
Production Location			
Craft Complexity	.00	.19**	.01
Craft Centrality	.01	.57***	.22
Contractor Size (log)	.00	-.12*	.16**
Labor Supply	.27***	.14*	.32***
R̄²	.05	.32	.12

*p < .10   p < .05   p < .01

often tradespeople find themselves out of work does warrant further consideration.

How often workers pursue nonunion employment opportunities (table 3.5, column 2) is sensitive to a wider set of factors. As would be expected, a large labor supply tends to encourage workers, regardless of their trade, to seek employment outside of the unionized sector. Working for homeowners in residential construction is one way building tradespeople try to supplement their incomes when aggregate unemployment in their trade is high. Other conditions, however, have stronger impacts on workers' attempts to cross over into nonunion areas.

Union and contractor size both tend to reduce nonunion employment for two basic reasons. First, residential construction tends to be less consequential for those trades where projects are relatively large (employing many workers) and unions have many members. That may be the result of greater market control by union firms. The second reason is related more to the personal resources required of individual tradespeople to secure regular employment. When general operations are fairly large, there are also large swings in the employment picture. This makes it more difficult for individual workers to switch between labor markets. It is too risky to commit oneself to a nonunion job when an imminent union project holds the promise of better wages and conditions. Also, when the union and contractor organizations are large, workers have to devote greater attention to maintaining as visible a presence as possible. Having been a member of both a small and large local union, I can attest to the dramatic differences between the two circumstances in this regard. It is too easy to get lost in the shuffle in large organizations. Thus, it is often unwise to remove yourself from the scene by taking on nonunion work. This is in contrast to the smaller scaled organizational environments, where it is much easier to maintain contact with both union officials and employers.

In the latter situation, individual workers doing nonunion work can, by telephone calls and socializing activities, keep in touch with the union officials and foremen. The other side of the coin is that workers in trades defined by smaller projects may more often be compelled to move into the nonunion sector more often, since the start of a new project does not bring with it the promise of employment for very many out-of-work tradespeople.

The regularity of site-to-site pressures on workers to ignore important aspects of the trade agreement in order to be hired or stay on the job (TA concessions) tends to reflect rather directly on the labor relations environment. First, contractors who employ relatively large workforces are more successful in avoiding complete compliance with the TA. They can use the promise of employment opportunities to pry work-rule concessions from union business agents and business managers or directly from the workers on the job site.

Similarly, labor supply has a strong impact on TA concessions. Other things being equal, the greater the labor supply relative to demand, as reflected by aggregate unemployment, the less protection workers have against infringements of their trade agreements. Conversely, when labor supply is low, job protections are enhanced. This, of course, corresponds to the previously discussed impact of labor supply on the balance of power in the union-contractor relationship.

Finally, members of more militant unions seem to experience less protection against pressures to grant on-site concessions to employers. On the surface this appears to contradict the intended goals of the union to increase protections for the membership. However, what it probably indicates is the greater vulnerability of members in local unions forced to rely on trade union militancy rather than production location as a source of power in its collective bargain relations. Core trades that do not rely on militant actions are in a better position to hold the line against project agreements.

The responses of union officials during interview sessions bolster this interpretation, as well as lend added insight to the mechanisms by which unions attempt to protect their rank-and-file. Asked to specify those issues they see as most important to their duties as a business manager or agent, most included contract negotiations, organizing nonunion contractors, and dealing with local political and governmental agencies. However, the single most important response was keeping members employed. Even more to the point, most see their ability to stay in elected office as largely contingent on their success in placing members on jobs, distributing employment opportunities, and keeping overall unemployment at an acceptable level (or at least giving the impression of doing everything possible to do so). In other words, the primary focus of union activity is the reduction of unemployment. In the bargaining process between union official and employing contractor, one way for the union representative to increase employment is to grant concessions on work rules and wages. Thus militancy aimed at reducing unemployment and maintaining low surplus labor thereby also results in more prevalent and regularly recurring substandard working conditions.

Such a pattern reflects rather poorly on the power of local building trade unions to protect the interests of their memberships. Other things being equal, strong local unions should be able to affect both low unemployment and contractor compliance with trade agreements. Having to trade-off between desirable goals suggests that local unions have far less control over market conditions and labor relations than many writers have generally assumed (for example, Applebaum 1983; Stark 1980; Burck 1979; Northrup and Foster 1975). The obvious alternative perspective is to view employing contractors as having the upper hand in labor relations.

A similar point must be made regarding the impact of occupational skill level. The complexity of work and locational centrality do offer individual protection against unemployment and greater employment opportunity in the residential non-union sector. On the other hand, even these effects are only small to moderate. Neither craft skill nor productive centrality is an overwhelming guarantee of quality employment. In particular, highly skilled craftspeople at central locations in the labor process are no more likely to avoid employers' pressures to lower their standards of work than their less advantaged counterparts.

Overall, the general weakness of the combination of union militancy, production location, and labor supply in explaining workers' employment opportunity structure is in itself worth noting. Their combined effects explain a small fraction of individual rates of unemployment and TA compliance in the statistical analysis described. It is thus obvious that relationships at the levels of occupational and interorganizational power processes do not suffice as an explanation of individually experienced employment opportunities. Other facets of the employment picture must be included.

Two individual level circumstances are most salient in this regard. The first is the differences in levels of participation in trade union activities. The rewards of union success may be unequally distributed among the membership. Benefits may selectively acrue to those who have stronger and more frequent attachments to the organization. Second, individual affiliation with contractors' management structures may supersede the importance of union affiliations. Assessing the role of the managerial location in expanding workers' employment opportunities should help determine whether union affiliations and employer loyalties are alternative, competing, or complementary organizational sources of employment.

Union and Contractor Attachments

Organizations are political systems and the local craft union is no exception. In fact, the political dimensions are perhaps stronger in local unions than in other organizations since the official leadership is elected by the membership. Employment opportunities as discussed earlier have important political implications for elected officials. For the members it is the converse that is true: political activity is consequential for employment. Active participation in union affairs, as well as close contact with the local's current administration can have significant impact on one's employment picture (table 3.6, column 1).[8]

As such, the leadership can use what control over employment opportunities they do have at their disposal to influence the direction of the active members' involvements. By selectively distributing work opportunities among membership, the administration in power can effectively coopt potential political threats. Active but politically uncommitted members can be brought in the fold of the machine by offering a steady supply of jobs. Such cooptation also creates in the process a degree of dependence on the machine. Members who rely on the union office for their work quickly become aware that continual

Table 3.6. Regressions of Individual Employment Variables including Trade Union Attachment Factors and Contractor Attachment Factors.

	Unemployment	Nonunion Employment	TA Concessions
Trade Union			
Union Militancy	-.00	.37**	.33**
Union Size (log)	-.02	-.81***	-.02
Production Location			
Craft Complexity	.01	.22**	.01
Craft Centrality	-.09	.59***	.02
Contractor Size (log)	-.07	-.11*	.15**
Labor Supply	.23**	.13	.19*
Trade Union Attachment			
Attendance	-.19***	.04	.21***
Stewardship	.13**	-.02	-.07
Contractor Attachment			
Foremanship	.00	-.10	.04
Administrative Consultation	-.17**	-.06	-.26***
On-Site Consultation	-.24***	.09	-.15**
$\bar{R}^2$	.18	.33	.24

*p<.10   **p<.05   ***p<.01

favorable (if not preferential) treatment is contingent on continual loyalty in political affairs.[9]

From the members' perspective, it is possible and not infrequent that political loyalty is for sale, so to speak. Members can consciously make it known to business agents that they will turn their union participation in directions acceptable to the machine in exchange for steady work. Of course, it is not automatic that such offers are accepted by the union leadership. The administration's political insecurity at the time is one factor influencing the ability of a particular member to trade for more work. The administration with a solid political base, or that foresees no major issues in the near future, may not be in the market for new adherents. Similarly, the personal qualities of the member is a major factor. The outspoken member who seems to be well respected by fellow members is a much more attractive candidate than less known and quieter members.

In both administration- and member-initiated circumstances there is a *quid pro quo* that reflects on a basic economic insecurity among building tradespeople. On the one hand, it makes control over employment opportunities an effective political resource. On the other hand, it makes union officials politically dependent on their ability to control them. It is thus ironic that the system breaks down under extreme employment conditions. Periods of full employment tend to reduce the political significance of job opportunities since members are less insecure. Seasonal or market surges in construction can create enough demand for labor that everybody works, regardless of union politics. Conversely, slack periods when unemployment is extremely high, while times of greater insecurity for workers, are also marked by little control for union officials. Extended periods of chronic unemployment therefore have a destabilizing effect on local union dynamics. Individual members, anxious about their personal circumstances, are more likely to make direct overtures to business agents or try to call in past favors and acts of political loyalty. But it is just at those times when union officials are least able to accomodate members by sending them out on jobs. Local union administrations are usually at their politically weakest when unemployment is very high for more than a short time. Participation can then take on political significance of it own.

The other economic consequence of political participation in union affairs seems to be less frequent work on projects that comply with the standards of the trade agreements (table 3.6, column 3). The politically active union member apparently does enhance his or her employment opportunities in a quantitative sense, but also experiences reduced job protections on the construction sites he or she works on. This contradictory outcome of union affiliation mirrors the previously discussed impact on union militancy. The similarity is not coincidental either. Since union officials try to manage unemployment partly by agreeing to work-rule concessions, those members who seek to increase their chances for employment through close affiliation with the local union must accept this pattern of exchange. Putting it bluntly, they must be willing to accept substandard conditions as a direct consequence of relying on the union for job opportunities.

The consequences of holding a union stewardship are slightly different, but no less contradictory to common expectations. Those who more often are appointed to be a steward tend to experience more weeks of unemployment. Being a steward, it seems, is a slight liability to an individual's employment pattern. One reason for this is that the formal functions of the union steward limit the kinds of job sites he or she will be sent to. The duties of the steward to oversee the contractually guaranteed rules of work safety, health, productivity, and remuneration tend to exclude the steward from employment on sites with informal project agreements. Contractors try to avoid having a steward placed on jobs where they have directly arranged with their workers to violate TA standards in some manner. Contractors can do that by not reporting the job to the union, or by camouflaging either its scale, or by scheduling in the report they do make.[10] Similarly, the union may decide that it serves no purpose to appoint a steward to a job on which a project agreement exists. Having come to some arrangement directly with the contractor, business managers or their agents are likely then to feel that there is no particular need for a steward, or that the presence of a steward actually would be cumbersome. In any event, such jobs where deals are made are not always covered by stewards.

At a more personal level, it is often the case that stewards are less willing personally to compromise working conditions, wages, and other protections guaranteed by their TAs. Unfortunately, it also means being less able to take advantage of those employment opportunities the trade union can provide. For some, it comes down to a choice on the basis of personal principles. There are many tradespeople for whom being knowledgeable about labor law, their union's constitution, by-laws, and trade agreement, and their attempts to uphold them as much as possible are true points of pride. For these people being a union steward is both an opportunity to exercise their beliefs and an official acknowledgement of their dedication to the union.

In addition, there are also indirect and long-run benefits of the steward position. This is specifically the case for those tradespeople with an eye toward elected union position. For the member who desires to advance within the union's political hierarchy, the stewardship offers the opportunity to demonstrate a strong union commitment, a desire to protect the members' rights on the job, and an ability to deal effectively with contractors and management. Moreover, the more often a person is appointed as steward, the more regular are the chances to demonstrate these qualities in front of fellow union members. That opportunity is a crucial factor in gaining recognition among the membership as an active and articulate advocate since most workers change both job sites and employers on a regular basis. Thus, the stewardship can be an important stepping stone to higher union office; although one that entails immediate and shortrun sacrifices in terms of employment.

Managerial Location and Employment:

The last chapter examined the correlates of the managerial location as regards on-site work structure. Here the factors of the official foremanship position and consultational relations hips with contracors are considered explicitly within the context of labor relations and employment opportunities. Their inclusion in the present analysis allows a direct contrast to the consequences of trade union affiliations.

Reference to table 3.6 shows quite clearly that being attached to contractors' organizations in some managerial capacity has consonant impacts on employment and TA compliance. It improves the employment picture for tradespeople by decreasing unemployment and increasing compliance with trade agreement provisions. Actually, more regular employment and superior working conditions are two rewards employers can and do offer to loyal and helpful tradespeople. From the other side, tradespeople attempt to ingratiate themselves with contractors by demonstrating a willingness and ability to perform various managerial functions. Both parties do continually seek an edge in their economic exchange.[11] Still, there is little doubt about the advantages that accrue to those whith close affiliations with contractors.

This, of course, is in stark contrast to the ambiguous consequences of trade union attachments. Workers who rely on their contact with the local union have to make the choice between immediate economic security and the quality of their conditions of work. It is a choice managerial tradespeople apparently do not as often have to make. This is an important point. For one thing it reflects on a basic difference between one group of tradespeople and another. Those dependent on their trade union for employment must trade-off between employment and the protections of the trade agreement. Those with a close relationship to contractors experience both less unemployment and fewer infringements on their conditions of work. But, in addition, this pattern implies a basic power differential between contractor and trade unions in the local market. Very simply, contractors' control over the employment opportunity structure is greater than that of the building trade unions. It is only for that reason that managerial tradespeople accrue greater employment advantages.

The question of personal choice thus occurs in the context of a set of industrial relations characterized by contractor domination of employment opportunities and relatively weaker trade unions forces to trade-off between desirable goals. Within this context, individual workers are usually forced to balance their short- and long-run economic needs, as well as choose between equally desirable but mutually exclusive options. Contradictory practices on the part of individual workers, reflecting a plaguing insecure marginality in the labor market, are often the result.

For example, one personal hedge against slack employment in the unionized sector is to establish connections to the nonunion residential sector. Doing so, however, entails certain costs. It may mean occasionally having to forego a union job because it overlaps with prior nonunion commitments. Regular nonunion employment also places individual workers in a weaker position with regard to union contractors who may not get the chance to get to know them, or to business agents who are antagonized by and unsympathetic to their nonunion relations. In consequence, workers who regularly split employment between sectors may end up having to grant various concessions to employers. Similarly, their union agents may place such workers on jobs covered by project agreements more frequently than more loyal union members.

A second factor influencing patterns of employment are the benefits to various parties when workers are paid with untaxed wages. Many workers see it to their advantage to derive a proportion ot their income off the books. Cash income that is not reported to the Internal Revenue Service means more spendable income than wages from which taxes are deducted. Since there are also significant advantages to having one's income from legitimate sources—such as social security contributions, unemployment insurance eligibility, health insurance, and retirement fringe benefits contributions—some union workers seek to maintain a balance between reported and unreported income. Such workers generally figure that the minimum level of legitimate wage income to be what is necessary to qualify for unemployment insurance and/or health insurance coverage. The two primary sources of unreported cash income are nonunion work and arrangements with union employers

One advantage of nonunion residential work is that it is an unregulated sector. There are numerous small independent contractors working on small projects ranging from spot building to house alterations for homeowners. The diffuseness and scale of activity in the residential sector make it easy for cash transactions to take place. The union member can obtain unreported income either by working for a nonunion contractor or, as some do, maintain his or her own small enterprise. Craftspeople from certain trades (such as, painters, paperhangers, electricians, carpet layers, and tile setters) are in enough demand in the residential sector that they can operate what amounts to independent contracting practices by working directly for homeowners. Because most of this nonunion activity is in areas considered to be unorganizable by union officials, craftspeople so engaged are tolerated as long as they do not encroach on organizable terrain (for example, commercial construction, or larger-scaled, tract residential building). The second source of cash incomes is much more problematic from numerous perspectives.

When wages are paid in cash, substantial advantages go to the contractor. Contractors do not make social security contributions, pay unemployment and workers' compensation, or contribute to the union welfare, insurance, and retirement fund on such wages. The savings can be significant when you consider that together they can amount to more than fifty percent of the gross payroll. Unionized contractors thus seek ways to pay their workers a portion of their wages off the books on some jobs as a direct addition to their profits. They can also use cash payment of wages to their advantage on jobs where unforeseen delays have upset scheduling or where cost overruns threaten profit margins. For instance, it is not uncommon for workers to agree to have their overtime premium paid in cash. Employers forced to resort to an overtime situation can at least save on the extra payroll taxes and fringe benefit contributions. Finally, it is also evident that contractors who can depend on their regular workers to come to some sort of agreement about getting paid in cash have a competitive bidding edge over legitimate contractors.[12]

While the above dynamics operating at the level of individual choice are partially independent of many of the factors associated with the formal judicial-political labor relations system, they should not be interpreted solely in terms of randomized individual differences. They have common motives rooted in personal uncertainties and insecurities about employment and income that are tied directly to market conditions; insecurities that are not eliminated by the protections of craft and union. The pressures of material insecurity on construction workers have never been fully recognized, nor their consequences fully appreciated. Nonetheless, they are significant enough to force workers to subvert the very conditions of craft work and union employment it is in their own objective interest to uphold.

The Issue of Employment

Having thus far looked at the array of factors that bear on

both the on-site work structure and the employment opportunity structure for building tradespeople, it is possible to focus in more closely on two related issues. First, the analysis will be extended to explore the interrelationships between construction site TA concessions and the other two facets of employment. Essentially, the dual-pronged question here is how unemployment and nonunion employment operate in the determination of job concessions and whether granting job concessions improves the chances for work on union projects. Second, the possibilities of direct interrelations between organizational and labor relations will be explored. In this regard the question is whether labor relations outcomes at the individual level, particularly patterns of job concessions, affect workers' opportunities for autonomy in their work. Generally speaking, inquiry into the interpenetration of organization of work and labor relations is only recently coming to the fore in the work of sociologists and labor economists; inspired by Harry Braverman's seminal *Labor and Monopoly Capital.* Such late blooming interest is somewhat ironic since these relationships are probably among the most significant for workers on the job.

As discussed earlier, workers' employment tends to reflect the impact of individual, market, and union conditions. But there are also significant relationships among the employment variables themselves. Thus far it has been implied, but not elaborated on, that there is a direct association between job concessions and unemployment. Frequently unemployed tradespeople are more likely to agree to various job concessions principally as a means of getting hired on union projects. Similarly, those working more frequently in nonunion areas are likely to resort to concessions to get union work (see table 3.7).[13] Presumably there is a reciprocity in these two relationships. The unemployed agree to concessions in order to reduce their unemployment. Those in nonunion residential areas make concessions to increase their unionized employment. Obviously, granting production concessions to employers is not the most desirable approach to raising one's chances for union work. On the other hand, for many tradespeople it comes down to a situation of it being better to do union work under substandard conditions than to do only nonunion work or to do no work at all.

Table 3.7. Regression of TA Concessions including Individual Unemployment and Nonunion Employment

	TA Concessions
Trade Union	
Union Militancy	.32**
Union Size (log)	-.01
Production Location	
Craft Complexity	-.01
Craft Centrality	.05
Contractor Size (log)	.17*
Labor Supply	.18**
Trade Union Attachment	
Attendance	.23***
Stewardship	-.08
Contractor Attachment	
Foremanship	.06
Administrative Consultation	-.22***
On-site Consultation	-.11*
Individual Employment	
Unemployment	.18***
Nonunion Employment	.17***
$\bar{R}^2$	.29

*p<.10   **p<.05   ***p<.01

In part, this stems from a lack of strong ties to the unionized labor market. Workers unable or unwilling to secure regular employment or who rely primarily on residential work generally have weaker ties to union and contractor organizations. One obvious way such tradespeople can generate employer interest in hiring them, of course, is by accepting less than the standard union conditions. Similarly, without close ties to the union, tradespeople who only occasionally appear in the dayroom to sign up for employment are more likely to be placed by their business agents on the less desirable jobs where project agreements have been arranged.

The bottom line is that granting job concessions is an attempt at increasing one's employment. Clearly, it is not a desirable way of getting jobs. However, tradespeople desperate to do at least enough union work to qualify for medical insurance coverage and to make pension contributions may feel they are at times faced with little or no alternative. The question then is whether it is a successful strategy. Since unemployed and residentially employed tradespeople more often accede to job concessions, the crux of the issue is whether doing so in turn reduces the amount of unemployment or frequency of residential nonunion work.

It is a difficult question to answer with any degree of certainty. In talking with workers on the job about this, it seemed that most do not so much focus on how effective it is, as much as they accept the concessions as part of their circumstances. Some feel they possibly do increase union employment. Others disagree, feeling instead that they are always stuck on the rotten jobs because of their lack of connections. To deal with the issue empirically would require reliable data about workers' employment patterns over a period of time. That would permit a look at shifts in unemployment as workers agree to employers' demands for concessions. The data at hand are not suitable for such an analysis.

However, the assessment of the likelihood of reciprocal connections between job concessions and unemployment and nonunion employment does not suggest significantly strong effects (analysis not shown). It is argued here that granting production concessions is an ineffective way of increasing employment. Similarly, job concessions have only an insignificant impact on nonunion employment. Here too the indication is that the primary relationship has job concessions being influenced by, but not necessarily influencing, unemployment and nonunion employment. The possibility of reciprocal influences cannot be dismissed on the basis of a cross-sectional analysis. However, it is suggested here that in the employment cycle unemployment and nonunion work operate to lower workers' protections on unionized jobs, while the potentially positive results for workers who grant concessions to employers are, at best minimal.

The second issue to be addressed in this section is the impact of the collective and individual facets of labor-management relations on the work structure at the construction site. Management's organizational response to actual or potential conflict with employees or their unions is often overlooked as an aspect of work at the point of production. Nevertheless, in the case of construction work, stronger managerial control over production is a defensive response to antagonisms over work rules on the job or as a way of preserving the integrity of the contractor's organization. Since foremen are also union members, contractors can easily feel it strategic to establish clear lines of demarcation between their firms and the union during periods of conflict. One way of accomplishing this is to limit the on-site autonomy of tradespeople belonging to unions with which it has conflictual relations. At the individual level, tradespeople with strong union loyalties or those compelled to agree to job concessions may in the eyes of contractors warrant extra attention on the job site.

The results of this research indicate that this indeed is the case. Granting job concessions to employers, a realistic albeit somewhat self-defeating response to unemployment, has detrimental effects on the structure of work by increasing the amount of supervision to which such workers are subject.[14] In other words, agreeing to work under substandard conditions with respect to wages and work rules brings with it the imposition of additional managerial surveillance; and consequently less individual autonomy in the labor process.

Contractors' need to maintain control over production is the evident reason for this. Workers' concessions tend to undermine notions that contractors and workers are partners in production. In other words, concessions have a delegitimizing effect that make it impossible for contractors to rely on unsupervised workers to do their jobs. Having gained the promise of greater economic advantage from production, the contractor must institute control mechanisms to ensure that outcomes reflect the promise. They therefore tend to strengthen their control over the labor process when labor relations in a specific circumstance increase the likelihood of noncooperation among the workforce. In the present case, greater direct supervision of the craft workforce maximize compliance when antagonistic interests in production come to the surface.

The direct impact of this economic aspect of labor relations on workers' autonomy in production bears on how the development of relations within work organizations like construction firms are to be understood. Jeffrey Riemer (1982) argues for a greater role in production for skilled building tradespeople. He posits that a greater active decision-making role for skilled building tradespeople would help to alleviate many of the production problems and inefficiencies that plague contruction. Motivational considerations should prompt changes in organizational arrangements on the contruction site. Constraints on workers that prevent them from fully exercising their skills and knowledge in the production process are sources of low morale, low productivity, and unnecessary waste. Consequently, he calls for a restructuring of the labor process to permit greater intrinsic rewards for building tradespeople.

The main problem, of course, is that organizations are not structured or restructured in a vacuum. To the contrary, they are shaped by the dynamic antagonisms and constraints inherent in labor and market relations. Riemer appropriately acknowledges the role of the political economy of capitalist market relations:

> The primary threat to worker autonomy in the skilled building trades is economic. Building-trade contractors continually attempt to maximize control over their workers to further their own economic gains. This is done daily through the manipulation of individual workers by certain managerial and supervisory personnel in an attempt to increase worker production. Similar attempts are made at the organizational level (1982, p. 231).

As long as employers benefit from their ability to extract extra economic concessions from workers they are also forced to seek ways to restrict workers' autonomy. The continual erosion of the areas of workers' self-direction and unsupervised activity is based on the potential for hostility, recalcitrance, or merely lack of motivation in production that result from concessions coerced from economically insecure tradespeople.

Consequently, there would appear to be little room for organizational innovations designed to enhance the role of skilled building tradespeople in the labor process. For one thing, the combination of localized markets and labor-intensive production have strong effects on subcontracting operations (see for example, Eccles 1981). For another, to the extent that contractors' ability to extract job concessions is tied to their capacity to structure on-site work arrangements to fit their control imperatives, they will resist efforts on the part of union or third parties to enlarge the autonomous sphere of worker activity in the labor process. Thus, as discussed more fully in chapter five, the introduction of alterations in the structure of construction work must be tied to restructuration of fundamental labor and product market relations. At minimum this implies the need to buffer industrial activity from the severest effects of the localized competitive market. At maximum it implies the need to transcend them altogether.

Becoming a Member: Apprenticeship, Access, and Discrimination

Many readers would have expected a chapter on trade unions to begin with an account of how workers first enter the union. I chose to deal with this topic last essentially for two reasons. First, as it should be clear at this juncture, mainstream social research and the popular media have tended to overstate the extent of local union control over the labor market. Thus, it was necessary to establish a more realistic basis for discussing the entrance process. Second, the issues of unequal access and discrimination against minorities and women by trade unions generally, and especially the building trades, are far too sensitive and important to broach without some preliminary discussion.

It is popularly believed that trade unions use their ability to restrict entrance to apprentice training programs and to constrain artificially the supply of labor by refusing to admit new members in order to control the labor market. This results in the father-to-son and uncle-to-nephew inheritance of the entitlements of union membership. In that context, discriminatory practices are thus considered to be simultaneously a key mechanism by which unions practice market control and one of its chief results.

However, the results of this research, as well as observations during years of association with one local's apprentice-training program suggest that many local unions do not exercise enough control to dominate, not to mention monopolize, the opportunities for entry.[15] Control of labor supply is, of course a central element in the labor relations dynamic. The availability of free labor within a trade affects both collective bargaining outcomes, as well as daily negotiations about work rules and project agreements. Locals do attempt to manage the size of the membership and especially to limit transient members who may deprive regular members of employment opportunities.[16] Such attempts notwithstanding, formal joint union-contractor apprentice programs apparently do not effectively serve such restrictive functions.

Table 3.8. Method of Entry to Workers' Building Trade. Distribution of Responses to the question, "How did you (member) break into your trade?"

	Number	*Percent*
Taught By Friend	50	19.6
Taught By Relative	82	32.2
Self-Taught	28	11.0
Union Apprenticeship	95	37.3
Missing	(5)	—
	260	100

For instance, data from the survey questionnaire indicate that only a minority of tradespeople broke into their trade through formal apprentice training programs (37.3 percent; table 3.8). Most either learned their skill on their own or were taught by a friend or relative (62.7 percent). For these building tradespeople, the union organization was not, strictly speaking, the primary conduit of entry to the industry. While many local unions have had formal provision for an apprentice membership status and wage scale in their contracts since their incep-

Table 3.9. Relationship Between Respondent's Age and Means of Entry into Their Building Trade

	Age		
	Younger (<45)	Older (≥45)	
Union Apprenticeship	69	22	91
	60%	16%	
Other	46	114	160
	40%	84%	
Total	115	136	251
	100%	100%	

Means of Entry (row label)

$X^2 = 51.95; p < .005$

tion, most only recently have initiated actual training programs. If younger (age less than 45 years) and older (age 45 and above) workers were compared with respect to their means of entry (table 3.9) it is seen that younger workers are much more likely to have gone through formal apprentice training programs; 60 percent versus 16 percent. The trend is toward implementing training programs across the trades. Of course, the higher skilled trades such as plumbing and electrical work have operated more fully developed programs for a longer time than the others. This no doubt reflects the greater importance of formal training in addition to on-the-job training for these crafts. Thus, while only 18 percent of lower-skilled and 32 percent of medium-skilled tradespeople broke into the industry through a formal apprentice program, fully 64 percent of the higher-skilled workers did so (table 3.10).

But even at this point in time a significant proportion of tradespeople do not go through formalized training for their craft. For many, entry is through extraorganizational channels. Personal relationships with friends and relations play the key role (Applebaum 1981). They can affect the chances to learn the skills of a building trade as well as to obtain steady work. Localized product and labor markets, labor intensive production, a preponderance of small subcontracting operations, and seasonal employment combine to accentuate the role of per-

Table 3.10. Relationship Between Respondent's Occupational Skill Level and Means of Entry to Their Building Trade.

			Skill		
		High	*Medium*	*Low*	
Means of Entry	Union Apprenticeship	36 64%	54 32%	5 18%	95
	Other	20 36%	117 68%	23 82%	160
	Total	56 100%	171 100%	28 100%	255

$X^2 = 21.78;$ $p < .001$

sonal contacts. It has already been seen how important it is for those seeking work to maintain close person relations with subcontractors and their regular foremen. It is even more improtant to have strong ties in the industry in order to break into a trade.

Aside from joint apprentice programs, there are no major organizational channels of entry for those not already in possession of the skills of the trade. There is little incentive for a contractor to take on a worker with unknown aptitude for a particular trade given the generally unstable employment relationships. The same contractor, however, is likely to be more willing to help a personal relative get started in the trade, or to accommodate a trusted tradesperson trying to break in a friend or relative. Similarly with union officials who may not be overly enthusiastic about a new member with no local connections. The elected official, always sensitive to political realities, may actually see such isolated members as short-term burdens with respect to finding them jobs, with little potential for significant political returns. The political impact of unemployment cautions many business managers to be very careful not to overload the organization, especially with untested, untrained, or inexperienced members.

Close relatives of contractors, union officials, and journeymen have a distinct advantage in this context. The obvious factor, of course, is access. Sons, grandsons, and nephews (and very minimally daughters, granddaughters, and nieces) are in the best position to benefit from social ties to the industry. But the advantage is more than merely providing access; it is the timing of that access which is of equal importance. Many tradespeople get their first exposure to construction work in their early teens as part-time helpers. Opportunities to do construction work over school holidays and summer recesses are of invaluable benefit. Most obviously, they are opportunities to learn the skills of the trade at an early age. Serving what amounts to a preapprenticeship helps later on when going through formal apprentice training. Most significant in this regard, such *pretrained* apprentices are a real bargain for the contractors who hire them. In effect they can pay apprentice wages to a worker who can produce at a much higher level than other apprentices.

There are also less obvious, but equally important, advantages to breaking into the industry early. For one thing, it means being introduced to the social networks that later will be necessary to making a living as an adult. The younger relation can ride the coattails of his or her sponsor while establishing connections of his or her own. In a related vein, there is the benefit of direct exposure to the culture of construction work. Like any other work environment, construction work has its own distinct flavor. Early socialization into the ways of a craft, the social dynamics between trades on the construction site, and the political machinations of the local union makes it much easier to contend successfully with the various obstacles to make a livng in the industry that arise from time to time. In particular, dealing with the recurrent cycles of unemployment that all building tradespeople experience is a problem that is much eased by early experience. The social and psychological correlates of working in an industry characterized by cycles of boom and bust—swings between periods of extended lay-offs and periods of overtime workdays and seven-day work weeks—can be debilitating if one is not properly prepared for them. Finally, there is a direct economic advantage to early entry under the wing of a close relation. Apprentice wages (usually beginning at forty or fifty percent of journeyman scale) are not particularly high to start with and, when combined with seasonal employment, do not amount to a substantial annual income. Maintaining independent means of transportation for getting from site to site and purchasing the necessary tools of the trade are costs over and above ordinary daily living expenses. The financial burden for apprentices on their own can be acute. On the other hand, serving out an apprenticeship under a member of one's own family (especially one who lives in the same house) is more easily afforded since transportation costs are either shared or provided and hand-me-down tools are more than adequate until they are gradually replaced with new ones. Much of the social and economic marginality of breaking into a trade and serving out the apprenticeship can be attenuated by the support of family and friendship social networks.

What can be said then about the opportunities for people with little or no social ties to the local industry, especially for minorities and women? The combination of several endemic industrial characteristics make it exceedingly difficult for such people to get access into the trade and then, just as importantly, manage to secure a livelihood in the long run. According to authors Bourdon and Levitt (1980) under-representation of minorities occurs in most of the building trades, although there are substantial differences. There is little or no evidence of discrimination, as reflected by under-representation indices, for the less skilled trades such as painters, roofers, plasterers, and cement masons. There is a much greater under-representation gap in such trades as carpenters, electrical workers, plumbers, and operating engineers. Bourdon and Levitt's conclusion about the problems of minority recruitment and training in contruction is instructive: "without extensive new analyses of the problems of minority recruitment and training in construction, it appears that whatever difficulties exist cannot be attributed to the influence of building trades unions alone" (73). In order to appreciate what those difficulties are, as well as the extent to which they permeate labor practices in the industry, it is necessary to look deeper than restrictive union practices.

Essentially, it is possible to speak of patterns of inequality of access as resulting from the interrelationship between individual-level racism and sexism and the social-structural characteristics of the localized labor market.[17] There can be little argument about the presence of racism and sexism; by which is meant people's actions and practices that are closely tied to their prejudiced beliefs, values, and ideas. Ethnic, racial, and gender awarenesses are fairly high among building tradespeople. They are such pervasive elements in their thinking that they infuse both friendly banter and more serious conversation among workers on the construction site. Working day after day on a construction site it is always possible to hear people making reference to their own or somebody else's ethnic or religious background. Much of it occurs as benign give and take while workers go about their jobs. It nevertheless reflects a high degree of racial and ethnic consciousness based on a good deal of stereotyped images of various groups. Similarly with respect to sexist orientations, in the male-dominated workplace it is almost impossible not to encounter off-handed remarks and conversations about women and male-female relationships that quite clearly express chauvinist and sexist attitudes. The girl-watching and wolf-whistling diversions for which male construction workers are so infamous are only the most obvious manifestations of such attitudes.

Clearly, such attitudes easily translate into behaviors. Minority and women apprentices can easily find themselves discouraged by the treatment they receive on the job. While it is not possible to offer any direct evidence of this, it is very likely that many decide to leave the industry on account of the prejudiced and discriminatory behaviors they experienced.

As a general observation, it can be said that the forms of individual prejudice run somewhat different courses for minority and female entrants. For males, it can be a case of hostility giving way to a gradual, if begrudging, acceptance. Those with the fortitude to withstand the early stages of initiation, to learn the skills of the trade, and secure a livelihood eventually gain a measure of respect from his fellow tradesmen. In the physically demanding and frequently dangerous workplace, construction workers will come to accept skilled mechanics who work hard and turn out quality jobs in spite of their prejudices. It is in this sense that the racial and ethnic prejudices and awarenesses get turned into forms of superficially cordial contact.

According to my observations, the circumstances are somewhat different for women. This researcher has witnessed less initial gut-level resistance to female apprentices. In fact, many male workers are quite solicitious and helpful. The obvious reason is that they tend to find the presence of women less threatening than that of Black and Hispanic men. It is possible that part of the explanation is that men can find a measure of security in their interactions with inexperienced female trainees. Having women act as gofers or instructing them in the skills of the trade, allows men casually and comfortably to assert a dominant role. Moreover, the opportunities to help women carrying bulky or heavy loads, or to steady the nerves of a novice unused to climbing and working from scaffolds, confirms the chauvinist beliefs many men hold. They are able, in the context of presumably friendly and helpful activities, to reaffirm for themselves their own superiority. The obvious long-run obstacle for women construction workers then is overcoming the patronizing and condescending orientations of their male coworkers if they are to be able to make a living in their trade. As long as such attitudes remain as prevalent as they are now, it will be difficult indeed for women to have reasonable expectations of being considered for managerial positions or union offices.

But the real problem for women and minorities attempting to break into construction are the connections between such individual prejudices and the social-structural arrangements of the labor market. As described, the local labor market favors those with strong social ties. By virtue of prior inequalities of access the very same characteristics thus loom as major barriers for those without them. With no established social networks to move into, individual women, Blacks, Hispanics, and other minorities are deprived of many crucial social supports. They cannot benefit from early industrial socialization, trade-related pretraining experiences, and the various financial economies associated with being part of a cohesive intraindustrial social network.

Moreover, the significance of the social network for the dynamics of breaking in is, in some respects, overshadowed by its role in helping individual workers to maintain connections during periods of unemployment. Those with friends and relatives in the industry can more easily hold onto their socal ties in the local market. Their de facto social integration means they are able to keep abreast of job openings through informal channels. Similarly, making regular appearances at the local union's dayroom for the unemployed, a political necessity if one hopes to get regular jobs through the union, is eased in large measure by the chance to socialize with friends and acquaintances. The task of holding onto social ties while unemployed is far more difficult for socially marginal individuals. By definition, there are fewer people to call on for information about future job prospects and a trip to the dayroom can be an alienating and stressful experience. Such difficulties for members of marginally represented groups may in part account for the high dropout rates for minority groups from apprentice training programs. In essence, minority and women building tradespeople have the heavy burden of working to build and then to maintain the strong social ties, essential to long-term survival in the industry, that white males more frequently can take for granted.

As long as estrangement, social distance, and hostility exist between white males on the one side and minorities and women on the other, such emotions and beliefs will have a determining influence on practices within social networks, just as exclusive networks may, by virtue of their homogeneity, reinforce psychological, emotional, and value prejudices. So long as black and Hispanic workers are viewed by white males with suspicion, hostility, or even just a degree of social uncomfortability, they will tend to be excluded from, or remain marginal to, the social network formations that lead to jobs. Women too will remain in a marginal position for as long as the men who dominate the microsocial structure presume them to be trespassers attempting to do a man's job, or see them as secondary contributors to their family's income. Thus, discrimination in the building and construction industry is institutionalized to the extent that opportunities for initial access and employment are channeled through structured microsocial networks.

Precisely because it is based on the conjuncture of the microsocial and individual-level values, this form of institutionalized racism and sexism is especially enduring. Affirmative-action legislation, originating outside the industry, is not able to address this source of employment inequality because it focuses on organizational behavior. Within the industry the combination of localized trade-specific labor markets, numerous small employers and highly politicized unions has been fertile ground for its perpetuation. In short, while racially and sexually based inequalities in construction are not necessarily any more extreme than in other aspects of American society, they are also not likely to be any less resistant to change.

4

ALIENATION
AND THE
LABOR PROCESS

At their heart, most studies of the workplace are primarily concerned with the effects of the labor process on the workers it directly touches. Whether the ultimate emphasis is on raising productivity by enhancing the workers' performance and attenuating the problems of turnover and absenteeism, the more humanitarian interest in workers' safety and health on the job, or the conflict of interests between labor and capital at the point of production, central questions revolve around workers' subjective, psychological, and social responses to their involvement in production.

Workers have known this from their first attempts to organize and defend their human dignity and collective interests against the imperatives of industrial capital. American management learned the lesson when F. W. Taylor's principles of scientific management first showed itself most successful at generating worker antipathy and resistance. In the same vein, replacing the stick of scientific management with the carrot of human relations management represents an understanding that how workers feel about themselves and their jobs is indeed a pivotal issue. By the earlier 1970s, the accurate perception of widespread malaise and disaffection prompted the appointment of a presidential commission to study the sources of the "white collar woes" and "blue collar blues" that seemed to be gripping workers in the United States. And, by the 1980s, western capital

121

was looking to the orient for the managerial panacea with the magic to cure the ills of mechanized, automated, bureaucratized, and class-dominated work organization. Indeed, it is even being recognized now, however belatedly, that the labor aristocrats in the building trades are subject to many of the same alienating and dissatisfying conditions. Recent studies of construction work have hinted at the need for changes that would give to building tradespeople a more central role in production and accordingly greater opportunities for intrinsic rewards from their work.

Amid the varied discourse on the meaning and significance of workers' participation in and responses to the labor process, Marx's theory of alienation to this day stands out as arguably the most viable and fruitful source of insight into the dynamic of production relations under capitalism. His theory of alienation endures as both an instrument of empirical analysis and moral galvanization. This has been so notwithstanding fundamental disagreements over its role in Marx's critique of capitalism, his theory of social transformation, and its applicability to an analysis of social relations of late twentieth-century capitalism.

In point of fact, it is a testament to its importance that alienation receives the attention it does. Non-Marxists have often found it to be a convenient focal point for attempting to refute Marxist theory; primarily by fabricating interpretations with only the slightest connections to Marx's original concepts.[1] But divergences have appeared among Marxist approaches as well. Structuralists (for example, Althusser) openly reject the concept as irrelevant or worse (religious, ideological, and unscientific: Althusser 1978). World systems theorists have not found it necessary to take it up at all. Those with a microsociological focus champion the cause of its continued relevance, but tend toward philosophical interpretations not amenable to empirical analysis (for example, Pappenheim 1959; Meszaros 1970; Ollman 1976). Thus, according to Peter Archibald, the theoretical and methodological are inherently intertwined: "In the first case we should do empirical research but throw out the theory of alienation . . . . In the second case we should keep alienation but not investigate its empirical validity" (1978, 120).

It is argued here, however, that the significance of alienation is found in a synthesis of both perspectives. Scientific Marxism and Critical Marxism are both partially correct, but only because both are also in themselves deficient. Alienation is the central element to Marxist theory because it emphasizes the interrelationships between subjective, psychological, and social structural processes. It encompasses distinguishable facets in its objective conditions of work (exploitation and the division of labor); in its subjective and phychological forms (feelings of powerlessness, estrangement, goal-expedience, intellectual dependence); in feelings of discontent; and in its social forms (estrangements in and from social associations). Their confluence, in turn, influences the social consciousness people develop about production and class relations.[2]

This analysis is based on a reading of Marx that gives full weight to the centrality of alienation in class-based systems of social production. On the one hand, it is the basis and means by which such systems operate. On the other, it is the foundation for collective social actions directed in opposition to them. As such, the social process of alienation explains the inherent dialectical instability of capitalist production, grounded as it is in the antagonisms of class relations.

Marx used his theory of alienation to counter the fetishist approach of classical political economy to the dynamics of capitalist production. He argued that in taking private property as the starting point of their analysis, classical economists merely asserted as a historical fact that which they should be trying to explain. Marx, in contrast, set out to understand private property in terms of the social relations underlying it: in effect, analyzing the abstract institution by revealing the concrete social relationships actually defining it. By replacing the ontological argument of politcal economy with the sociological and historical analysis of alienated social relations "private property is thus derived from the analysis of alienated labor." Accordingly, "only in the final stage of the development of private property is its secret revealed, namely,that it is on one hand the 'product' of alienated labor, and on the other hand the 'means' by which labour is alienated, 'the realization of this alienation' " (1956, 131).

Capitalism is built on a foundation of alienated labor and advances through the continual alienation of the worker. At the same time, people experience in their daily lives these systemically conditioned arrangements in varying degrees of directness. Thus, if alienated labor is the basis of capitalist production, it is also its most significant outcome. The relations of property and the division of labor mutually inform peoples' relationship to the product of their labor, to themselves, and to the other members of society. The demands of efficiency and capitalist control in production, as has been discussed, presuppose an extreme division of labor wherever possible. The worker is thus alienated from his/her products in that he/she becomes dependent on the product "in that he receives an object of work . . . and secondly, in that he receives means of subsistence" (1963, p. 127). Workers are forced to offer their labor in exchange for means of subsistence. They therefore work for rewards extrinsic to their activities; not for those directly related to the tasks themselves. Secondly, the progress in the division of labor is manifested as the compartmentalization of tasks. Jobs become simpler, more repetitive and more uniform in their content. Eventually this results in the ultimate division between mental and material labor.

It is here, in the division between the physical and intellectual elements of work, that the conjuncture of alienated labor as social condition and as social consequent occurs. Alienation from the object and process of production influences distinct aspects of the subjective and objective circumstances for the worker. As work becomes increasingly characterized by one portion of human activity at the expense of the other—essentially becoming simpler and more strictly manual—so do one's social relations. The bifurcation of labor directly restricts the opportunities workers have for exercising the full range of their abilities. In the extreme, alienation is that form of work whereby the worker is unable to develop both mental and physical attributes to the fullest, "but is left physically exhausted and metally debased" (Marx 1963, p. 125). The culmination of repeated divisions of labor in this regard results in acutal and perceived losses in the labor process.

Subjective Alienation

The subjective elements of alienated labor include the self-attributions and reflective orientations people hold corresponding to a daily routine of fragmented and externally directed work activity; what Marx referred to as estrangements in the worker's relationship to self. "The performance of work appears in the sphere of political economy as vitiation of the worker, objectification as a loss and as servitude to the object, and appropriation as alienation" (1963, 122). Work thus has a dual result in capitalism, not only producing an object, but objectifying the producer. The worker ultimately "does not fulfill himself in his work but denies himself, has a feeling of misery rather than well-being, does not freely develop his mental and physical energies" and ends up feeling "homeless" while at work. According to Marx, labor within capitalism is "labour in which man alienated himself, is a labour of self sacrifice, of mortification" (1963, 125).

Workers, in other words, arrive at self-evaluations commensurate with their objective situations. The worker comes to view herself as—related to herself in terms of—the dependent "object" of the production process. Rather than seeing herself as the active agent applying knowledge, expertise, and manual skill as judged appropriate and necessary, she comes to view her role as merely being an adjunct to the physical machinery.

For Marx, workers react against the subjective side of alienation as much as against the objectively alienated conditions of work to which it is tied. Thus, alienation, as both social condition and social consequent, is also the medium of social change. In their collective efforts to rid themselves of the oppression of the alienated condition, workers must confront the institutional arrangements by which their labor is alienated. In other words, they must first come to question and then to act against the *system* of alienation. The social contradictions of capitalist production at micro- and macrosociological levels, while not limited to subjective and psychological dynamics, certainly do include them. In fact, the subjective element of alienated class relations gives political uncertainty to the Marxist dialectic.[3] Five facets, or dimensions, of alienation are especially relevant to an understanding of alienation as an intergral component of capitalist relations: powerlessness, self-estrangement, goal expedience, intellectual dependence, discontent. Each has an important connection as a consequence of involvement in the labor process and as a determinant of action within the class structure.

Powerlessness:

Powerlessness refers to one's perception of the expectancy of not being able to influence the outcomes of events concerning one's own life. It reflects the self-perception of the relative capacity to affect social circumstances and not the actual capacity for doing so. While the two factors are distinct, albeit interrelated, it is essential to bear in mind that there is no necessary correspondence between them. People are not always aware of the resources at their disposal which could be brought to bear in their social interactions and structured associations.[4] For instance, objective conditions may change without an immediate or apparent effect on self-perceived efficacies. This can be viewed as a temporally relevant factor according to which there is a significant lag between alterations in social-structrual relations and awarenesses of them. Bertell Ollman (1976) draws on this insight in his discussion of character structure as the internalization of beliefs and action practices rooted in past experiences and prior social conditions. Workers' character structures, being both product and principal cause of alienation, mean that "workers must be viewed not only as prisoners of their conditions, but as prisoners of themselves, of their own character structures which are the product of previous conditions" (1976,248–249). It is thus, according to Ollman, the exceptional situation in which people who are alienated act in direct accordance with new conditions.[5]

Of course, this raises the entire question of the relationship between human perceptual capacities and external reality. It is necessary to understand that both objective and subjective efficacies bear on social practices; but at the same time there are factors affecting an enduring gap between awareness and actuality. In consequence, perceived efficacy remains in itself a key element in the processes of social action. People, collectively or as individuals, must have some measure of belief in their ability to be successful. Those who see themselves as totally powerless are likely to remain inactive in the face of given sets of social conditions.

The question, of course, is how the various aspects of workers' involvement in the labor process affect their feelings of relative efficacy. The results of this research suggest that organization, managerial position, and work structure have significant influences on the facet of alienation (table 4.1). Being self-directed in production and more frequently holding the formal position as foreman on the construction site instill a greater sense of personal capacity to affect desired social outcomes (low subjective powerlessness). Conversely, tradespeople who make few production decisions and who are never or only infrequently selected by contractors to be foremen tend to feel more powerless than their self-directed and managerial counterparts.

In addition, the bureaucratization of the contractor's on-site organization (number of managerial positions) is also related to powerlessness. While many theorists have assumed a negative impact of bureaucracy on workers' sense of alienation, here the opposite result is seen. Working in the more complex organizational arrangement seems to give a greater, not lesser, sense of personal efficacy. Of course, this is in reference to relatively small bureaucratic structure. Nevertheless, it should be recognized that, in construction, a greater formalization of the organizational authority structure is less alienating for both managerial and nonmanagerial tradespeople.

Self-estrangement:

Among the meanings of estrangement supplied by *Webster's Dictionary* is "to turn from an affectionate or friendly attitude to an indifferent, unfriendly, or hostile one." In its most literal interpretation, self-estrangement means to hold a negative or hostile attitude toward oneself. Albert Memmi developed the notion of "self-rejection" as the principal subjective dimension of being oppressed or dominated. "[I]n every dominated man, there is a certain degree of *self-rejection*, born mostly of his downcast condition and exclusion" (1968, p. 86). Memmi here

Table 4.1. Regressions of Subjective Alienation Variables with Craft Labor Process Factors

	Powerlessness	Self-Estrangement	Goal Expedience	Intellectual Dependence	Job Satisfaction
Production Location					
Onsite Size (log)	.09	.12	.02	.11	-.05
Duration	.04	.03	-.27***	-.08	.00
Bureaucracy	-.15*	-.15*	.15***	.11	.01
Contractor Size (log)	-.15	-.19**	-.02	-.07	-.00
Craft: Complexity	.10	-.00	-.09	-.21**	-.06
Mentality	-.05	-.15*	-.08	-.21**	-.06
Centrality	.13	.10	-.12	.03	-.01
Labor Supply	-.00	.28**	.14	.11	-.11
Managerial Location					
Foremanship	-.18**	-.14	-.17**	.13	.15*
Administrative Consultation	.07	.05	-.07	.09	.02
Onsite Consultation	-.03	.12	.03	-.01	-.11
Trade Union					
Militancy	.18	.27	-.22	.03	-.01
Size (log)	.01	.12	.00	-.11	.03
Attendance	-.01	-.08	-.11	-.06	.13*
Stewardship	-.04	-.05	-.03	-.02	.14**

Table 4.1. Regressions of Subjective Alienation Variables with Craft Labor Process Factors (Cont'd.)

	Powerlessness	Self-Estrangement	Goal Expedience	Intellectual Dependence	Job Satisfaction
Work Autonomy					
Self Direction	-.14*	-.09	.31***	-.03	-.08
Supervision	.03	.19**	.07	-.03	.02
Individual Employment					
Unemployment	.03	-.03	.07	.01	-.26***
Nonunion Employment	.12	.10	.03	-.03	-.02
TA Concessions	-.01	-.01	.08	-.04	-.21***
Individual Controls					
Age	.07	.02	-.04	.09	.07
Education	-.13*	-.03	-.09	-.09	.07
$\bar{R}^2$	.03	.13	.19	.02	.17

*p<.10   **p<.05   ***p<.01

ties the subjective—self-rejection—to the objective condition of allienation. Focusing on the colonial relationship, he contends that the complement of the colonizer's attempt to subjectively justify his dominant and exploitative position through a negative mythology of the colonized is the latter's partial acceptance of that negative self image:

> Constantly confronted with this image of himself, set forth and imposed on all institutions and in every human contact, how could the colonized help reacting to his portrait. . . . He ends up recognizing it as one would a detested nickname which has become a familiar description. . . . Willfully created and spread by the colonizer, this mythical and degrading portrait ends up by being accepted and lived with to a certain extent by the colonized (1965, p. 87).

And further, self-rejection even infuses the attempts of the colonized to escape their dominated circumstances. Incorporation of the self-denigrating image informs the efforts of those seeking release through assimilation with the colonizers:

> By this step, which actually presupposes admiration for the colonizer, one can infer approval of the colonization. But by obvious logic . . . *he rejects himself* with most tenacity. Love of the colonizer as subtended by a complex of feelings *ranging from shame to self-hate* (1965, p. 121; emphasis added.)

In *Dominated Man*, Memmi extended the notion of self-rejection to other social forms of oppression, including those faced by workers (on this also see Marcuse 1964; 1972). Similar analyses have been made by Franz Fanon and, concerning the situation of Afro-Americans, by Malcolm X. In the social psychological studies made by Melvin Seeman, it refers to one's inability to find and engage in self-rewarding activities. And Melvin Kohn (1976), in a study of American workers, extended the implications of self-estrangement to include feelings of purposelessness, boredom, and a willingness to take life as it comes.

As self-estrangement is interpreted here, such sentiments are rooted in a personal state of self-denigration associated with a perception of having one's life events determined by external forces. In other words, self-estrangement engenders feelings of boredom, passivity, and fatalism. Passivity in the face of external pressure—uncontested acceptance of imposed conditions—leads to boredom, ennui, and an absence of a sense of purpose. There is thus a strong logical connection between sentiments of powerlessness and self-estrangement.

The logical connection between them notwithstanding, they are not identical. Subjective powerlessness and self-estrangement may be sensitive to different structural components of the labor process or relate to chronic conditions of work within different temporal contexts. It is possible, for instance, that only after prolonged exposure to conditions of subjective powerlessness does one come to accept that powerlessness: in the sense of internalizing it as a belief, or as coming to view that state as something to be lived with. Shorter periods of perceived powerlessness, not leading to self-estranged attributions may have different consequences. Thus, the subjective loss of social power in the short run may be sufficient to inspire actions designed to restore it; actions which given the proper historical conjuncture may prove to be revolutionary in character.

On the other hand, and this is the principal significance of the distinction, the likelihood that people will engage in various oppositional actions declines as one begins to accept as real, and incorporate as legitimate, the subjective appraisal of being without action capacities appropriate to address social circumstances. The person who views himself as powerless and contemptible is not the person most likely to manifest the personal and social resources for undertaking socially significant actions. Rather, he is more prone to express his self-hatred for being powerless in terms of passivity, fatalism, or inwardly directed violence (Fanon 1965).

It is not necessary, of course, that powerlessness precede and give rise to self-contempt. The latter may occur either prior to or simply in the absence of feelings of powerlessness. Boredom and feelings of purposelessness may be present while retaining in some measure a sense of efficacy. In fact, one source of a person's low self-esteem may be the failure to manifest the power he or she believes to be in his or her possession. Such a person may be prompted, by that self-rejection, to do more about external conditions than merely acquiesce to them. In other words, action not inaction, rejection not acceptance, and determination not fatalism may result from the feelings of distaste and denigration held by the not entirely powerless. Albert Memmi brings this point to the fore by linking self-rejection, engendered by the social structures of domination, to hatred of those conditions. The strong (subjectively or otherwise) will seek to resolve self-estrangement through the active rejection of the structure of social domination.

In fact, the empirical analysis shows that powerlessness and self-estrangement are not for the most part sensitive to the same facets of work and employment (table 4.1). The only exception is the impact of bureaucratization, which appears to be associated with both dimensions. Similar to its impact on powerlessness, workers in the more bureaucratized operations are less alienated on the self-extrangement dimension.

Similarly, workers employed by larger contractors and who have the opportunity to deal with written materials as a regular part of their job also report less boredom, passivity, and purposelessness. A reasonable interpretation of these results is that a more complex work environment—a larger and more formalized work organization, and tasks that require both mental and physical labor—is more inherently interesting and involving of the workers' energies, with commensurate impact on their general self-perceptions.

In contrast, two other variables have incremental effects on workers' self-estrangement. Those who are more frequently supervised in the course of their work tend to report greater feelings of estrangement than those who experience looser supervision. Constant surveillance by managerial personnel undercuts a worker's sense of active involvement, leaving in its place a sense of boredom and passivity. Similar feelings are engendered by the presence of a relatively high level of aggregate unemployment in a worker's trade (labor supply). This is a surprising pattern, because individual unemployment does not appear to affect alienation along any of the four dimensions. Seemingly, workers' sense of alienation is affected by structural, but not personal, unemployment. This may be explained by the very nature of aggregate unemployment as a factor over which individual workers have no direct control. Yet, as has been seen, aggregate unemployment is also a pivotal factor influencing individual-level employment conditions (for example, unemployment and job concessions). The combination of its significance and insensitivity to any individual actions seems to breed a sense of self-estrangement among those building tradespeople in labor markets characterized by a high labor supply.

Goal Expedience:

In its broadest sense, this facet of alienation taps a person's perceptions of appropriate means-ends relations. It reflects one's perception of the relative necessity of adopting, or the relative willingness to adopt, a posture which places priority on ends over means; that is, using, to some extent, the ends to justify the means employed to achieve them. The focus on goals rather than means has obvious connections to the capacity for social-transcending action. To escape from oppression (for the moment it does not matter of what form) often requires the adoption of innovative and risky modes of action. Logically, it is only by breaking the bounds of current societal normative prescriptions, subjectively even if not behaviorally, that significant change can be affected.

Goal expedience may be a rational and legitimate personal response to structural social conditions. Sociologist Robert Merton (1968) has argued that this is viewed best in terms of how social structures generate pressures for both conformity and nonconformity. He locates the sources of innovative and rebellious behavior in the frequent discrepancies between socially valued goals and the socially structured opportunities for achieving them. An expedient orientation may, according to Merton, result from the combination of cultural emphasis on certain values and the social structure.

The inherent anarchy of the competitive market engenders innovation, risk taking, and normative boundary stretching. According to Merton:

> Recourse to legitimate channels . . . is limited by a class structure which is not fully open at each level to men of good capacity. Despite our persisting open-class ideology, advance toward the success-goal is relatively rare and notably difficult

for those armed with little formal education and few economic resources. The dominant pressure leads toward the gradual attenuation of legitimate, but by and large ineffectual, strivings and the increasing use of illegitimate, but more or less effective expedients (1968, pp. 199–200).

The adoption of one mode of behavior over another is a more or less predictable function of particular social conditions. And further, modes of behavior, such as innovation and rebellion, pertain not to those who are ineffective and normlessly without direction, but to those who adhere to the adoption of a relatively pragmatic perspective on the relations between means and ends.

Thus, in contrast to those (for example, Archibald 1978) who links it to Durkheim's theory of anomie and thereby dismisses it, goal expedience is a salient and significant facet of Marx's theory of alienation. Goal-expedient values are the subjective complements to actions, often attributed to those seeking relief from oppressive social structures, which are considered innovative or revolutionary.

Among building tradespeople, there are fairly strong connections between the labor process and this form of alienation. Once again, the nature of the contractor's on-site organization is of direct consequence. More transitory work organizations (a short duration on the construction site) and more bureaucratized organizations independently enhance goal-expedient values. In both situations workers tend toward personally enterprising orientations as a means of survival. For example, lining up the next job is always in the fore of workers' minds in trades characteristically on construction sites for relatively short times. Unstable employment circumstances instill in these workers an entrepreneurial or ambitious spirit. They are always seeking to make the most of the job they are on at the time. One way to do this is to simply work as slow as possible, thereby stretching out the duration of the project. Another is to justify a small workforce to the contractor on one basis or another which would have the effect of creating more days of employment for those already on the job. Still another is to *find* new tasks or to justify to the general contractor the need to redo work previously performed. This occurs most often among the finishing trades. There is always a certain amount of damage that occurs during construction. Wallboards get gouged or dented; wood mouldings get scruffed or broken. Occasionally, work done according to the architectual blueprints calls for electrical outlets in inappropriate places, or neglects to specify outlets where there is an obvious need for them. Such changes from original prints are usually added in as extras in the subcontractor's contract. Thus, the enterprising worker who is able to justify the need for re-dos or changes can stretch out his or her employment without jeopardizing the situation of his or her employer.

A slightly different variant of this orientation occurs among pieceworkers. For wallpaperhangers, one of the few trades in which wages are paid according to a piece-rate, the orientation is toward innovations that shorten rather than lengthen the duration of the job. Two goal expedients are generally used by paperhangers. Since they are paid only for the amount of material they hang, paperhangers seek to justify changes in architectural plans that eliminate parts of the job that require excessive time to install an insufficient quantity of wallcovering. Being a paperhanger myself, I have both listened to and engaged in such attempts. The lengths to which a paperhanger will go to convince an architect or decorator not to follow their original designs is truly amazing. The abilities to talk fast, demonstrate the insight of a craftperson, and to meld technical and aesthetic issues into an apparently convincing argument are great assets. Of course, from the paperhanger's point of view, the goal is to convince the architect or decorator not to do the work, regardless of the actual merits of the argument.

In contrast to hourly workers who are assured of their day's pay once they are on the job, pieceworkers always have an eye toward how much they are getting done. Because paperhangers are generally on the site for a short time, the pressures to maintain a goal orientation are fairly constant, and time is always of the essence. Consequently, they look for ways to increase their production. This very often entails using techniques that are not necessarily the most appropriate, but are the most expedient.

It is also worth considering the influences of being a foreman (table 4.1). In this research a negative association was found between holding a foremanship and goal expediency. Being a foreman implies a job security, to the extent that it exists in the industry, that nonmanagerial workers do not have. Tradespeople who are frequently foremen on jobs are thus relieved to some degree from the pressures of finding new jobs or making the most of the one they are on. In addition, foremen are responsible to the contractors and subcontractors for whom they carry out managerial functions. They are thereby restrained from adopting strictly self-serving goal orientations. Rather, they are much more likely to play by the rules, so to speak. That, of course, is of no great surprise since their managerial position allows them to benefit from those rules in ways that nonmanagerial persons cannot. On the other hand, craftworkers, other things being equal, lack that measure of security provided by the managerial location. They therefore tend toward a goal-expedient orientation.

Intellectual Dependence:

The fourth form of subjective alienation to be considered, intellectual dependence, refers to a person's degree of ability to crystalize his or her ideas and to distinguish them from those of other people. One aspect of subjective alienation is not being able to contrast clearly one's own opinions against those expressed by others. To be independent, on the other hand, implies a more clearly defined image of self in that the person views him/herself as holding specific views on important matters that can be articulated and communicated. It also denotes a measure of positive self-valuation to the extent that an independent point of view frequently means holding on to it in the face of disagreement from others. Such disagreement actually may carry with it various kinds of negative social sanctions. For instance, independent thinkers may run the risk of losing the approval and acceptance of valued social associates, such as friends or relatives. At a more significant level, perceiving oneself to possess opinions at odds with the mainstream may also mean awareness of placing in jeopardy material social rewards, such as monetary income and job security. This is precisely the case as regards trade-union awareness and its development. Whatever its limitations, it was and still is contrary to predominant capitalist ideologies and has carried with it substantial risks for those accepting it.

The notion of intellectual dependence has a long tradition in Marxist social analysis. It pertains directly to Marx's treatment of class consciousness, ideological class domination, and the movement from class in-itself to class for-itself. It also informs current neo-Marxist New Class analyses which explicitly concern themselves with linguistic, communicative, intellectual, and ideological processes. For Marx, the alienation of the worker encompassed the inability to separate long-term inherent interests from the operation of capitalist social relations. At an abstract level, Marx referred to the fact that the dominant ideas were those of the dominant class; the material domination of production relations being directly complemented and supported through ideological and intellectual domination. At the more concrete levels it is reflected in methods of production that leave workers mentally debased, and as accepting of reified conceptions of productive and commodity relations.

Lenin took up the problematic of alienation as intellectual dependence implicitly in discussing the limitations of trade union consciousness. His argument that processes of trade union relations with capitalists will not in and of themselves lead workers to a revolutionary awareness rests, in essence, on the underlying premise that the trade unionist has accepted the logic of the capitalist system. The quintessential trade unionists' demand for more merely reflects a belief in the system's capacity for granting more. The purely quantitative demand precludes by its very logic consideration of the qualitative questions about the nature of the productive/distributive system and alternatives to it. Lenin's critique of purely working-class originated action and his advocacy of the professionally guided vanguard party derives from an implicit appreciation of the intellectual consequences of alienated labor.[6]

Similarly, processes of identification with the oppressor (Marcuse 1972; Fanon 1965; Memmi 1968) engenders affectation of cultural and social mannerisms. But they also mean the partial acceptance of the system of domination itself. The processes of intellectual alienation thus give partial explanation to the reproduction of such relations of domination. In this sense, the colonial mechanisms of indirect rule can be understood not only in terms of material advantages which accrue to elite segments of the oppressed, but also in terms of the unavoidable mental, cognitive, and logical identification resulting from systemic structures of domination. Thus, even in the process of liberation the incapacity to escape the bounds of the logic of the system of their subjugation conditions, at least in part, repetitions of earlier patterns and reconstructions of prior structures.

New Class theorists have drawn heavily on the concept of intellectual capacity (Ehrenreich and Ehrenreich 1979; Gouldner 1978a; 1978b; 1976; Mallet 1975). Gouldner states rather boldly that the basis of the emergent social class is rooted in the relationship to the means of production, but informed by distinctive productive functions. Besides playing a unique role in production, Gouldner argues that it is distinguishable by virtue of cultural capital. The New Class' cultural capital largely resides in its ideological commitment to the practical involvement in a speech community defined by a "culture of critical discourse" having distinctive ties to the concept of alienation (also see Habermas 1971). "The culture of critical discourse is characterized by speech that is relatively more situation-free, more context or field 'independent.' This speech culture thus values expressly legislated meaning and devalues tacit, context-limited meanings" (Gouldner 1978a, 177). Among the most significant of its consequences, the culture of critical discourse promotes the capacity to conceive and thereby pursue not only "what is," but "what can be"; in other words, a theoretical and practical commitment to social alternatives.

The ability to formulate opinions and view them in juxtaposition to those held by others, bears directly on the capacity for overcoming the aspects of work which serve as potential barriers to intellectual development. This is highlighted by Bernstein's (1971) work on class-related patterns of language acquisition and the origins and consequences of restricted and elaborated linguistic codes. Connecting the localized context-bound speech of the working class to the debilitating effects of the conditions of work and authority on the job, he locates one important facet of how class structures are maintained and perpetuated. Similarly, Melvin Kohn and Carmi Schooler, in a series of studies have demonstrated the reciprocal connections between structural components of life on the job—particularly the opportunities for self-direction, autonomy, and the substantive complexity of work—and intellectual flexibility (Kohn 1976, 1983; Kohn and Schooler 1973; 1978; Schooler 1976). They have found that circumstances of working life may have impact on workers' cognitive functioning; consequences that shape their subsequent changes for jobs with more desirable characteristics and less debilitating correlates.

Hence, there is a direct theoretical connection between alienating components of the labor process and workers' cognitive and intellectual capabilities. However, this research shows only weak indications of such connections. Only occupational complexity emerges from the analysis as having an impact on workers' intellectual dependence. Workers in the higher skilled trades tend to have a clearer notion of how their own ideas differ from those of their close associates. On the other hand, workers in the lower skilled trades report little in the way of differentiation between their ideas and opinions about important issues and those of their friends and relatives. This result is in substantial agreement with the work of sociologists working in much broader occupational contexts (for example, see Kohn 1976; 1983; Kohn and Schooler 1978). It is of interest to note though that commensurate relationships were obtained from the building trades; so often associated with uniformly skilled and advantaged craft occupations.

Discontent

The social sources and consequences of discontent have been analyzed both by theorists focusing narrowly on the labor process and more broadly on the dynamics of collective behavior and social movements. Interest in the circumstances of work and employment that relate to workers' satisfactions and dissatisfactions has a long tradition. It derives from the philosophical and sociological questions posed by St. Simon, Spencer, and Durkheim, among others, about the relationship between individual and societal well-being and the process of modernization.

Emile Durkheim viewed the problems in terms of the consequences of an advancing division of labor which simultaneously performs economic functions that "raise societies to luxury" but also impinge on the members of society in defining the most significant "conditions of their existence" (1933, p. 63). Durkheim was distinctly concerned with the potential for the destruction of the necessary social bonds between important segments of society, not the least of which being the moral and normative ties among society's members. If the total system becomes too vague and distant from the daily activities or if the daily experiences of work become too onerous and without apparent purpose the individual loses the feeling that he is serving something. This result is "due, in part to the fact that the working classes are not really satisfied with the conditions under which they live, but very often accept them only as constrained and forced, since they have not the means to change them" (p. 356). Durkheim thus presented satisfying workers' needs at least in a minimal fashion as a societal matter of some importance since broadly felt discontent among the general workforce can have serious ramifications for the health of the entire social body.

Modern proponents of this perspective concerned with the effects of the postindustrial mass society have accepted Durkheim's notion of worker satisfaction as a social problem (for example, Galbraith 1967; Bell 1973; 1960). Even a post-scarcity society requires that workers be productive, however, and unhappy workers, as it has often been demonstrated, usually manifest their discontent in terms of low productivity, high turnover, absenteeism, and even sabotage. To cite the HEW Task Force on Work in America, "if the nature of work is dissatisfying (or worse), severe repercussions are likely to be experienced in other parts of the social system" (O'Toole et al. 1973, p. xv). Similarly, sociologist Neal Smelser argues that job dissatisfaction, like other social aspects, "feed back into and influence the productive process." Consequently, workers' sense of satisfaction is one of the more salient variables which "determine the amount of work offered by a laborer" (1976, 103–105).

The literature on work-related discontent is so vast and so complex it will not be discussed here. Instead, I will consider the issue of job discontent in terms of its relationship within the alienation problematic. This means identifying those aspects of employment and the labor process that influence workers' relative job satisfaction. It also means an examination of the interrelationships between job satisfaction and the elements of alienation.

Overall, construction workers' sense of satisfaction with their job is influenced by a somewhat wider range of factors than the other facets of subjective alienation. Occupational, managerial, and union employment characteristics have a significant impact. Not too surprisingly, workers who are more frequently unemployed and those who report a greater incidence of jobs on which they make concessions tend to be more dissatisfied than those with a better employment picture. Obviously, neither being out of work nor working under substandard conditions is an objectively desirable circumstance. Their impact on workers' discontent, however, indicates that workers do not complacently accept them as unfortunate yet inevitable aspects of their lives in the industry.

The fact that unemployment and job concessions are such strong dissatisfiers also helps to explain why union officials and contractors are so concerned about the political ramifications. If workers were complacent in the face of periodic unemployment, for instance, there would be no problems for those holding union office during periods of slack market demand. However, as it stands, a high rate of unemployment among a local's membership means a high proportion of dissatisfied members who tend to direct their dissatisfaction at their elected leadership. In short, union members unhappy about their employment circumstances voice their discontent by voting their present administration out of office.

By the same token, it is only because workers have a negative reaction to job concessions that contractors must accept additional managerial burdens when winning such concessions. The discontent job concessions creates may be manifest in a poorly motivated workforce that has to be monitored on a fairly constant basis. In the extreme, contractors have to employ stricter supervision in order to protect themselves from resentful workers who may purposefully waste material or who may choose to work at a level well below acceptable qualitative and quantitative standards.

Other sources of satisfaction for building tradespeople are grounded in their attachments to contractor and union organizations. The managerial position is a significant area of satisfaction, apart from the employment advantages to which it is closely allied. Fulfilling the duties for the on-site operation of a contractor's production responsibilities bring with it the true pleasure of accomplishment. Of course, there is also the sense of satisfaction of achieving the position in a contractor's managerial hierarchy. Many workers strive for years to attain a regular spot as foreman, and success in doing so becomes a point of satisfaction in itself.

Similarly with becoming a steward and actively participating in the union. In an industry where the intrinsic rewards of work are increasingly difficult to come by, tradespeople can still turn to their local union. On the construction site, stewards with responsibility for upholding work rules and resolving minor grievances are engaged in a satisfying sphere of activity independent of their strictly production-related duties in the labor process. Off the job, too, there is a lot of gratification for tradespeople who help to maintain a strong union. Commitment to the union is a point of pride and identification. In fact, some express it in the way they view a member who is a foreman or who adopts the employer's perspective as *a boss's man*. The perjorative connotations of the term reflect the basic importance and correctness they feel to be associated with being a good union man.

Social Alienation

As mentioned earlier, the complement to subjective and psychological dynamics of alienation and discontent is alienation as a social-structural condition rather than as a perceived state. Social alienation refers to the quantitative and qualitative estrangements people experience in their social associations. At the macrosociological level it pertains to the characteristic relationship within and between social classes during particular historical junctures. At the microsociological level it refers to the significant aspects of the relations people have that reflect a relative degree of social isolation.

As with other forms of alienation, the kernal of Marx's analysis appears in a rudimentary form; provocative but not developed to a degree that would permit direct empirical applications without further elaboration. Marx's focus on the objective alienation of social life is rooted in his materialist view of historical social forms and social transformation. It is in and through their social relations that people carry out their socially productive functions. If in the act of production people produce their conditions of existence, a significant aspect of those conditions are the patterns to their interpersonal relationships. The historical forms of production are defined by the social relations corresponding to them: "In all these forms [of production], the reproduction of presupposed relations are the foundations of development" (1973, p. 487). Thus, alienation within capitalism encompasses more than the conditions of work, it also includes relations between people. "What is true of man's relationship to his work, to the product of his work and to himself, is also true of his relationship to other men" (1963, p. 129). The capitalist division of labor engenders a material estrangement in people's interpersonal relations. A direct consequence of the labor process is that "man is alienated from other men."

The alienation generated between people in the labor process includes both circumstances by which people are alienated *in* their relationships and *from* them. The former refers to the content of the social exchange between people. Simply, social relationships neither demand equal contributions nor return equal rewards to those engaged in them (Blau 1964). Reciprocal relations, in which both parties contribute, are more involving than unilateral ones, in which the flow of communication is one directional. In other words, people whose social relations and group affiliations are characterized by a greater proportion of reciprocal associations are less alienated in their relationships than those who experience a preponderance of unilateral associations. For example, it is the difference between participative and autocratic forms of decision making. In the first, workers have direct input and actively contribute to the exchange of ideas, information, and opinion, which leads to the actual decision or policy. In the second, workers merely receive the result of the decision process—instructions from management—and are faced with the relatively less complicated task of compliance.

Among building tradespeople, those who have the opportunity to engage in consultations with contractors about production problems on the site or who coordinate the activities of different trades are less alienated in their productive relations than those who only receive instructions and carry them out. Consider, too, the intricate interactions required to coordinate the efforts of ironworkers and operating engineers working to erect a building's steel skeletal structure. Hoisting a steel I-beam weighing several thousand pounds to the proper level and then jockeying it into position demands close communication employing both visual and auditory signals. On very large structures the operating engineer may be completely dependent on communicated information as he may not be able to actually see the area where the I-beam he is lifting is being placed.

This element of the quality of social relationships, as a structural factor, informs, at least in part, Basil Bernstein's (1971) distinction between restricted and elaborated linguistic codes. It also appears in theories of the New Class as a speech community sharing a culture of critical discourse (Gouldner 1978a; 1978b) or a common interest in communicative competencies (Habermas 1973). Analysis of the content of social exchange gives sociological relevance to the origins and development of speech variants and grounds the New Class in objective social relations, not just subjective interests and normative value commitments.

To be alienated from social relationships means to experience a relatively paucity of social contacts or structured relationships. Georg Simmel (1955) saw the development of society and the growth of individuality as reciprocal phenomena in that complex social forms allow for, but also are defined by, the multiple relationships and group affiliations of the individual members of society. For Simmel, this defined the inherent dialectic of objective and subjective processes and of the individual and societal relationships. Simmel tied quantitative processes of association and group affiliation to a sociologically relevant conceptualization of individuality and to a conditioned need for personal resources. "Thus one can say that society arises from the individual and that the individual arises out of association" (1955, p. 163). The extent to which people are alienated from social associations is a function of the opportunities for their development.

For instance, Kornblum's (1974) study of industrial and social organization in a Chicago working-class community deals with the significance of structured community-level personal and organizational affiliations. He notes that people from ethnic groups having a territorial base in the mill neighborhood can increase or maintain prestige in the community through participation in the union. Groups not having representation at the community level cannot benefit from union participation in the same way. The latter are not able to translate power in the steel mills into political influence in the local community. James Geschwender (1977) makes a similar observation in his study of an organization of black workers in the automobile industry. The Detroit-based organization held strengths and weaknesses largely by virtue of the presence or absence of community and political linkages.

At the individual level, social alienation tends to interact with subjective forms of alienation. As noted earlier, the confluence of subjective and objective factors may be of primary importance in determining the actualization of action potentialities. To the extent that this insight has been recognized, the general trend is to posit a facilitating effect of social integration on personal intellectual flexibility and comprehension (Bernstein 1971; Coser 1975; Kohn and Schooler 1978) and career attainment. Arthur Stinchcomb (1974) suggests that bureaucratic organizations are positively related to intellectual flexibility and creativeness partly because they structure cosmopolitan-type social associations. Rose Coser sums up this orientation generally by concluding that, "a social structure that is more complex seems to be associated with the development of intellectual flexibility and self-direction" (1975, p. 258).

To these observations it is possible to add the perspective

that social and subjective alienative forms may have opposing influences. The complex social situation most likely contains both elements that provide the structural opportunities for growth, intellectual development, and the exercise of personal efficacy and those that impinge on the person's capacity for taking advantage of them. For example, Robert Blauner (1964) found that the variability and self-direction associated with craft trades in the printing industry led to low subjective powerlessness and strong feelings of personal self-worth; in other words, low subjective alienation. On the other hand, also focusing on the printing crafts, Lipset, Trowe, and Coleman (1956) found that the demands of the printing industry tended to foster intimate primary group affiliations; in other words, social alienation.

In this study of building tradespeople, I have tried to analyze four aspects of people's interpersonal associations: the number of interpersonal contacts people held off the job ("Social Network Size"), the proportion of their network made up of people from their same trade ("Percent Network Same Trade"), the proportion of their network made up of members of their family ("Percent Network Relatives"), and their number of organizational affiliations ("Organization Network Size"). Similar to the subjective forms of alienation, the primary question is whether the social aspects of alienation are related to the various components of the labor process.

It can be seen from table 4.2 that, while not overwhelming, there are a few significant connections between a person's role in the labor process and his general social relationships. For one, working in larger firms at a skilled trade appears to foster somewhat smaller social networks comprised of a higher proportion of people from one's own trade. These factors tend to bind workers into a slightly more uniform and smaller set of social contacts.

In contrast, participation in contractor and union organizations appear to have more cosmopolitanizing influences. Foremen tend to have larger social networks than non-managerial tradespeople. Moreover, their social contacts off the job are tied less to kinship than is the case for other construction workers. Consonently, on-site consultative relations with employers and formal union duties as a steward are associated with broader organizational memberships. In other words, those who regularly assume formal organizational responsibilities on the job also participate more often in organizations off the job.

Such connections between tradespeople's working experiences and their nonworking lives provides a clue as to the social meaning of craft work. Popular beliefs about the life of the craftsman, mostly fueled by mistaken academic analogies that equate craft occupations with the professions, tend to emphasize its socially integrated and mainstream nature. It is more than a little ironic then to find that the typical factors of craft work—high levels of skill and the freedom to be self-directing on the job—condition a more local rather than cosmopolitan social network. People in trades that engage them in skilled and self-directing work tend to socialize with fewer people and more often with family members than other construction workers. In other words, they tend to have more local and, in terms used her, more alienated, social network formations.

Frequently ignored aspects of craft production are the ones with cosmopolitanizing social influences. In particular, formal duties in bureaucratic organizations. Taken together, fulfilling managerial functions in contractors' firms and shop steward functions in the union are associated with larger, more varied, and organizationally oriented patterns of social association off the job. In fact, the impact of the managerial location on tradespeople's subjective and social alienation is pervasive.

Holding an official foremanship position appears to be the factor with the most telling consequences for individual tradespeople. Those foremen with consultative relations with their employers have a greater sense of personal efficacy, a stronger sense of playing by the rules, and higher job satisfactions. They also tend to have larger and more varied social networks. The social, normative, and subjective consequences of managerial location in the building and construction industry are not dissimilar to those attached to more broadly conceived class categories.

This point is relevant directly to an understanding of the relationship between occupations and the class structure of advanced capitalism. Some theorists have argued for the limited

Table 4.2. Regressions of Social Alienation Variables with Craft Labor Process Factors

	Social Network Size	Percent Network Same Trade	Percent Network Relatives	Organization Network Size
Production Location				
Onsite Size (log)	.02	.01	.07	.04
Duration	-.14	.12	.06	.16
Bureaucracy	.13	.04	.00	.05
Contractor Size (log)	-.29***	.27***	-.05	.12
Craft: Complexity	-.04	.32***	.14	.07
Mentality	.10	-.02	-.02	.10
Centrality	.03	.18	.07	.13
Labor Supply	.13	-.04	-.01	.03
Managerial Location				
Foremanship	.15*	.10	-.19**	.08
Administrative Consultation	.00	.06	.03	-.14
Onsite Consultation	-.02	-.01	-.03	.27***
Trade Union				
Militancy	.21	-.07	.16	.24
Size (log)	-.11	.10	.04	-.17
Attendance	-.10	.17	.06	-.04
Stewardship	.13	-.09	-.05	.18**

Table 4.2. Regressions of Social Alienation Variables with Craft Labor Process Factors (Cont'd.)

	Social Network Size	Percent Network Same Trade	Percent Network Relatives	Organization Network Size
Work Autonomy				
Self Direction	-.20**	-.05	-.01	-.06
Supervision	-.07	.01	.05	-.02
Individual Employment				
Unemployment	-.11	.02	.06	.00
Nonunion Employment	-.08	-.10	-.12	.03
TA Concessions	-.02	.10	-.04	.04
Individual Controls				
Age	-.21**	.04	.01	.26***
Education	.05	.13	-.02	.17**
$\bar{R}^2$	.10	.27	.00	.12

*p<.10   **p<.05   ***p<.01

relevance of a class analysis. Instead they seek to interpose organizational relations of authority and occupational characteristics bearing on autonomy and self-direction. In the words of sociologist Melvin Kohn, "insofar as ownership and hierarchical position affect alienation, it is mainly because owners and people high in the supervisory structure are able to be self-directed in their work" (Kohn 1976, p. 122). From this perspective, it is not class but occupation that underlies alienation. Owners and supervisors are less alienated partly because their jobs have the right characteristics. Changes can be made in the division of labor such that workers' tasks are also more self-directing and allowing for greater participation in organizational decision processes. Solutions to the problems of dissatisfaction and alienation in work are thus assumed to be attainable through alterations in organizational arrangements within existing property relations. On the other hand, as Kohn (1985) has recently pointed out, such approaches do protect against the notion that shifts away from capitalist forms of ownership automatically mean unalienated conditions on the job for workers.

Why then is the managerial class element, in construction, so easily distinguishable, not only in terms of unalienated work structure and superior employment, but also as regards the unalienated subjective and social correlates of its involvement in the labor process? For one thing, it is a mistake to substitute occupational conditions for class location. Rather, class structure and occupational structure are such that the distributions of occupational and task characteristics occur within and are partially determined by the broader class arrangement. Alienation, then, is one direct manifestation of class location, but also of the occupationally mediated process through which people experience the working out of class relations in the labor process. For instance, various factors play a role in determining the amount of self-direction, closeness of supervision, or the substantive complexity of work. Many of them reflect the imperatives of efficiency and control in class-dominated work organizations that expand or contract workers' opportunities for autonomy. Many others are intrinsically linked to managerial class location.

Thus, in the case of construction, those in positions of management, who benefit from the labor of their coworkers through forms of coexploitation, also avoid the alienation more closely linked to the noncontradictory working class. True, foremen in the building trades are less alienated partly because their class position provides them the advantages of more self-directed and unsupervised work. But circumstances unrelated to task and job characteristics are significant as well. There are connections between formal managerial location and feelings of personal efficacy, satisfaction, and social integration apart from the influences of occupation, task content, and employment structure. In other words, the class location has social significance over and above the specific material and social advantages associated with it.[7]

A second reason for the salience of class position in the building industry is the organizational context of the building labor process. As Max Weber argued, the structural complexity of bureaucratic work organizations has a direct impact on class antagonisms. Not that bureaucratic industrial capitalism transcends the material bases of class conflict; only that the greater distance between exploiting capitalist and exploited worker makes the conflict of class interests that bind them much less visible. Emergence of class antagonisms are most likely when the production relations are most direct and uncomplicated by bureaucratic and managerial differentiation.

In construction, production is conducted on a relatively small scale and the labor process is relatively less bureaucratized than in fixed-plant mass production. The comparatively short and simplified hierarchical structure thus enhances the social salience of the managerial position in the labor process. The direct correspondence between management position and various rewards and advantages enhances the significance of the formal position. It comes to represent in and of itself a reward; the attainment or nonattainment of which having implications for people's self-perceptions and social orientations.

Under more complex organizational arrangements, wherein there are greater differentiation among management positions themselves, the relationship between formal position and various rewards is less apparent and the formal position loses inherent significance. Mediational processes thus become more prominent in the more complex organizations. To the extent that this is the case, it suggests that circumstances at the organizational level inform whether productive relations develop in antagonistic or cooperative directions. In other words, organizational processes and structures may play an important intervening role in the development of class relations. In any event, there is the somewhat ironic circumstance that in the construction industry's less hierarchically structured labor process the formal class position retains direct associations to alienation not necessarily present in circumstances of greater organizational complexity.

Alienation, Labor Process, and Class Consciousness

As a general observation, the structure of the labor process in construction influences both subjective and behavioral forms of alienation. To some extent, different aspects of the labor process affect different facets of alienation and discontent. As has been discussed, workers' discontent is more sensitive to their conditions of employment (for example, unemployment and job concessions) and organizational attachments than it is to on-site organization and work structure. Subjective alienation, on the other hand, is conditioned more by work-related factors and less by employment. And third, social alienation is largely affected by occupational conditions and managerial location in contractors' firms.

The absence of uniform effects on workers' alienation raises issues bearing on the significance of alienation in the social dynamic. For one, workers' self-reported job satisfaction does not always reflect the totality of their individual responsiveness to the conditions of labor. People do not, of course, have to be aware of or accurately assess the relationships of production to be affected by them, either positively or negatively. To the contrary, there is a degree to which aspects of the relationships that workers feel to be satisfying, or at least not dissatisfying, can actually have harmful or negative consequences. The mechanisms by which people come to perceive their social circumstances are tied to alienated relationships of which they are not entirely congnizant.

This line of reasoning further implies that the alienation-class consciousness relationships should be treated as highly problematic. Workers' alienation is not merely a measuring stick of the goodness or badness of society; it is integral to the process of social change itself.

Marx and Engels held alienation to be the essential ingredient in the processes determining whether the class *in itself* becomes a class *for itself*. Their treatment is complex and somewhat ambiguous; entertaining the likelihood of contradictory tendencies. On the one hand, they associated alienation with rejection of the capitalist system. Experiences in and of a system of alienation directly influence workers to perceive alienation as both condition and process and then to revolt against it. The often-noted romanticist element to their writings surfaces here, for underlying this part of the analysis is the premise that the truth of material existence (real social relations) prevails over the myths of bourgeoise ideology (false consciousness). Most alienation and discontent theorists adopt this logic by positing positive correlations between discontent or alienation on one side, and oppositional or negation consciousness on the other. The basic argument is that since active rejection of current circumstances derives from deep-seated dissatisfaction or alienation, then greater alienation or discontent should associate with more strenuous rejection of the social order. Such subjective emiseration theories complement material emiseration theories that posit linear relationships between objective social conditions and collective revolt.

On the other hand, however, Marx and Engels also saw alienation as debilitation and limitation for the working class. Commodity fetishism, for example, is the subjective correlate of objectively alienated productive relations in which workers have lost control of the objects of their own labor. Workers come to place inordinate value on the inanimate results of their labor as a result of their own alienation. The inversion of subject and object in alienated production helps to fuel its continuity by instilling passivity and acquiescence among workers. This part

of their analysis then rests on their understanding of how alienation can promote conservative or reactionary outcomes.

First of all, greater alienation may interact with situation-
specific sources of discontent to reduce class consciousness.
The various dimensions of alienation that have been discussed
can be viewed as subjective and social resources that an individual draws on when seeking to address areas of dissatisfaction. Insufficient personal resources (such as, feeling oneself to
be powerless or estranged from life events) can, over time,
prompt re-evaluations of the initial feelings of dissatisfaction.
Capacities not up to the task of social action are more likely to
lead to a change in affective state.

Thus, the extremely alienated, lacking subjective resources,
may not be able to act in reaction to their discontent other than
to adapt to extant circumstances, possibly by refusing to focus
on unpleasant conditions or cognitively restructuring personal
priorities. In contrast, those who are less alienated subjectively
may be more likely to take actions in their own behalf. Self-
perceptions of social efficacy and self-worth are the precondi-
tions for actively rejecting unsatisfactory relationships of work
and employment.

This, in any event, appears to be the case among the
building tradespeople in this study.[8] One item from the survey
questionnaire asked respondents the degree to which they
agreed or disagreed with the statement, "In my trade the relationship between workers and contractors is like a
partnership." Disagreement with the statement was taken as a
class conscious position. Agreement with the statement indicated acceptance of a bourgeoise belief in the cooperative
nature of production relationships. A single item such as this obviously does not capture more than a portion of so complex a
concept as class consciousness. It does not tap attitudes about
individual versus structural determinants of social position,
recognition of classes as cohesive social actors, or perceptions
of the form of the class structure and its susceptibility to basic
alteration. It is but one dimension, albeit a central one. Whether
one rejects the ideology of the dominant class—in this case rejecting the idea of cooperative, partnership-like employment
relations—reflects a class conscious orientation.

Also shown in table 4.3, this restricted measure of class consciousness has substantial connections to workers' objective circumstances in the labor process as well as their subjective alienation. Among all the various production relationship

Table 4.3. Zero-Order Correlations and Regression of Class Consciousness Variable with Alienation Variables and Select Production Relationship Variables

	(1)[a]	(2)[b]
Alienation		
Powerlessness	.11**	.06
Self-Estrangement	.15***	.07
Goal-Expedience	.20***	.04
Intellectual Dependence	-.06	-.07
Job Satisfaction	-.27***	-.13*
Social Network Size	.06	.04
Percent Network Same Trade	-.14***	-.11*
Percent Network Family	-.00	-.14*
Organization Network Size	-.06	-.05
Production Relationships		
Foremanship	-.33***	-.15*
Bureaucracy	.31***	.22***
Stewardship	.13**	.18**
Job Concessions	.26***	.16**
Individual		
Age	-.16***	-.05***
Education	.02	.05
R²	—	.22

*p<.10   **p<.05   ***p<.01

[a]Zero-order corrlations. The class consciousness variable is scored in the positive direction. Strong disagreement with the belief in a worker-contractor partnership reflects the high end of the scale.

[b]OLS regression analysis.

variables considered thus far, the four appearing in the table were the ones with significant empirical associations to the class consciousness indicator. Union shop stewards and their managerial counterparts, foremen, tend to have opposing perceptions of the employment relationship. Of course, it is not too surprising to find that union stewards have a more class conscious orientation than foremen. Nevertheless, it is worth noting that performing formal duties in contractor or union organization is something more than just an instrumental means to employment ends for building tradespeople. If nothing else, it would seem that foremen are boss's men in sentiment as well as deed.

In addition, giving in to job concessions also has a predictable impact on class consciousness. Those tradespeople who more frequently find themselves on jobs where they work under substandard conditions are much more likely to view their relations with employers in conflictual rather than cooperative terms. While discussing this question on the job, one tradesman put it succinctly, if a bit facetiously, "Sure we're partners. My boss makes me his partner on every job he is in trouble on. I'm a partner in all his problems. On the good jobs, I'm just a worker." It does not seem too far afield to surmise that, as a general rule, involvement in work relationships such as those being discussed—where workers are regularly approached and quite often forced to accede to concessions about work rules and remuneration—leads workers to an accurate appreciation of the conflict of interests between themselves and those seeking the concessions.

The link between the on-site work organization's hierarchical structure and workers' perceptions of the contractor-tradesperson relationship rests on the same basic premise. The presence of a defined managerial structure on the construction site, represented by a greater number of formal positions, no doubt heightens the impression among workers that there is divergence of interest in the labor process. Having worked on both relatively bureaucratized and nonbureaucratized sites for extended periods, I have been able to appreciate the different orientations they instill. Tradespeople accustomed to the non-bureaucratic work arrangement tend to assume greater responsibility for producing a job of good quality. They are also more directly involved in the various production and political (that is, union-related) problems that may arise on the job. The more bureaucratic site, however, tends to remove most workers from such points of involvement. Production problems are handled through the managerial chain of command involving supervisors, foremen, and crew chiefs. Union-contractor problems are handled between union stewards and contractor-managers. Usually, workers are merely informed as to the results of a decision process in which they have no direct input.

Probably the most telling indication of the differences between the two types of work settings is that which occurs when tradespeople who are usually on nonbureaucratized sites are employed on the other. More than once I have seen a chagrined worker walk away from a conference between a supervisor and a foreman after being told his input was neither expected nor appreciated. These same tradespeople were often heard during coffee break and lunchtime converstations declare their distaste for "this kind of work" on jobs where there was no appreciable difference in the physical tasks required of them. The difference was in the lower levels of mental and social involvement asked of workers by management in the more bureaucratized setting.

Analysis of the determinants of class consciousness in the labor process also affords an opportunity to explore the meaning of social alienation. Thus far the social alienation dimensions have been interpreted in terms of the distinction between local and cosmopolitan social networks. The underlying premise is that the local social network, comprised of few associations of little status differentiation, reflects a less desirable configuration of social affiliations and reflects the alienated condition. The cosmopolitan network, represented by numerous social contacts with a more varied composition, has an unalienated characteristic.

The local-cosmopolitan comparison figures prominently in modernization and functionalist theories of social development, but only inplicitly in Marxist and neo-Marxist theories. This leaves the issue of the relevance of social alienation to an analysis of class consciousness open to question.

The complexity of the social alienation-consciousness relationship resides in the fact that the social structural dimensions bear on both subjective and psychological disaffection and of resource acquisition. Those with the most reason for opposing existing social conditions (because they have the least in the way of social resources) also tend to have the fewest social structurally related opportunities for doing so. This implies a structural determination which informs the development of social awarenesses apart from strictly subjective processes. Marx made this point in his analysis of class struggles in nineteenth-century France. What distinguished the rural peasentry from the urban proletariat was not so much their respective economic and material privations as it was their differential social structures. The former were not a revolutionary class for Marx, not because they suffered no hardship within a developing capitalism, but because they did so in relative social isolation. Social alienation is a structural source of acquiescence because "there is merely a local interconnection" from which "the identity of their interests begets no community, no national bond and no political organization" (Marx 1963, p. 124). People with only local connections that promote "no diversity of development, no variety of talent, no wealth of social relations" are not in a position to articulate on oppositional consciousness.

To the contrary, consciousness is conditioned by the nature of social connections such that rejection of the dominant ideology requires the cosmopolitan social associations that foster individuality. The working class was the nineteenth-century revolutionary class partly because its members experienced their social conditions in direct association with and in contact to members of the class with antagonistic interests. In other words, for the individual it is the differentiated cosmopolitan social network and not the alienated local network that permits the development of a perceptive understanding of the bases of productive relations. To quote again from Marx, "private property can be abolished only on condition of an all-round development of individuals" (1970, p. 117).

The contradictory nature of the relationship between social alienation and class consciousness is seen here. On the one hand, the development of an oppositional orientation (or at least the partial rejection of bourgeoise ideology) is predicated on the establishment of a "wealth of social relations." On the other hand, the nature of capitalist production generally militates against such opportunities for workers. According to sociologist Rose Coser:

> To the proposition that the worker is deprived of the means of production and the product of his labor must be added the proposition that the worker is deprived, when at work, of some vital social-structural prerequisites for the development of his individuality (1976, p. 241).

The differentiated complex social network defines, for Coser, the necessary social-structural prerequisite. One's social experiences in the labor process that preclude broadly based social networks undercut the development of individuality and social autonomy. This places the potential growth of working class consciousness in relatively unalienated social circumstances. The socially alienated, in contrast, reflecting capitalism's suppression of individuality among workers, may be less likely to visualize themselves in opposition to bourgeoise notions of production.

Similar tendencies have been noted among building tradespeople (table 4.3). The composition of their social networks is directly relevant to how they see their employment relationship, independent of the influences of organizational complexity, employment conditions, and managerial and union roles in production. Specifically, tradespeople whose social networks are comprised of a greater proportion of relatives and of people from the same building trade as themselves tend to hold to a less class-aware view of their relationships to their employers. Social associations bounded by occupation and family have a provincial quality evoking Marx's view of rural peasantry. The infusion of imposed circumstances into workers' off-the-job associations (namely, occupational and familial ties) is in this sense the social analogue to adopting a societally prevalent ideology. Coupled with localized competitive market conditions and variable production sites, social alienation reflects a restricted and segmented social existence that makes it difficult for a construction worker to see beyond the present state of labor relations. Of course, any interpretation of the connection between workers' microsocial structures and value-belief structures is open to argument. However, I was often struck during conversations with other workers about their relationships to their employers by their tendency to accept most aspects as givens which they have little capacity to alter. And, secondly, there is a tendency to personalize the relationship. The acceptance of a specific and unequal role in a personalized relationship lends a certain kinship, or primary-group, quality to the perception of the employment relationship. Workers in the same trade often discuss their respective bosses and supervisors in very much the same general tone as would speak of a patriarchal family relation. It is possible that workers will tend to see their employment relationship through lenses colored by their broader range of nonworking relationships. Workers who socialize mostly with those to whom they are tied through occupation and family visualize their employment relationship in similar terms. Those with diverse social relationships less determined by external circumstances, accordingly may be better able to see beyond socially acceptable images to what perhaps is a more accurate reading of the situation, but one that requires a less personalized, forgiving, and acquiescent perception.

Thus a few aspects emerge from the analysis as salient in the overall dialectic of alienation. Most obviously, subjective alienation and social alienation, as social consequents, are significantly affected by objective conditions in production. Many researchers, especially from a managerial vantage, have looked at the problem of alienation in terms of ways to manipulate workers' sense of discontent and malaise through slight alterations in the organization of the workplace. In this sense, part of the task is to manage workers' sentiments about their work. However, because the impact of the labor process is not uniform for all forms of alienation and because not all aspects of the labor process is an interrelated organizational totality that includes the economic and political relations with workers' unions, attempts to impose changes run into inherent difficulty. For one thing, both unemployment and job concessions, as determinants of workers' alienation, are untouched by strictly organizational redesign. To the contrary, as discussed in chapter three, work structures commonly associated with workers' alienation are frequently tied to managerial positions or are influenced by market circumstances and labor-management conflict.

Similar points have to be made as well with regard to the relationship between alienation and class consciousness. To some degree, workers' perceptions of production relations are tied to the objective conditions they meet with on the job and in their relationships to their employers and their union. In conjunction, however, they are also tied to their own personal alienation. The confluence of alienated conditions of work and workers' emotional and social responses to them characterize the development, or nondevelopment, of a class-based perspective on production relationships. Thus, in trying to come to grips with the problematic of alienation and class consciousness, it is necessary to speak in terms of the configuration of alienated circumstances, rather than of independent linkages. The latter approach would be justifiable if only one or two factors had overarching significance, or if a multiplicity of variables had uniform consequences. But as has been discussed, the influences are much more complex. Some are complementary, but many others are contradictory or conditional. Moreover, many of the relationships are better understood in terms of their reciprocal and mutually dependent connections as opposed to simple unidirectional cause-effect relations.[9]

If this analysis is extrapolated to the broadest levels, it can be seen why "most oppressed" theses of class protest and revolution are consistently shown to be inadequate. Segments of society that suffer the severest deprivations are least likely to have the material, social, psychological, or emotional resources for successful mobilization. Consequently, they may actually be relatively unresponsive or reactive to the sources of discontent in comparison to less alienated groups. In line with this reasoning, there is a hint at why classes "of the middle sort" (Rude 1980; E.P. Thompson 1963) have played such an integral role in militant social movements during earlier historical stages of productive development. As groups suffering the losses of greater alienation in and from the sum of societal relations, they react quicker, more definitively, and more pointedly to changes in their social circumstances than do those for whom alienated relations are already a way of existence.

At the much narrower levels, perhaps a bit more directly

relavant to the focus on building tradespeople, it is also possible to begin to understand how alienation can be the foundation for progressive revolt in the eighteenth and nineteenth centuries and for the apparent opposite in the late twentieth. Subcontracting and technological changes in production have deskilled and framented most building crafts. Consequently, labor markets have come to be more competitive through the last century. Simultaneously, basic changes in the national and world economies have given to corporations with national and global interests an overwhelming impact on local and regional markets. Nowhere is the ever greater dependence of local economies more directly felt than in the construction industry. The loss of control at the point of production as well as in the broader realm of the market, occurring over many decades, has been real. Thus, if we reconsider the basis of the hard hat mentality so commonly associated with the building trades—the conservatism, overblown patriotism, jingoism, and social rigidity—in the light of this analysis, something other than affluence and embourgoisement is discovered. We find instead a defensive and somewhat limited response to the marginalities, insecurities, and areas of powerlessness that characterize workers' lives on and off the construction site.

5

CRISIS IN CONSTRUCTION

Toward a Strategy for Overcoming Market Forces in Labor Relations and Housing Production

Crisis is a term central in the lexicon of social analysis. From a structuralist perspective it signifies a convergence of conditions that reflect as well as precipitate major social changes. Its use is ideally suited to those seeking some form of social intervention, evoking as it does the sense of imminent disaster. Yet is is precisely in this sense that the construction industry can be said to be in a state of crisis.

The explicit focus here has been on the work and organization of production in construction and their consequences for building tradespeople. The preceding chapters have described how the general industrial and organizational conditions affect the lives of tradespeople on and off the job. Subcontracting and task specialization have undermined workers' control in the labor process. The building trades unions are in the midst of entrenched battles against nonunion contractors, even in their former strongholds in the northeast. Against their own unionized contractors they struggle to resist concessions on the job site, give-backs in collective bargaining, and the growth of double-breasted shops. It often seems that at their best, local unions manage to buffer their members from the worst aspects of a variable, uncertain, and tenuous labor market. At their worst, they actively or passively collaborate with employers who seek to secure their own economic and organizational control. Unemployment, for instance, was in excess of 20 percent during the depressionary period of 1982 to 1983. During 1985, unemployment in the construction industry has consistently run at a level just under 14 percent—almost twice the national average. Such trends have contributed to an increasingly severe division of labor, loss of workers' power in the labor process, less economic security, and a weaker position in collective bargaining. Generally speaking, this has fostered a greater dependence on the entrepreneurial initiatives of real estate developers and builders in order to sustain employment opportunities.

The focus of attention here on the production side of construction notwithstanding, it should be evident that much more is at stake. One of construction's principal products, housing, is a social necessity. Thus, to address issues concerning the organization, production, and labor relations in the building trades is also to raise questions about how well societal mechanisms provide for a crucial material need. While analysts speak of a crisis with respect to construction's labor market, it is also true that they see a crisis as regards its product market.

Affordable housing, both rental units and privately owned homes, are increasingly in short supply. Between 1980 and 1982 housing starts hit their lowest levels since 1946. For example, single-unit starts dropped to 663,000 in 1982. Their current level (an annual rate of just over one million for the first six months of 1985) remains far below what is necessary to provide adequate shelter for everyone. The tightness in the housing market can be illustrated by looking at when in the construction process people buy their new home. In 1974, a majority of houses were sold after they were built (51 percent). By 1984, that figure had dropped to 31 percent. In other words, in 1984, 69 percent of homes sold were purchased either while they were under construction, (43 percent), or before they were even started, (26 percent). The bottom line, of course, is the impact on affordability. The median price of a new structure in

December 1985 was $89,300. This represents a 249 percent increase of the 1974 median price. As a more dramatic representation of the crisis, consider that in 1974 92 percent of new homes sold for less than $60,000. The figure for December 1985 was 12 percent. At the other end of the scale, the Bureau of the Census' *Construction Reports* did not even compute a separate figure for the houses costing more than $120,000 in 1974. Yet, by 1985 29 percent of the houses sold were for prices in excess of $120,000.

The prices of both new and existing homes have undergone such an inflationary surge that only a minute fraction of the population can actually afford to buy their own home. According to Michael Stone (1983), "during the 1950s, about two-thirds of all families could have afforded the typical new house; by 1970 the proportion had declined to one-half . . . , and by 1981 to less than one-tenth." The American dream of homeownership is fast becoming a dream deferred.

A Twofold Crisis

Conditions within the labor and product markets are inherently intertwined. Residential shelter is among the chief products of the building industry's labor process; while it is the social need for housing that sustains the livelihoods of thousands of building tradespeople. This interpenetration of the issues of housing provision and labor relations, in fact, has long been recognized by those practically involved in the industry.[1] The contradictory position this dual crisis leaves people in is almost painful. Older people bemoan the housing shortages that make it impossible for their children to find houses they can afford to buy and rents that take an ever greater proportion of their children's incomes. Yet these same people, if they are lucky enough to be homeowners, rely on their civic associations to steadfastly oppose low or middle-income developments that they think will threaten property values in their neighborhoods. Similarly, building tradespeople, equally concerned about the future for their offspring will speak out of one side of their mouths about the need for affordable housing. Yet, almost to a person, they can be counted on to support any and all development schemes for high-priced residential or commercial construction from which they expect to gain employment.

Both facets of the crisis, moreover, have been exacerbated by market sensitivity to factors within and without the industry. Federal monetary policy through control of money supply and interest rates has a double effect on construction (Mills 1972). It raises the costs of the money needed to build and it raises the costs of mortgages needed to buy. At the local level, the politics of self-interest rather than of social need often result in zoning laws that restrict, if not totally preclude, low- and middle-income housing. Local suburban political machines, notoriously conservative, use large-plot, single-family zoning requirements to ensure an equally conservative high-income constituency. Middle-income homeowners, for whom their houses represent a hard-earned prospect of economic protection against inflation as much as a comfortable place to live, are threatened by any talk of subsidized or rental housing they think will lower the market value of their own houses. Within the industry, the activities of real estate developers, builders, and especially those building and purchasing on speculation inflate prices while restricting socially needed supply.

The confluence of such problems is such to prompt us to speak of a crisis *of* the market. Simply put, market relations, through which labor and its products are commodities to be bought and sold have been woefully inadequate suppliers of housing under anything other than ideal profit-making circumstances. Yet most policies aimed at the problems of housing treat it as a crisis *in* the market. In other words, the situation is generally viewed within the context of an immutable market circumstance that possibly can be prodded, stimulated, or redirected, but not altered in any fundamental way. Thus, market-oriented policies are the ones applied: monetary stimulation through low-interest building loans and mortgages; homesteading programs by local governments which lure middle- and upper-income people to blighted or marginal urban areas; entrepreneurial incentives offered by municipalities in the form of tax abatements, easements, and agreements with builders which approve permits for highly profitable commercial or high-income residential construction in exchange for the promise to set aside a fraction of the project for specially targeted groups such as the elderly. Generally, though, they fall short of what is necessary.

They tend to be inadequate largely because they accept the limits of what the market can provide even when stimulated from without. For instance, as long as control of interest rates is a cornerstone of federal monetary policy, low-interest housing loan programs connot be so widespread as to disrupt that policy. Rather, they tend to send prospective homebuyers stampeeding to lending institutions, provide favorable publicity for local politicians, and yield only token relief for those caught in the housing crunch. Builder and consumer incentives generally operate on a small scale that, by definition, exclude those most in need of better housing. Where such programs have been more successful, as in the gentrification processes taking place in urban areas, the results are essentially unequal and unfair. They benefit consumers with enough capital to make improvements sufficient to turn dilapidated buildings into quality living spaces. They benefit the small for-profit nonunion contractors who get the contracts from homesteaders. And they benefit speculation builders and real estate traders who are quick to react when local market values begin to climb. In contrast, middle- and lower-income people find themselves either unaffected or displaced by gentrification. Moreover, since much of the home alteration and private residential work is dominated by nonunion contractors, union tradespeople get little or no benefit from urban gentrification. Actually, it could be argued that such builder- and consumer-oriented programs, in conjunction with weakened federal enforcement of Davis-Bacon protections, have abetted the growth of the nonunion sector and thus have contributed to the erosion of conditions for building tradespeople generally.

Thus, for those wedded to the market, it comes down to a matter of adequate housing for those who can afford it and belt-tightening for the rest. In the words of one such market analyst, "probably the greatest weakness in U.S. housing policy has been its failure to acknowledge the power . . . of the adaptive process in the urban housing market" (Mayer 1978, p. 430). The worst thing we could do, according to Mayer, would be to seek now to alleviate housing shortages that the market and slower population growth will handle by the end of the century:

> There will still be a shortage—there will always be a "housing shortage"—but there will not be a crisis we can create for ourselves if we tolerate increasingly frivolous (regulatory) behavior by an increasingly pervasive government (p. 430).

But is it simply a matter of living with the sloppiness of market mechanisms, only made worse by government regulation? I think not. To reiterate an earlier point housing is in a crisis *of* the market. Lasting solutions, if they are to be found, probably lie outside its bounds. Policies must be developed that, at minimum, buffer the housing industry from the socially dysfunctional dynamics of the market. At best, such policies should lead eventually to the elimination of the so-called free market as the dominant factor affecting the provision of housing needs.

To those ends some housing analysts have argued for a social program that decommodifies housing. Sketched in broad outline, such a programmatic objective "is to limit the role of profit from decisions affecting housing, substituting instead the basic principle of socially determined need" (Achtenberg and Marcuse 1983, p. 221). A bit more specifically Achtenberg and Marcuse advocate a program that includes several basic principles of housing policy. The cornerstones of their program are social ownership of housing; social production; and social control of land; and public financing. Social ownership and control over housing and land have two purposes. The first is to limit and eventually eliminate speculation that needlessly raises costs to housing consumers. The secnd is to ensure the socially responsible maintenance and upgrading of existing housing as well as the future uses to which are put presently undeveloped land. According to Achtenberg and Marcuse,

> social ownership can take a variety of forms, including direct ownership by government or non-profit entities, collective ownership by resident-controlled corporations or neighbor-

hood councils, non-equity or limited-equity cooperatives, or non-speculative resident ownership of single-family homes. What matters is not the precise legal ownership structure, but that the housing has the attributes described above and is permanently removed from the speculative market (p. 222).

The decommodification of housing also demands social production to increase both rental and ownership housing supply. This will meet the needs of new families and replace outmoded units beyond repair. Socially guided housing production would thus enable individual freedom of choice and mobility without playing into the hands of speculators and for-profit traders who thrive on a market characterized by tight supply.

Finally, the authors advocate public financing policies that would rid the housing sector of its dependence on private sources of credit. Short term public policies would "allocate more private credit to housing and alternative public housing credit should be developed (such as state housing banks and public funds)" (p. 223). Long-term policies include direct government spending and direct grants to community developers. Obviously, such moves entail a shift in the allocation of social resources. Reordering priorities away from defense spending would make large sums available for socially needed housing. Tax restructuration, including revitalization of the corporate income tax and a truly progressive individual income tax system, would also yield revenues for socially useful spending. In any event, the decommodification of housing conceivably can be an integral feature of a revitalized domestic economy.

It is in the same vein that it is necessary to speak of the need to protect labor from market forces. The competitive elements of the craft labor market (numerous small firms; seasonal employment; industry rather than firm employment; cyclical unemployment; subcontracting) tend to accentuate the instability of private sector for-profit housing.[2] They tend to inflate labor costs during periods of peak activity and full employment. During slack periods they equate market revitalization with wage and work-rule concessions by tradespeople and unions. It is necessary to move away from housing and labor policies that treat entrepreneurial profit-from-labor as the inviolable principle. Yet adequate treatment of this labor facet of the issue is often absent.

To this end, a policy of social production should, at minimum, include three basic programs: worker management of the labor process; worker investment in housing production; and community/labor program coordination. These principles of social production would move us toward an overall housing policy that is socially as well as economically efficient and which unifies the interest of workers with their communities.

Worker Management

Worker management essentially refers to a system of housing production according to which the building trade unions would assume direct responsibilities for production. In point of fact, the craft mode of production in the building industry is ideally suited to the successful application of worker management. Basic organizational and production relationships already in existence could serve as the foundation of a worker-managed labor process.[3] Relatively small-scaled, site-specific production in which authority relationships are channeled through a truncated bureaucratic structure, and a division of labor along the lines of a trade-specific subcontracting structure have given most workers direct exposure to a full range of production tasks within their trade. Even the strictly managerial functions—such as material delivery, estimation, layout, and work allocation—are not unknown to most tradespeople. Christopher Gunn (1984), for example, outlines six guidelines for the facilitation of workers' self-management (moderate capital intensity; economies of scale with fewer than 300 workers; a labor process compatible with collective work relations; ecologically sound products; technologies with requisite knowledge obtainable by workers; possibility of implementing appropriate orgnizational forms in multiple locations). Even a quite superficial consideration of the organizational and economic conditions in the building industry reveal the great extent to which they satisfy self-management guidelines.

Moreover, the present role of the trade union in the localized craft labor market makes it adaptable to handle production responsibilities in a worker-managed system. Its present responsibilities for storing and allocating labor, as well as organizing nonunion projects, demands a good deal of working knowledge of the labor process on the part of business agents. Equally important, the union's office staff and facilities are already able to handle most facets of trade operations. Full participation in joint union-contractor programs (for example, apprentice training, insurance and welfare funds) further equips both the union's office staff and it's elected officials to handle production-related tasks of record keeping, material procurement, and the general monitoring of the progress on job sites.

We can point to several economies that would potentially be realized from worker-managed housing contruction. The most obvious, of course, is the potential for raising the efficiency and productivity of workers involved in a democratic worker-managed labor process (Russell 1985; 1982; Simmons and Mare 1983; Hammer, Stern, and Gurdon 1982; Johnson and Whyte 1977).[4] But economies derive from structural efficiencies, as well. The assumption by the local union of direct production duties reduces or eliminates the need for subcontractors as intermediary agents. This in itself represents a subtantial savings. For one thing, it replaces a subcontractor's overhead and profit margin with proportional salary and office costs. Since the unions' office facilities and staff are already in place, the administrative overhead of allocating time for worker-managed projects is minimized. Second, the subcontracting structure, notable for distributing financial risks among numerous firms, is equally known for production inefficiency due to failures of communication between multiple small firms, poor scheduling and miscoordination on the construction sites between workers from different firms (Cherry 1974).

In contrast, the worker-managed construction system facilitates coordination between trades. Representatives of the various building trades, free from the distorting effects of entrepreneurial profit seeking, can emphasize intertrade cooperation necessary for efficient overall production. Naturally, errors of judgment and mistakes in estimation and scheduling will occur, but a worker-managed project would nevertheless be less encumbered by the problems generated by profit-oriented entrepreneurs who tend to fall behind schedule by taking on more work than they can handle, or by neglecting the less profitable contracts in favor of those on which they are making out better. Similarly, tradespeople integrated in a worker-managed project are much more likely to work cooperatively among themselves. In the context of the worker-managed project the inducements are for workers in different trades to find ways to coordinate their tasks in order to maintain as smooth and rapid a production schedule as possible.

The localized nature of housing creates far too many factors for there to be a single organizational model of worker management. Geography, climate, existing housing conditions, current trade union structure, and community political arrangements all will shape the form of any applied program. Thus, there will be numerous forms of worker management. Yet it is clear that some basic changes would be required in the structure of trade union operations. This is true especially as regards interorganizational relations among building trades locals. Close coordination is crucial if worker management is to be successful. An organizational mechanism is necessary to link the trades. In all likelihood the Building Trades Councel can be adapted to this purpose.

For example, a worker-management council could be established with responsibility for overseeing worker-managed projects within its jurisdiction. The council, in turn, would appoint project coordinators to direct specific job sites. The council and coordinators must have authority to call on labor power where and when needed. Individual trade union officials from each trade would be responsible to the project coordinators for supplying job sites with material and equipment, as well as labor. In the short term, such new organizational ties between trades can be the stepping stone to closer cooperation in collective bargaining and labor relations (for example, unified contract termination dates; reduction in jurisdictional disputes) that would improve production relations within the local industry. In the long term, better organizational ties could mean industrial reorganization within local economies that would yield greater flexibility, stability, and security for labor. We could see, for instance, unions liberated from the knee-jerk response to any technological change as a threat to employment presently engendered by craft market relations. Closer ties among craft unions on an industrial basis would permit human adjustments to major technological changes that may increase demand for labor in one trade at the expense of another. Programs for retraining overly abundant tradespeople for a craft where employment is more likely, obviously of benefit to the workers adversely affected by technological change, would also help the unions themselves move into a more proactive role in the industry. Union officials could thus be encouraged to participate in developing, planning for, and anticipating adaptions to new technologies. It is a possibility that only can emerge if the social diseconomies of craft unemployment are not the immediate price to be paid for various economies in production. Worker-management of housing production at the local level is a first step to general policies that unify social and financial economies.

Worker Investment in Housing

Current market relationships leave unions vulnerable to the demands of developers and builders who use their private financial backing and the promise of employment to glean concessions from union labor or to avoid it altogether. Private control and use of credit also have an inevitable effect of concentrating activity in highly profitable areas of commercial, industrial, and high-income residential construction. Thus private credit is diverted away from socially needed contruction for low- and middle-income housing (Michael Stone 1983; Achtenberg and Marcuse 1983; Schur and Phelan 1981). Union dependence on developers with private credit has also meant a commensurate pattern of political alliances in obtaining approval from local and county governments for their development schemes. With jobs as the factor outweighing most other considerations, union officials have been enmeshed in a set of political and economic relationships in which they play a dependent and subservient role.

A unified pension investment strategy (in the form of low and moderate interest building loans and mortgages) would substantially strengthen and enlarge the unions' role in the earlier planning stages of the building process. Freed somewhat from their dependence on market speculators and entrepreneurs, they would be able to move into areas of the houing industry where the social need is present, but sufficient promise of economic return for profit-oriented builders is not. The social investment of pension funds, in conjunction with the superior efficiency of a worker-managed labor process, unlocks the door to new paths out of the housing crisis. Direct labor investment may provide the basis for a local financial pool of credit targeted for socially owned or not-for-profit privately owned residences. Local credit, under local control can be applied flexibly in ways that conform to local community needs (for example, see Rifkin and Barber 1978). But it also means a break from policies that make poorer conditions of employment and lower wage scales the price to be paid for housing affordability.

Of course, there are various problems confronting the installment of such a plan. For one, the Employee Retirement Investment Security Act and other federal and state labor laws restrict the uses to which pension money can be put. Direct investment in housing construction would require changes in statutes that would facilitate such strategies while maintaining appropriate safeguards against mismanagement and abuse. For a second, presently defined fiduciary responsibilities of pension fund trustees have a dampening effect on their willingness to apply assets to innovative programs. Here, too, appropriate legislation may be necessary.

Finally, since pension funds are jointly administered by unions and their contractors, resistance on the part of the contractors may have to be overcome. This may actually represent the most difficult problem, especially in those cases where a worker-management design is also put into operation. Employers have shown little hesitancy to use employee pension funds for investments from which they see direct benefit for themselves.[5] On the other hand, because worker management in construction may reduce the need for subcontractors, employer trustees may be unwilling to support uses of pension funds that undermine their own position. Winning their support may require short-term compromises that protect employers' position by restricting investments so as not to put contractors into direct competition with worker-managed projects.

Community/Labor Coordination

Whatever their advantages, investment strategies and alternative forms of production can only be partial solutions to a problem that is as much political as it is economic. Social production of housing will require that the efforts of local governments be synchronized with those of local building trades. A joint community/union effort would, of course, be necessary to manage the building projects which are developed. There are direct economies associated with organizational linkage. It would eliminate, for instance, costly contract bidding systems (and their well-known abuses) and minimize the public costs of ensuring compliance with building codes. It would also enhance community control over production and encourage active community involvement. Most significantly, it would facilitate the development of long-term community and regional planning for housing and general residential needs. Community planners can work in conjunction with trade union officials to identify neighborhood areas for redevelopment and areas of new housing. One promising area of fruitful endeavor is the redesign or rehabilitation of abandoned or underutilized municipal buildings. Closed school buildings, for instance, could be converted to recreational or residential uses.

Two additional benefits of joint commutiy-labor efforts are worth mentioning. First, planning efforts that eventually go beyond individual piecemeal projects to a long range vision of renewal and new development conceivably can yield additional savings. Multiyear plans that encompass several sequential projects would benefit from the use of standarizcd designs for efficient use of material and equipment. Most important in this regard are the substantial savings in labor that can be realized. Long-range planning and execution would permit the establishment of a relatively stable multitrade workforce. This minimizes dead time and means that social production of housing could achieve cost reductions similar to those realized by large firms that reallocate labor time to minimize the expense of unproductive labor because of misscheduling or unforeseen delays. But probably more telling in the long run, a building trades wage scale eventually could be established that reflected employment stability. Presently, the building trades unions sign what are termed "maintenance contracts" with employers who hire members on a full-time, permanent basis rather than on a per project basis (for example, sports facilities, shopping malls, colleges). The execution of long-term housing construction programs would likely qualify for similar status. In other words, social prduction of housing would escape the costs that the for-profit market adds to a construction by virtue of its instability.

A second benefit of close community/labor alliance is the opportunity to coordinate the building trades' apprentice training programs with the employment needs of poor communities. Joint community/labor housing contruction projects could provide training in a building trade for community people in need of an industrial skill. Thus, community people would be invited to join the apprentice programs the trade unions administer, while the community's own building projects would provide the training ground.

As far-reaching as the potential ramifications of housing and labor decommodification are, much must be done to actualize that potential. If worker management is to be an effective and efficient basis of social production, then building tradespeople must be educated about its principles and practices. The significance of the shift in locus of control from contractor to workers connot be taken lightly. A failure to fully prepare workers to assume direct production responsibilities could prove disasterous. It is no great insight to observe that American workers are schooled in the realities of production and market relations in which conflict with employers is fairly pervasive. A worker-managed construction site simply would not function if workers brought with them those same orientations born of private profit-from-labor production. On the other hand, a workforce with a solid grounding in self-management and a commitment to social production of housing would be a great advantage.

Finally, it should be clear, I think, that for local building trades unions to engage in housing production along the lines of socially guided worker-managed programs will require basic changes from present practices. These policies represent such a marked departure that it is necessary to think in terms of a transformation in the nature of trade unionism in the industry. It is, essentially, a move from business unionism to social unionism (McDermott 1981). The narrowly conceived objectives of the business trade union—the bread and butter issues of wages, hours, and working conditions—must be integrated with a broader array of social issues.

The very focus of this entire book reflects the limitations of business unionist practices. In the arenas of collective bargaining and local politics, the building trades are generally forced into subservient and defensive positions vis-a-vis developers, builders, and politicians. Business unionist practices over the decades established an almost total dependence on market relations and profit-from-labor construction in which the guiding principle is the labor relations analogue of trickle down economics. Unstable employment patterns and the direct linkage between union politics and membership unemployment compel unions to seek to accommodate market entrepreneurs and strike almost any bargain in exchange for jobs. On the job, business unionism has meant a division of labor that maximizes contractor control over the labor process while ensuring needed flexibility under variable circumstances. The prevalence of project agreements and the failure of unions and individual tradespeople to resist on-site concessions reflect the weakness of business unionism in protecting workers' rights.

In contrast, a social unionist practice means taking up a dual challenge. For one, it requires moving from the present dependence on building market entrepreneurs and subcontractors to an alliance with progressive community elements and local politicians. Whatever its shortcomings, business unionism is fully entrenched in the minds of union officials. To many of them, it has been the road to personal success as elected officials. It has also been a comfortable type of relationship in which to act as union leader. To shift to the relatively un-chartered waters of social production is thus politically very risky. It means trying to sell a new idea to a membership equally immersed in old ways. It also requires that union officials forge new working alliances among their fellow trade union officials. The division of labor in construction is extreme enough that no one trade can truly stand by itself in the industry's labor rela-tions. Thus, as mentioned, it may even be that socially oriented trade union locals will have to cede some autonomy to a cen-tralized coordinating unit. Nonetheless, it is a risk that if not taken will lead eventually to almost certain collapse. In the words of one local union official, the present trade union struc-ture is "a dinosaur" (personal interview). If they are not willing and able to adapt to the demands of a new environment of restrictive labor law and aggressive unionbusting contractor associations, balkanized trade unions will soon find themselves on a list of endangered species.

Social unionism also means taking up the challenge of iden-tifying the interests of union members with the social needs of the communities in the local's jurisdiction. To the degree that business unionism has meant jobs ahead of social needs, social unionism can mean jobs and social needs. Housing has been discussed as the major illustration, but there are others. Con-sider mass transportation, for example, where major social in-vestment in the development and rehabilitation of urban and suburban networks could be substituted for the boondoggle highway construction and repaving programs that benefit some building trades and a select few heavy construction contractors. Social unionist input would be an invaluable aid to such efforts. Similarly, the building trades have been such staunch supporters of nuclear power largely because of the massive number of jobs created by the construction of large nuclear reactors. Never-theless, there is no political imperative that binds the trades to nuclear power. Equally strong support from their corner could be garnered for safe, environmentally sound sources of energy. The problem in the past has been that controversial projects, such as nuclear reactors, were the ones put on the agenda. Therefore, that was where people in the trades saw their jobs for the future. They rallied behind those concrete proposals from which they anticipated needed employment. They also saw those opposing construction as threatening their livelihoods. The building trades thus have tended to close ranks even more tightly and to hold on all the more strenuously to their dependence on market entrepreneurs. The problem for the future will be to develop, articulate, and wage the political battles for construction programs that are socially useful. Here, too, the building trades can be an indispensible partner. The key obstacle, though, is overcoming long-established political and economic dependencies.

The final question then is whence the initiatives that will facilitate the necessary redirection toward social unionism in the building trades? As the previous discussion indicates, it would be misplaced optimism to expect them to originate in the building trades alone. There have been too many years of rearguard actions against market trends and too much conflict and distrust among the trades. Most discouraging, perhaps, is that local leaders, in the best position to redirect organizational resources and reorient the political consciousness of the membership, are possibly the least likely to initiate politically risky ventures.

Yet, many of these same characteristics make the trades receptive to carefully detailed proposals from local housing and workers' rights advocates. For one thing, they are not quick to turn their backs on any serious proposal that holds the prospect of new jobs. But for another, long-term association with the industry has made me aware of an underlying awareness on the part of the building tradespeople of the weaknesses of practices within the present structure. Conversations with business agents, local officials, and coworkers repeatedly return to the need for greater cooperation among the trades, a more unified approach to local politics, and a general sense that traditional approaches to union organizing are insufficient and increasingly ineffective.

Without a doubt, there will be resistance, and in some quarters outright hostility, to alternative policies with a progressive vision. But much of that resistance can be met by tailoring local strategies to meet local political and economic experiences. Supporters from the building trades must be enlisted to facilitate the fairly rapid implementation of pilot projects that will give evidence of their feasibility, as well as give them necessary experience in worker management. Care also must be taken to minimize the threat to the more sensitive of the existing political and labor relations while keeping intact the long-term goals and objectives of the social production program.

In other words, even if a solidarity and commitment to seek alternatives to for-profit construction and business unionism are not present among the building trades, there is an openness, however begrudging, to new possibilities. Natural flux in the industry's localized markets and recent declines in union membership and labor market control create fertile soil for cultivating alternative labor and housing policies. Thus, progressive union and community activists should not be quite as quick as they have been in the past to dismiss the hard hats and labor aristocrats as a hopelessly reactionary element. Certainly bridges have to be built and some hatchets buried. But the effort will prove to be, not merely justified, but necessary.

America in the last quarter of the twentieth century is a land of deepening divisions and widening contrasts: explosive growth in high-tech and low-wage service industries versus the near collapse of unionized smokestack industries; corporate flight to the southwest sunbelt and beyond versus unemployment and deindustrialization in the northeast; proliferation of luxury condominium communities and gentrified enclaves of young urban professionals surrounded by the squalor and a paucity of over-priced rental and ownership housing for the working class, middle income, and poor.

In this context the labor movement is still the major source of hope for most working people. Yet it cannot be a labor movement of business unions and of workers with eyes only on their paychecks. It must be a movement of social unions and workers with a political and economic morality that blends their personal needs for a secure livelihood with a commitment to meeting social needs in all sectors and at all levels.

Signs of this vital movement are emerging. Industrial unions, such as the International Association of Machinists under the leadership of William Winnpisinger, are developing policies for industrial conversion from the production of military goods to socially useful goods. The United Mine Workers and the Oil, Chemical, and Atomic Workers have fought for the safety and health of their members through policies of medical, educational, and family support that go beyond the workplace to workers' communities. District 925 of the Service Employees International, District 65 of the UAW, and District 1199 have similarly sought to meet the needs of women and minority workers that are not contained in traditional bread and butter issues by developing programs that offer social as well as economic support.

This movement toward social unionism must be nurtured and strengthened in those areas where it already exists and encouraged to develop in those areas, such as construction, where it is not as yet apparent. Everyday, working alongside other building tradespeople, I see the potential for that ideal to take root and blossom. I see it in the skills and knowledge they apply in their work. I see it in their willingness to cooperate with one another inspite of subcontracting and trade union structures that divide them and force them to compete. And I see it in the pride many take in the lasting product of their labors.

The trick, of course, is getting there. Much of my analysis throughout is evidence of how long and difficult is the road to the realization of that potential. But the entire history of working people in America is one of struggle. If this relatively small battle can be waged, perhaps in the years to come we will begin to see the men and women of the building trades supporting, advocating, and supplying the social production of sufficient quality shelter for all.

APPENDIX A_____

Research Methodology

This appendix is devoted to a description of the research design: sampling procedures, data collection process, and the operational measures of the important variables. The first section presents a general description of the area in which the research was conducted. The second and third sections describe the methods of data collection, focusing primarily on the mail survey, sampling, and respondent contracts.

The Research Locale

The empirical investigation focused on the conditions of work and employment within the territorial jurisdiction of a building and construction trades council (BTC) spanning two suburban counties of a major metropolitan area in the northeastern United States. The research was undertaken in this area because of my personal access to individual local union organizations. Its recent economic and political history, however, also makes it well suited for a strategic assessment of the general conditions in the industry. Conditions in this area in many respects have followed national trends in building activity and labor relations since 1948. The first decade following World War II was marked by the well-known boom in residential construction. Large-tract developers, in the context of a sellers' market, were quick to sign union contracts and thereby avoid costly work stoppages in the course of organizing drives. This rapid development of what was formerly mostly farmland contributed much to the early organizing success of the building unions.

By 1960 residential activity had dropped off markedly, but was balanced by sharp increases in commercial construction—characterized in this area by light manufacturing industry and office buildings. This pattern mirrored national shifts in building activity during this period (Mills 1972). Throughout the sixties commercial activitiy remained fairly stable, helped by the construction of a number of large shopping malls and continued growth in light manufacturing industrial parks, whild residential activity experienced a mild

183

resurgence. Building activity slumped badly in the first three years of the seventies, preceding and continuing through the nationwide recession of 1973–1974. Activity in the bi-county region showed signs of recovery in the 1975–1976 period. Since then the industry has been moderately active in the commercial sector but remained somewhat depressed with respect to the residential market until 1983. The weakness of the housing market, of course, can be attributed in large measure to the high interest rates associated with the tight money supply and restrictive federal monetary policy (Mills 1972). An exception to this is the development of the condominium market since 1977. In this suburban area, it took the form of small residential townhouse parks and planned microcommunities.

Thus, during the time of the study, construction activity in the area was at a middle-level point. Commercial activity had recovered almost fully from the recession by this time (of course, it has never regained the level of activity experienced during the postwar boom). The newly established condominium market had revitalized unionized employment in the residential sector, which had fallen off with the decline of the tract developers and complementary rise of the small nonunion spot builders. Large projects still in the planning stages at the time of the study offer the prospects of sustained activity into the near future.

Finally, the labor relations environment in the two counties has also followed national trends. In particular, there has been a marked decline in the proportion of building activity under union contract. From a high point in the mid- to late-fifties of approximately 80 to 85 percent share of the construction market, the unionized sector has fallen to about a 50 percent share. Again, this decline reflects similar patterns throughout the northeast and north central regions where a union presence traditionally had been quite high (Bourden and Levitt 1980; Burck 1979; Northrup and Foster 1975).

The coordination agency for the building trade unions is the BTC. Overall, the BCT is composed of sixty local trade unions, representing twenty-three different trades. All ten local unions cooperating with the research belong to the BTC. The council is a loosely knit umbrella organization for the affiliated local unions and trade-specific district councils. Its functions are primarily those of interunion coordination, communications, sharing of information, and political linkage with interest groups and governmental agencies. It is important to point out that all affiliated local unions retain complete autonomy with relation to the BTC. No formal sanctioning powers reside in the council and, for the most part, affiliates participate on a voluntary basis. Moreover, the territories of many of the local unions are wider than that of the BTC itself and thus many locals are also affiliated with other councils. Of the ten locals in the study, four have jurisdictions which extend beyond that of the BTC. This should not be considered a source of bias, however, since all locals are autonomous from the council. These organizations participate in the BTC as fully as other affiliates, and I found no evidence to suggest that their business agents handle problems in the territory differently from agents representing locals with smaller territories.

A final point of reference is that the study focuses solely on the building sector of the construction industry. No attempt was made to collect information on other forms of activity within the industry, such as highway construction or marine construction. Accordingly, all the unions represented in the study pertain to trades with direct and persistent presence on the construction site. This excludes from consideration those occupations concerned strictly with the handling and shipping of material and supplies to and from the site (for example, truck drivers, warehousemen, and those working at contractors' offices or storage facilities). It does include those occupations which do the handling of material on the building site as part of their trade functions (such as, helper and laborer trades).

Data Collection: Participant Observation

In an attempt to facilitate assessments of the organization and consequence of construction work in a greater depth than would be possible with the questionnaire alone, a series of on-site inspections was undertaken from the vantage of a participant-observer. I worked on different buildings as a journeyman from one of the trade unions in the study. In addition to fulfilling the duties of the job at hand, I took the opportunity while at work to observe the interactions that took place throughout the workday among the people on the site. I took note of worker-worker, worker-foreman, and foreman-foreman interactions. When the occasion presented itself, I was also able to observe the relations between union officials and rank-and-file members working on the site. I took advantage of rest breaks and lunches to engage workers from various crafts in discussions about their experiences in the industry, and to listen to conversations that arose spontaneously within the group.

Complementing the on-site observations, I participated in three job actions—organizing attempts at sites with nonunion workers (one a small housing development, one a motel under renovation, and one a small commercial manufacturing building)—and regularly accompanied one business agent on his tour of duties. In the three picketing actions, I observed, listened, and informally interviewed the people with whom I walked the picket line. The time spent with the business agent (about one or two days per week) permitted me to record first-hand typical relationships between contractors and union agents and between the agents from different local unions.

In none of the situations where I played a participant-observer role did I attempt to conceal my research. Business agents and coworkers on the site I talked to knew of my purpose for being on the job. Nor did I try to hide my long-standing attachment to the trade I was working in in order to solicit responses to supposedly naive questions. In all cases, I was straightforward with the people on the construction site about what the research was about, how it would be used, and what sorts of information I was interested in obtaining from them.

I did not keep a detailed diary of all events taking place on the site. Since my interests were not in the day-to-day study of life at the workplace, or in a detailed accounting of the craft culture, no attempt was made to record all on-site activities and interpersonal interactions in a systematic manner. Instead, specific incidents and interesting conversations were noted when and where they seemed to provide additional insight or highlighted in a graphic manner a general tendency or predominant condition on the construction site. Since the purpose of the on-site investigations and observations of business agent functions was to provide supplementary information of a qualitative nature to complement data from the mail survey, I made little attempt to systematize my observations as an on-going report or put them in a quantifiable form for analysis.

Data Collection: Mail Survey

As stated, the primary source of the data for statistical analyses is a survey done of active unions members from ten craft unions in the research locale. The progress of the survey can be detailed in three stages: local union initial contract and agreement to participate; sampling of individual respondents; respondent contracts, questionnaire distribution, and follow-up contacts.

The attempt was made to gain the cooperation of as many local unions representing trades directly involved in the building production process as possible. Initial contacts were begun in the fall of 1978 in order to establish a likelihood of access to a sufficient number of organizations. These early contacts, along with the judgment of the secretary of the BTC, suggested that access would be feasible in enough cases to warrant continuation of the project. Actual contacts were recommenced in the early spring of 1979 when the seasonal slump in activity during the winter months was ending. As expected, access to local union organizations by an outsider was an extremely sensitive matter. Many union officials were wary of participation in the survey, although all were quite willing to be interviewed directly and were very forthcoming in their discussions. The largest obstacle was their sensitivity to the reactions from the rank and file. Most were concerned that their members would object to the union giving out names and addresses to an outside agent, which, in turn, would adversely affect the agent's own political position.

In addition, political conflicts within local union organizations, relationships with international offices, and union-management relations did affect the ultimate pool of local unions. The original pool included four craft occupations not present in the final group which had to drop their offer of cooperation for a variety of reasons. One local union administration lost its bid for reelection and the new one felt it unwise to participate at such an early point after coming into office. One local became embroiled in a conflict with its international and had to withdraw its offer of participation. Two local unions, representing different trades but belonging to the same International union claimed they were forbidden to provide any organizational information to outside agencies by the general executive board of the international association.

The ten local organizations which remained in the pool do represent the range of skills, productive functions, and general organizational characteristics present among the building crafts generally. They also represent the distributions between structural and finishing trades and those with productive functions in the beginning, middle, and late stages of the building process.

Individual respondents were sampled from within each local union. Only active union members were eligible for selection—that is, nonretired and dues-paying members. Union officials who performed full-time duties and received salary from the union were excluded from the sampling frame (although they did respond to a separate questionnaire about labor relations and union conditions). Union officers who actually work in their trade on the construction site and derive their income from employment with contractors and not the union were included. For example, elected members of local unions' executive boards do not receive salary. Many officers (for example, president, treasurer, and so on) receive no salary or only a token honorarium for performing the duties of their elected office and remain full-time workers. Also, since the sample was drawn from membership listings, the sampling procedures did not distinguish current employment condition (such as, presently working versus presently unemployed), nor did it distinguish between apprentices and journeymen. This allowed construction craftspeople with a range of past experiences and current conditions to be eligible as respondents.

One of the conditions of access to membership rosters was local union control over the sample mailing list. In general, the mailing lists were kept in union offices for security (although there were three exceptions) and in four cases the union office handled the actual distribution of contact letters and questionnaires. As will be discussed later, this security provision obviously restricted the capacity to assess nonrespondents for possible sources of sample and response biases.

The final sample contains 246 construction craftspeople. The distribution of respondents was somewhat uneven, however. The highest response rates were obtained among the middle-level skilled trades (the best rate was 64 percent). Both the upper- and lower-level skill occupational categories showed fewer responses (the lowest rate was 33 percent). The response rate difference for high-skill and low-skill trades is not statistically greater than zero. Thus, while the distribution of union organizations represent a fairly even range of skill level (two low-skilled, two semiskilled, four medium-skilled, two high-skilled trade unions), the distribution of individuals is biased to some degree to the center of the skill distribution. This should not present a major problem, however, since this reflects the industrywide occupational skill distribution if all building trades are taken into account.

Nonrespondents and sample representativeness

The aforementioned restriction on control over the mailing lists placed by the conditions of access directly affected the capacity to assess potential nonresponse sources of bias in the sample. Union officials would not allow supplementary procedures, such as direct telephone contacts, either in an attempt to increase the number of responses or as a means of collecting information from nonrespondents. In addition, they were not disposed to permit the use of their records (for example, from the welfare and insurance office) to provide demographic and general background information about non-respondents as a way of comparing respondents with nonre-spondents.

Given that the obtained response rate is far less than complete, it is still necessary to determine the degree to which the sample can be considered representative of a population of construction crafts-people. I have already mentioned the general representativeness of the sample at the occupational level. Nonetheless, some estimation at the individual respondent level is also required. The absence of information directly about nonrespondents means that inferences have to be drawn from the characteristics of respondents actually in the sample.

Fortunately, there are external sources of information which can be used to establish a comparative estimation of the composition of the group of workers in the sample. Marshall and Glover (1975) examined differences in occupational experiences between construction craftsmen with and without formal apprenticeship training. They report data on six building trades (bricklayers, carpenters, electricians, ironworkers, plumber and pipefitters, and sheetmetal workers) from nine cities from all major continental regions. Their report contains selected characteristics of the responding journeymen in their sample. Second, the Institute for Social Research, 1977 Quality of Employment Study (Quinn and Staines 1979) provides summary statistics for education attainment levels for employed persons in their national sample, as does the Current Population Survey (*Employment and Training Report of the President* 1979). I compared five characteristics of the sample's composition: the proportion of those in the sample having completed formal apprenticeship training, mean number of years in the trade, mean number of years as a union member, mean age of respondents, and levels of educational attainment. These comparisons are shown in table A.1.

The first four rows in table A.1 contrast the present sample with the Marshall and Glover study. In terms of average age, years in respondent's trade, and years as a member in respondent's current union the two samples compare very favorably. There is some indication that the present sample contains craftspeople who are slightly older (45 to 42 years). Once the minimal age differential is taken into account the two samples are also virtually identical with respect to occupational experience (21.58 to 20 years) and union tenure (18.75 to 17.8 years). Thus, it appears that the present sample, drawn from a localized population in the northeast and encompassing a somewhat different distribution of construction trades, is very similar in composition to an independent national sample of tradespeople from six

Table A.1. Sample Representativeness: Interstudy Comparisons

	Silver	Marshall & Glover	QES	CPS*
1. Proportion of Sample with Apprentice Training	.38	.49		
2. Mean Number of Years in Trade	21.58	20.00		
3. Mean Nubmer of Years as a Union Member	18.75	17.80		
4. Mean Age	44.85	41.90		
5. Educational Attainment				
a. Less than High School	29.2%	31%	21.7%	26.3%
b. High School Diploma	48.6	43	38.2	39.6
c. Some College	19.3	23	22.8	17.0
d. Completed College or Higher	2.9	02	17.4	17.9
	100%	100%	100%	100%

*U.S. Department of Labor, *Employment and Training of the President, 1979*, (Current Population Survey).

construction occupations. The only exception to this pattern is the larger difference in the respective proportions of apprentice graduates (38 percent to 49 percent). This discrepancy can be accounted for, however, by references to the slightly different mix of building crafts in the two samples. Specifically, the present sample contains a wider range of skill levels, as Marshall and Glover did not include the laborer and helper trades present in this case. Their data on the differences between trades—ranging from a high of 61 percent for bricklayers and plumbers/pipefitters to a low of 25 percent for ironworkers—does suggest the ligitimacy of this interpretation. When the lower-skilled trades are excluded, the proportion of apprenticeship graduates in my sample increases to a level more commensurate with Marshall and Glover's findings (44 percent).

The case with respect to levels of educational attainment is much the same (table A.1, rows 5a–5d). The sample is almost identical to Marshall and Glover's, having a slightly higher proportion of high school graduates but relatively few respondents with some college experience. They essentially have the same proportions of those with less than high school diploma and with at least a college degree. Accordingly, they also show similar discrepancies with QES and CPS national samples, being overrepresented at the low end and underrepresented at the high end of the attainment scale. This is as expected, of course, since the QES and CPS national surveys also include a much wider range of occupations. They contain persons in professional, administrative, and management occupations (30 percent and 25.8 percent of the respective samples), which ostensibly require more years of formal educational preparation. A closer correspondence between the present and QES and CPS samples would have indicated serious distortions.

Overall, then, the random sample I drew from the rosters of ten local trade unions based in a single geographic area in the northeastern United States compares favorably with a nationwide sample of union construction tradespeople (Marshall and Glover 1975) on a number of highly indicative characteristics. They are of similar age, educational background, and with roughly equal amounts of experience in their construction craft and as union members. Differences in educational background from national data are explainable in terms of the restricted occupational population from which persons were selected. It would seem fairly safe to conclude that as a group, the focal sample of craftworkers is representative of the construction workforce, but not, and there is no reason why they should, of the national population of employed adults.

On the other hand, although the aggregate demographic characteristics suggest a high degree of representativeness among respondents, it remains somewhat problematic whether nonrespondent biases still exist. Favorable comparisons among respondents do not exist between respondents and nonrespondents. Simply, the same type of construction craftworkers may have been nonrespondents in the samples used for comparison, as well. Of course, there is no direct way to assess this possibility, but the potential distortions in the findings have to be acknowledged. This is especially important for the analyses of the personal alienation and satisfaction consequences of craft work. While it is probably safe to assume that respondent representativeness has allowed an accurate assessment of the structural and contextual factors inherent in the building construction process, this is less so for the other.

The attempt to analyze the subjective and microlevel social correlates of employment and work in construction on the basis of a survey sample such as this must be viewed cautiously as long as the personal attributes of those who have refused participation remain unknown. More to the point, nonparticipation in the research may be correlated with the outcome relationships which are the focus of the study. Nonetheless, to the extent that we can make a priori assessments of these connections at least it is possible to proceed. In the present case, it seems reasonable to speculate that whatever biases exist on the basis of nonrespondent personal characteristics exert a conservative influence; reflecting more strongly the responses of those not necessarily experiencing the most adverse conditions and suffering the most extreme states of alienation of discontent. In other works, to the degree that there is a tendency for the most alienated, disaffected, and estranged to be nonparticipants, the results probably underestimate some of the key relationships between the quality of work and employment and the subjective and microsocial conditions.

We can illustrate this point by reference to two subgroups of construction workers most likely to be underrepresented in the sample. The first group contains those persons who for one reason or another take a passive, apathetic, and generally nonparticipative approach to social life. My personal observations over the course of many years in the industry include many people who do not attend union functions (regularly scheduled membership meetings or special meetings held for voting on financial decisions or in general elections). On the job, there are those who show a reluctance about lodging formal grievances or questioning their union representatives about specific arrangements on projects, but rather tend to accept whatever situation is presented to them. It is possible, although I have no direct confirmation, that such persons also declined the opportunity to participate in the study by returning a completed questionnaire.

The second group of potential nonresponders are those either with poor verbal skills or recent immigrants with a relatively poor command of English as a second language. Historically, the construction industry, like other labor-intensive sectors of the economy, has served as a haven for both of these groups. In the latter case especially, the construction crafts have provided linkage to economic integration. Successive waves of Irish, Italian, East European, and, more recently, Greek and Hispanic groups have found their access to the American economic structure through work in the construction trades. Such groups tend to suffer the disadvantages of the language barrier. To a degree they are barred from assuming the managerial functions (and thus correlative advantages) which require the ability to read and write with facility. They also are at a disadvantage when it comes to articulating grievances either in the union meetings or on the construction site. In short, they may be more easily taken advantage of: both as union member and as craft employee. At the same time and for the same reason, they are also most likely not to have responded to the questionnaire. In consequence, the persons likely to experience the most adverse conditions of work and employment are probably underrepresented in the sample. This means that the results of the analysis may overstate to some degree the quality of conditions in the industry and specify patterned relationships which hold only for the more secure and socially integrated middle ranges of the population of craft construction workers. The analyses presented should thus be viewed in the light of this overarching qualification. In sum, while the sample indicates a high degree of general representativeness of the construction worker population, the exclusion of some segments does limit to a degree the generalizability of the findings.

APPENDIX B _____
Glossary of Terms
and Variables

This glossary contains definitions for the operational variables utilized in the analyses. The numbers in parentheses refer to the location of the item in the appropriate questionnaire (appendix C). Unless noted otherwise, the item appears in the *Craft-Worker Questionnaire*. Those taken from the *Business-Agent Questionnaire* are indicated by the BA code; those from the *Local Union Fact Sheet* have the LUFS code. These three instruments appear in appendix C.

Craft Location

Craft Centrality: The placement of the building trade in the production process. It is measured by the earliness in the process the tradespeople appear on the construction site (LUFS, 13).

Craft Complexity: The degree on intricate involvement an occupation's characteristics demand from the worker with respect to relationships to data, people, and things. It is measured by the Dictionary of Occupational Titles, U.S. Department of Labor (1977).

Craft Mentality: The extent of mental calculation required of the craftperson. It is measured as the frequency of having to refer to written material (3.7).

Contractor Size: The characteristic number of workers employed by subcontractors specific to respondent's trade. Measured by the mean number of workers on construction sites reported by all respondents from a single trade. See "On-site Size" (3.1).

Table B.1. Operational Variables by Conceptual Category

Craft Location	Age	*Organization*
Craft Complexity*	Education	On-Site Size
Craft Mentality		Duration
Craft Centrality		Bureaucracy
Contractor Size	*Managerial*	
	Location	*Alienation*
Work Autonomy	Foremanship	Powerlessness
Self-Direction*	Administrative	Self-Estrangement*
Supervision	Consultation	Pragmatism*
	On-Site Consultation	Intellectual
Employment		Dependence
Labor Supply	*Craft Union*	Job Satisfaction
Unemployment	Militancy	Social Network Size
Nonunion	Union Size	Percent Network
Employment	Attendance	Same Trade
Job Concessions	Stewardship	Percent Network
		Family
Individual		Organization
Characteristics	*On-Site*	Network Size

*Measured by a multi-item scale.

Managerial Location

Foremanship: The regularity of holding an official appointment as a contractor's foreman on the construction site (1.5).

Administrative Consultation: The regularity of direct, person-to-person consultations between the craftsperson and contractors (5.1).

On-site Consultation: The regularity of direct contact between the craftsperson and contractor about the progress of the job (3.7).

On-site Organization

On-site Size: The number of people in the respondent's trade on the job site (3.1).

Duration: The number of total weeks workers from respondent's trade will be on the job site from beginning to end of the project (3.8).

Bureacracy: The number of official management positions (foremen, supervisors, crew chiefs) in the respondent's superordinate authority structure (3.5).

Intertrade Contacts: The number of different other trades respondent must deal with directly as part of performing the tasks of his/her own job (3.10).

Work Autonomy

Self-Direction: The amount of freedom respondent reports having about making technical and procedural decisions in the production process (1.7; 3.9).

Supervision: The frequency of evaluative contracts from superordinates on the construction site (3.7).

Craft Union

Militancy: The degree of oppositional posture vis-a-vis contractors adopted by the union organizationa as reflected in strike propensity (LUFS, union-management conflict (BA, 1.3).

Union Size: The number of members of the local union (LUFS, 1).

Attendance: The degree of individual affiliation to the local union organization as reflected by frequency of attendance at official local union meetings (2.5).

Stewardship: The degree of official individual attachment to the local union organization as reflected by frequency of official appointment to a steward's position on the construction site (1.5).

Alienation

Powerlessness: Subjective feelings of confidence in one's own ability to deal effectively with social events (4.1).

Self-Estrangement: Self-perceptions of a denigrating nature; self-rejection. Measured by reports of boredom and feelings of purposelessness about one's life (4.2;4.2).

Goal Expedience. The adoption of a stronger focus on goals than methods in the means-ends relationship. Measured by social orientations about having to be ready to break the rules in order to maintain your position (4.1) and it being acceptable to do anything you want as long as you stay out of trouble (4.1).

Table B.2. Dependent Variables: Subjective Alienation

Powerlessness*
1. In general, I have confidence that when I make plans I will be able to carry them out (agree-disagree).

Self-Estrangement*
1. How often do you feel that the things you do have no real purpose (never-always).
2. How often do you feel bored with everything (never-always).

Goal Expedience*
1. It's all right to do anything you want as long as you stay out of trouble (agree-disagree).
2. To maintain their place in society, everybody finds it necessary to "break the law" at one time or another (agree-disagree).

Intellectual-Dependence*
1. How often do your ideas and opinions on important matters differ from those of your relatives (never-always).
2. How often do your ideas and opinions on important matters differ from those of your friends (never-always).
3. How often do your ideas and opinions on important matters differ from those of your neighbors (never-always).

*All items are to be scored on a five-point scale.

Intellectual Dependence: The capacity for distinguishing between one's ideas and opinions about important issues and those held by frequent social contacts. Measured by the frequency of disagreement with relatives, friends, and neighbors (4.2).

Job Satisfaction: The relative degree of satisfaction with which one views his or her job. Measured by an overall assessment (1.11).

Social Network Size: The number of different occupationally distinct social contacts one has off the job (4.3).

Percent Network Same-Trade: The proportion of one's social network comprised of members of one's occupation (4.3).

Percent Network Family: The proportion of one's network comprised of members of one's own family (4.3).

Organization Network Size: The number of different organizational affiliations one has in addition to union membership (such as, community service, recreational, political) (4.4).

Employment

Labor Supply: The availability of workers for hire within a given trade. Measured as the average (mean) weeks of unemployment among respondents for a specific trade (see Unemployment).

Unemployment: The number of weeks during the preceding twelve months for which the respondent was not employed (1.10).

Nonunion Employment: The regularity of working in the nonunion residential sector. Measured as the reported frequency of working for homeowners when union work is not available (1.5).

Job Concessions: The relative amount of protection the craftsperson has from compelled acceptance of substandard conditions of work. Measured as the job-to-job frequency of having to ignore aspects of the trade agreement in order to be hired or stay on a job (1.5).

Individual Characteristics

Age: The number of years since birth (5.1).

Education: The highest level of educational attainment reached by the respondent (5.10).

Multi-Items Variables:

The variables appearing in table B.1 that are composed of multiple items combined into a single scale are noted by an asterisk. For each one I note the items comprising the scale and a statistical assement of the scale's reliability.

Craft Complexity: Occupational complexity is measured at the occupational level, and refers to the degree of skill required to perform the tasks associated with that occupation. It is measured by the degree of mental, interpersonal, and manipulative complexity inherent in a job. The scale is comprised of three distinct facets: the complexity of work with data, with people, and with things. Ratings of the occupations represented in the sample were taken directly from the 4th edition of the *Dictionary of Occupations Titles* (DOT) (U.S. Department of Labor 1977). The DOT ratings are based on field observations in actual work settings of over 13,000 job titles (see Spenner 1979 for detailed discussions of the DOT ratings) and include assessment of the complexity of the job's activities with respect to these three facets. The scores for each occupation on each facet were combined in an additive scale. The reliability coefficient, Cronbach's Alpha, while not exceptionally high, is at an acceptable level (alpha = .62).

Self-Direction: Self-direction measures the degree of decision-making involvement on the part of respondent with respect to what tasks are performed and how they are accomplished. The scale is composed of two items, one referring to respondent's general job experience and one referring to his or her current job condition. In both cases the responses were on a five-point scale from which respondent selected a single statement which best described their situation:
1. I am told what to do and how to do it.
2. I am told what to do and the conditions of the job determine how I do it.
3. I am told what to do and I decide how I do it.
4. I have some freedom to decide what I do and how I do it.
5. I am on my own as long as the work gets done.

For both items the higher value corresponds to greater self-direction. The two items are strongly related to each other (r = .73) and the scales reliability coefficient is acceptable (alpha = .85).

Militancy: Two items were combined in an additive scale to measure craft union's militancy. One is the number of years since the local union conducted an official strike against its contractors' association. This variable is taken to represent the degree of conflictual dynamics which characterize the collective bargaining over contract negotiations. The second variable is the rating of the union official of the relative degree of conflict versus cooperation which characterizes the union and contractors. Official responded to the item, "How would you describe the relationship between your local union and employers?" on a five-point scale. The range of possible responses were "pure conflict," "mostly conflict," "some conflict and some cooperation," "mostly cooperation," and "pure cooperation." In cases where responses were obtained from more than one official from a single local union they were averaged prior to coding. This item was taken to represent the pattern of relative conflict in the ongoing dynamic between the local union and employers not related to the organization's propensity to strike as a means of resolving contract disputes. The two separate items were standardized and added to form the union militancy variable. The items are correlated reasonably strongly ($r = .45$) and the scale has a reliability coefficient of 0.63.

Alienation variables (table B.2): The attempt was made to measure all four variables of subjective alienation with milti-item scales. Successful scales were developed for three of the dimensions.

Self-estrangement: Two items comprise this variable. One assesses the degree of purposelessness one feels about his or her life in general. The other measures the extent of boredom which one feels pervades his or her life. The two items have a bivariate correlation of 0.42; the scale's reliability measure is 0.69.

Goal Expedience: As noted in chapter four this dimension corresponds to what other researchers have labelled "normlessness." The two items in the scale (alpha = .58) reflect respondent's degree of agreement-disagreement, on five-point scales, to one statement about getting into trouble—"It's all right to do anything you want as long as you stay out of trouble"—and on a statement about the necessity of having to violate social rules—"In our society you have to be ready to break the rule in order to maintain your position."

Intellectual dependence: Kohn refers to this dimension, comprised of identical items, as cultural estrangement. As I discussed this dimension measures the degree to which people distinguish between their ideas and opinions and the positions taken by people with whom they have regular contact. Identical questions were asked of respondents' perceptions in relation to relatives, friends, and neighbors. The first has correlation coefficients with the other two of 0.35 and 0.36, respectively. The other two items are correlated more strongly ($r = .63$). The combined scale has a reliability coefficient of 0.71.

All the alienation variables are coded so that the higher values indicate a greater degree of alienation; for example, feelings of more powerlessness, a more pragmatic orientation to the means-ends relationship. This holds for all operational variables, as well. To facilitate interpretations of the statistical analyses all variables have been coded (either in the initial coding process or through subsequent transformations) to vary in a positive direction.

APPENDIX C _____

Survey Instruments

Building Trades Survey

April, 1979

Dear Fellow Construction Worker,

    As you know, I am conducting an investigation into the day-to-day conditions we face in the construction industry. My own experience tells me that the people with the most information are the people who do the work. I believe that a study conducted by a construction worker and based on the viewpoints of construction workers is the best way to get an accurate picture of our situation. By answering the items in the booklet you will play an important role in the study.

    The questions are very straight-forward. For most of them you only have to check a box in order to select your answer. I designed the questions this way to get a lot of information, with minimal inconvenience to you. They ask for information about aspects of our work experiences such as our employers, unions, job-site conditions and some individual background. All these areas are important, so please fill out all the questions.

    The questionnaire is entirely confidential, so please do not put your name on the booklet. The return envelope contains a card with your name so I will know who returns the questionnaires, but not anyone's specific answers. This way I will not ask you to return the questionnaire after you have already returned it to me. Of course, you may remove the card if you wish. After filling out the booklet just place it in the return envelope (I have stamped and addressed it) and drop it in the mail.

    I greatly appreciate your cooperation in this project, and thank you for participating. Your judgements will make this study a success. Will you please fill out and return the questionnaire as soon as possible?

Fraternally yours,

Marc Silver
LU 1727
IBPAT

1.GENERAL EXPERIENCE

1. How long have you been working in your trade? _____

2. How did you break into your trade (check one)?

☐1. A relative taught me.   ☐3. Through union apprenticeship.
☐2. A friend taught me.   ☐4. I taught myself.

3. Which statement describes the conditions of the various work-sites you go on?

☐1. They are all the same.   ☐3. They are mostly different.
☐2. They are mostly the same.   ☐4. They are all different.

4. In general, which statement describes the attitudes of employers toward your work?

☐1. Fast production is the only thing that counts.
☐2. Fast production is most important, but good-quality work counts a little.
☐3. Good-quality work is most important, but fast production counts a little.
☐4. Good-quality work is the only thing that counts.

5. Please answer the following questions by checking the appropriate box:

	Every Job	Most Jobs	Some Jobs	Rare Jobs	No Jobs
How often do your employers talk with you about a job before it starts?	☐	☐	☐	☐	☐
How often do your employers talk with you about the progress of a job under way?	☐	☐	☐	☐	☐
How often are you a foreman or super on the job?	☐	☐	☐	☐	☐
How often are you pressured by your employers to ignore the rules of the Trade Agreement in order to stay on the job (or be hired)?	☐	☐	☐	☐	☐
How often do you work direct for home-owners when no union work is available?	☐	☐	☐	☐	☐
How often are you appointed a "union steward" on a job?	☐	☐	☐	☐	☐

6. On the next question please check how much you agree or disagree:

	Strongly Agree	Mostly Agree	Undecided	Mostly Disagree	Strongly Disagree
In my trade, the relationship between worker and employer is like a partnership	☐	☐	☐	☐	☐

7. Which statement best describes your general experience on the job?

☐1. I am told what to do and how to do it.
☐2. I am told what to do and the conditions of the job determine how I do it.
☐3. I am told what to do and I decide how I do it.
☐4. I have some freedom to decide what I do and how I do it.
☐5. I am on my own as long as the work gets done.

8. On the next question please check how much you agree or disagree·

	Strongly Agree	Mostly Agree	Undecided	Mostly Disagree	Strongly Disagree
I depend on my employer to get the jobs and he depends on me to give a good day's work	☐	☐	☐	☐	☐

9. How many different employers did you work for last year? _____

10. How many weeks of unemployment did you have last year? _____

11. Overall, how satisfied are you with the type of work you do?

Very Satisfied	Mostly Satisfied	Undecided	Mostly Dissatisfied	Very Dissatisfied
☐	☐	☐	☐	☐

2. UNION EXPERIENCE

In this section I am asking about your experience in your local union.

1. How long have you been a member of your local union? _____

2. Did you vote in the last election for union officers? ☐NO ☐YES

3. Do you now hold an elected position in your local? ☐NO ☐YES

4. Have you ever held an elected position before? ☐NO ☐YES

5. How often do you attend union meetings?

☐1. Every meeting   ☐3. Some meetings   ☐5. No meetings
☐2. Most meetings   ☐4. Occasional meetings

6. In your opinion, how effective is your local union in protecting you in dealings with employers?

Very Effective	Mostly Effective	Undecided	Mostly Ineffective	Very Ineffective
☐	☐	☐	☐	☐

3. CURRENT JOB CONDITIONS

In this section I am asking about the conditions on your present job, or last job if you are now out of work.

1. How many people in your trade are on the job-site? _____

2. Do you work alone, or in a group? ☐ Group   ☐ Alone

3. If you work in a group, how many are there in your team including yourself? _____

4. For the following questions please check yes or no:

		YES	NO
1.	Are you a Union Steward on this job?	☐	☐
2.	Are you a Foreman on this job?	☐	☐
3.	Are you a Crew Chief on this job?	☐	☐
4.	Are you a Super on this job?	☐	☐

5. How many Stewards from your union are on this job? _____

6. How many official positions are there above you (Crew Chief, Foreman, Super, GC Super)? _____

7. For the following questions please check how often each situation occurs:

	Constantly in the day	Somtimes in the day	Once per day	2-3 times per week	Once a week/less	Never
How often does somebody check on your performance? ...	☐	☐	☐	☐	☐	☐
How often does the Foreman or Super ask your advice?	☐	☐	☐	☐	☐	☐
How often do you talk with your employer about the progress of the job?	☐	☐	☐	☐	☐	☐
How often do you have to refer to written material (instructions or blueprints)?	☐	☐	☐	☐	☐	☐

8. How many total weeks will workers in your trade be on the job? _____

9. For this job, which statement is most accurate?

   ☐ 1. I am told what to do and how to do it.
   ☐ 2. I am told what to do and the conditions of the job determine how I do it.
   ☐ 3. I am told what to do and I decide how I do it.
   ☐ 4. I have some freedom to decide what I do and how I do it.
   ☐ 5. I am on my own as long as the work gets done.

10. On the lines below, please list the trades of the workers on the job you have to deal with in carrying out your own job. Start with your most frequent contact.

_____ _____ _____ _____

_____ _____ _____ _____

4. GENERAL OPINIONS

In this section I am asking about some of your opinions about things on and off the job.

1. For the next few statements please check how much you agree or disagree:

	Strongly Agree	Mostly Agree	Undecided	Mostly Disagree	Strongly Disagree
In general I have confidence that when I make plans I will be able to carry them out	☐	☐	☐	☐	☐
Generally, most of the things that happen to me are the result of things I have no control over	☐	☐	☐	☐	☐
There are things I can do that might influence national policy	☐	☐	☐	☐	☐
The best policy to follow is to take life as it comes	☐	☐	☐	☐	☐
If something works it doesn't matter if it's right or wrong	☐	☐	☐	☐	☐
In our society you have to be ready to break the rules in order to maintain your position	☐	☐	☐	☐	☐
It's all right to do anything you want as long as you stay out of trouble ..	☐	☐	☐	☐	☐

2. For the next few statements please check how often each situation occurs:

	Always	Almost Always	Sometimes	Almost Never	Never
How often do you feel that the things you do have no real purpose?	☐	☐	☐	☐	☐
How often do you feel bored with everything?	☐	☐	☐	☐	☐
How often do your ideas and opinions on important matters differ from those of your relatives?	☐	☐	☐	☐	☐
How often do they differ from those of your friends?	☐	☐	☐	☐	☐
How often do they differ from those of your neighbors?	☐	☐	☐	☐	☐

3. On the lines below, please list the occupations of the people you see socially most often off the job. Please check if the person is a Relative or Friend.

	R	F		R	F		R	F
_____	☐	☐	_____	☐	☐	_____	☐	☐
_____	☐	☐	_____	☐	☐	_____	☐	☐

5. BIOGRAPHY

Here are some questions often found to be related to people's job experience.

1. What is your present age? _____   2. Are you married?   ☐YES   ☐NO

3. Do you identify with any particular national background? ☐YES   ☐NO
    a. If YES, which one? _____

4. Do you identify with a particular religion? ☐YES   ☐NO   (Which one? _____)

5. How many children do you have to who work in your trade? _____

6. How many of your children work in another construction trade? _____

7. What's your father's main occupation? _____

8. How many other relatives do you have who are in your trade? _____

9. How many other relatives do you have who are in another construction trade? _____

10. How many years of education have you completed:

    ☐1. Less than high school   ☐3. Some college
    ☐2. Finished high school   ☐4. Finished college

LU_____

LOCAL UNION FACT SHEET

1. Total number of members....................................._____

2. Presence of an Employer Association.................__YES; __NO

3. Total number of signed employers.........................._____

4. Total number of counties under jurisdiction of local......._____

5. Total number of paid, full-time officials.................._____

6. Total number of full-time officials "on the road"........._____

7. Length of term of office for elected officials (in years).._____

8. Total number of positions on the Executive Board.........._____

9. Number of Executive Board meetings per month..............._____

10. Number of membership meetings per month...................._____

11. Average attendance at membership meetings (# of members)..._____

12. Category of Trade................___ Structural; ___ Finishing

13. Point in building process when Trade enters the job site:
    __1st Quarter___ 2nd Quarter___3rd Quarter__4th Quarter

14. Percentage of membership who work for homeowners when not
    employed in union work...................................._____%

15. Average number of weeks of unemployment for workers in a
    year.._____

16. Total number of members not employed at the present time..._____

17. Number of years since Local conducted a strike............._____

18. Category of signed contractors:
    ___ General Contractors   ___ Sub-Contractors   ___ Both

19. Local Union affiliation.........___District Council;___Autonomous

NOTES _____

Chapter 1. Introduction

1. The various multimodel and contingency theories of organization have lost much of their grip on the field in recent years in favor of ecological, external control and political economy perspectives. That has meant a greater sensitivity to the loosely coupled nature of organizational systems and to the importance of political factors influencing organizational behavior. Nevertheless, a rational-technical determinism remains as an implicit foundation of much of managerially oriented theory. American management's recent love affair with the Japanese model is a case in point.

2. The analysis of the role of power in organizational settings derives from the works of both Marx and Weber. Those working in the Marxist tradition have focused on the inherent sources of contradiction and conflict in relations within and between organizations. Analyses based on Weber's work have attended to the various organizational bases on which power may rest (for example, Poole 1975, 1981; Roos and Hall 1980; Bacharach and Lawler 1980; Etzioni 1975; French and Raven 1968). Authority vested in the organizational position is one such form; expertise authority is another. Empirically they are often intertwined, but they are conceptually distinct. In the present case, for example, the contractor's power as superordinate in the work organization is counterbalanced by the craftperson's power as expert in the production process.

3. I am not arguing that Braverman's position here stems from a flaw in his larger analysis that technologies reflect capital's dual logic of domination of and efficiency in production. The problem is his failure to apply that broader analysis accurately in this instance. I will return to this issue at greater length later in the chapter.

4. For example, three of the better known observational case studies, Meyers (1946), Riemer (1979), and Applebaum (1981), take for granted the accuracy of the craft administration model. None of the three sought to test its adequacy against their observations.

5. The guild structure was not very egalitarian. Rather than guarantee affluence for all members, it usually secured the position of those few at the top of the guild's hierarchy (the masters) while leaving the bulk of craftsmen in the trade (journeymen) to hire out for wages. According to Francis B. Andrews' account of the building industry in medieval Europe, "the master no longer worked himself, he took oversight only and walked about in a nice gown and gave direction, and finally in the Renaissance he became a 'professional' man" (1974, 8). The primary distinction between master and journeyman is the former's entrepreneurial ability to obtain building contracts and the industry's need for large workforces. In the view of historian Louis Salzman:

> One reason for the rather exceptional position of the master in the building crafts was the unusually large proportion of journeymen—men working by the day—in these crafts, necessitated by the conditions of their employment. In what we may call the resident crafts there were numbers of small masters with their own workshops, employing few, or even no, workmen; in building . . . labour was fluid and a large body of men had often to work under one master . . . . [T]he building of a castle would be in the hands of one master mason, controlling perhaps fifty masons, *of whom a fair proportion would be fully qualified for the rank of master* (1952, 48–49, my emphasis).

6. I have relied heavily on William Haber's authoritative account of industrial relations in the American building industry. I have drawn freely from his work for much of the material in this section.

7. According to Haber, "in power and effectiveness it [the Contractors' Council of Chicago] was at least equal to the Chicago Building Trades Council" (447). Haber makes a similar observation with respect to the situation in New York City. Concerning contractors' associations in other cities, Haber observes that most had been able to unify the labor policies of their affiliated firms by 1910.

8. Strict divisions of academic labor within the social sciences have been weakening in the past decade, particularly with respect to sociology, economics, history, and labor studies. The work of Braverman, and labor market theorists such as Averitt (1968) and Deoringer and Piore (1971) and the revitalization of Marxist theory have provided the foundation for this change by focusing on the inherent interconnections between the economic and the sociopolitical imperatives within capitalist firms.

9. Conflict over control at the workplace has been a dominant

aspect of labor relations in the United States. For some, the development of industrial organization is the dynamic struggle between
owners and their managers on the one side, and workers, on the other,
for control over decision making on the shop floor and at firm levels
(for example, see Clawson 1980; Edwards 1979; Montgomery 1979;
Stone 1974; Marglin 1974; Gorz 1967). Significantly, those who have
recently argued for political strategies that shift away from strictly production issues to include social, environmental, and consumer issues
have done so from an analysis of the outcomes of class struggles for
controls at the workplace (McDermott 1981; Edwards 1979; Gorz
1980).

10. My position here contrasts markedly with that of the
organizational theorists who see the operation and structure of
organizations as stemming for the most part, from the imperatives of
technology alone. From a technological perspective, developments
pertain to the unavoidable movement of modern industrial society (for
example, Bell 1973; Galbraith 1967; Touraine 1971; Ellul 1964). From
another, but related, perspective technology derives from the ra-
tional/economic motives of advanced capital which emphasizes the
continual improvement of techniques of production in the pursuit of
profit (for example, Woodward 1965; Blauner 1964; Weber 1978). My
position does not preclude consideration of the independent
technological influences, but rather encourages an expanded vision
that includes those pertaining to structures of domination and control
(for example, Noble 1977; Gouldner 1976). The direction in which
this dialectic works itself out also depends on numerous other factors,
including market control, labor market characteristics, firm
characteristics, and competition in the international market.

11. Notwithstanding numerous differences of emphasis and interpretation among multimodel approaches, they share a rather
mechanistic causal model in which work structure is for the most part
determined by casually prior variables. This holds even for Chandler's
analysis which differs substantially from the others by focusing on the
impact of managerial planning strategies of growth, diversification,
and financial investment rather than technology and environment.

12. William H. Whyte (1959) recognized the importance of normative compliance in his treatment of the organization man. People
who live their lives within and find individual expression only through
their organizations are the logical result of effective normative control.
In a similar vein, Etzioni's (1975) compliance theory stressed the role
of normative power under certain organizational conditions. From a

different theoretical vantage, Michael Burawoy (1980) offers insight into how normative control finds expression on the factory shop floor. According to Burawoy, a major consequence of normative control is the self-exploitative activities workers engage in on the job.

13. Subcontracting in the building industry dates back as far as feudal Europe (Salzman 1952; Andrews 1974). On larger projects during the middle ages, the master mason, or master carpenter at times, would take the primary contract for the building. He in turn would hire journeymen from his craft as well as subcontract specific parts of the construction process to masters of other crafts. They would, of course, be responsible for hiring their own journeymen. It is ironic that it is the subcontracting system, but not the guild system, that has survived the centuries.

14. Although it is not necessarily a common practice, it does happen that foremen with hiring and firing powers exact a premium from other tradespeople for putting them on a job. In some cases, foremen do in fact act as inside contractors. Situations most conducive to these unfortunate practices of coexploitation are those where external monitoring of foremen's activities by the union are difficult (for example, small projects; in the absence of a shop steward; under piece-rate systems). In his ethnographic treatment of construction work, Herbert Applebaum (1981) identifies how some aspects of craft-labor markets facilitate foremen acting as independent contractors (see 64–66). However, by conceptualizing it as an instance of individual autonomy for tradespeople, he fails to appreciate the coexploitative elements attached to the situation.

15. As historian William Haber (1930) correctly points out, union restrictions on productivity and the use of apprentices, as well as rules against piece-rate work, are intended primarily to minimize the practice of lumping and other forms of inside contracting.

Chapter 2. Working at the Construction Site

1. The common tendency to view building construction as a craft-dominated process is best exemplified by Stinchcombe's (1959) craft-administration thesis. The business press has always blamed problems in the industry on the stranglehold of the building trades unions (for example, Burcke 1979). Sociologist Jeffrey Riemer (1979) presents an extreme, and promanagement, version of the craft-administration thesis in his academic study. According to Riemer, "building tradesmen know their work and are generally free to perform it as they

choose" (161). Moreover, he argues that craft administration gives rise to potential social problems.

> But what happens when workers gain inordinate control over their working conditions? The freedom and initiative of the construction workers to modify their work . . . suggests some of the problems that society faces when workers have this freedom (137).

Riemer's answer to his own question (unsupported by any direct evidence) is that builders and consumers are the ones who bear the costs when workers have significant control of production. Herbert Applebaum (1981) is similarly complacent about the nature of construction work from an anthropological perspective.

2. On this point my observations are in essential agreement with Goldthorpe et al. (1969). They locate craftworker dissatisfaction over current working conditions in their inability to exercise significant control in the labor process.

> It could be said, then, that the main emphasis in the craftsmen's replies was, in effect, on changes which would in their veiw lead to greater efficiency and which would at the same time increase their own involvement in, and control over, the work process with which they were concerned (21).

In this vein, it is important to note that the tables include the responses of foremen and workers. As I will discuss later in the chapter, the relationship between managerial location and autonomy is substantial.

3.. The literature on the topic extends back to the founders of sociology. It has been central to the interests of such classical theorists as St. Simon, Marx, Durkheim, and Weber, as well as contemporary social scientists working in their traditions. Accordingly, the interest has been so broad—spanning theoretical, political, and metholodological orientations—and the sheer volume of work so enormous the literature resists any brief attempt at summarizing it here.

4. For the purposes of quantitative analysis, I operationalized the substantive complexity of building craft work as the additive scales of the Department of Labor's ratios of the complexity of work with people, data, and things *(Dictionary of Occupational Titles)*. The mental involvement required of the building craftperson is measured by an

item from the survey questionnaire. Respondents were asked to report the relative frequency of referring to written material in their work (from "never" to "constantly in the day").

5. The relationship is an inverse one between size and the *relative* administrative size. As those familiar with the organization studies literature well know, size is among the most frequently researched variable. As John Kimberly (1976) pointed out, however, efforts have not always been sufficiently informed as to its theoretical significance to yield useful results. As organizational sociologist Howard Aldrich (1972) made abundantly clear, murky theorizing and methodological fetishism are a futile, if not disastrous, combination for organizational research.

6. There is a large variation among the building trades in the characteristic length of time tradespeople remain on a single construction site. Site duration ranged from less than one week to almost two years for individual workers in the sample. At the occupational level, the shortest average duration (mean) was 2.7 weeks; the longest was 42.1 weeks.

7. The logic of the analysis, for those so interested, follows the path analysis model; although I have not utilized a path diagram. Bureaucracy is thus an endogenous variable, causally situated between the organizational and occupational exogenous predictors and the work autonomy dependent variables. I should also point out that while I have not included a table of correlation coefficients, no evidence of multicolinearity exists for any of the subsequent regressions.

8. Human relations adherents, for example, have for many years stressed the importance of cooperation and reciprocal interactions between managers and their subordinates. The diverse interpretations of the Hawthorne Studies are congruent at least in their common acknowledgement of the significance of participative and consultational elements as structured aspects of the work organization (Roethlisberger and Dickson 1939; Landsberger 1958; Blumberg 1968).

9. Common recognition of these factors, however, should not be confused with common interpretations or applications. Management-oriented human relations and Japanese-style theories are arguably attempts at manipulating workers' perceptions and attitudes for purposes that ultimately are exploitative and against workers' interests.

10. It is important not to overstate the dependence of subcon-

tractors on craft employees in this regard. It is not unusual(although it is becoming more so) for subcontractors to start out as craftpeople themselves. This is especially the case in the specialty trades and finishing trades which tend to be less capital intensive. With little capital outlay a former union worker can start a business and become a union contractor. This means that many employers have substantial craft knowledge of their own. They are not solely dependent on the advice they receive from workers. On the other hand, they may find it difficult to keep abreast of production innovations as regards how easy or difficult they are to handle on the job, or to keep in touch with enough workers to be a good judge of performance capabilities. Anecdotally, I have often heard from union workers their complaints about working for exmembers who have recently turned contractor because they tend to be tougher on their employees. Workers find such bosses more difficult to work for partly because, drawing on recent experience as workers, they know too much to be taken advantage of by workers trying to limit their contributions to production.

11. A cost-plus contract specifies no set price for the contract, but permits the subcontractor to add on a fixed percentage over whatever costs the project entails. This type of contract is especially useful to the contractor, as in the case here, when potential variabilities or uncertainties make a firm bidding price very risky. Cost-plus contracts were fairly common during the post-war building boom and, in the area in which the study was conducted, during the middle sixties. Periods of extremely active building promotes cost-plus agreements because builders expect to have no trouble passing along the added price to consumers in the sellers' market. They have also been an important, but often unrecognized source of inflationary trends in building. Intercontractor arrangements such as this also encourage employer associations to not contest trade union demands during negotiations. One reason for this is that higher settlements do not cost them anything when they can pass on their wage costs to the builder. A second, is that contractors actually can benefit from higher labor costs in the cost-plus situation; their profit, being tied to overhead, merely increases proportionally.

12. A common technique used by small subcontractors (and even larger ones) to handle cash-flow problems is to delay payments to the local union insurance benefits funds. While wages have to be paid weekly, fringe benefits are not quite so easily kept trace of by the union officers. The indirect transaction—payment on a per project basis covering many workers and paying through the mail to a bureaucratic office—allows a certain slack for employers with money

problems. This method can lead the subcontractor into more problems than he started with, however. First of all, withholding fringe
benefits is illegal. This in many ways is a secondary consideration, for
in practice, the violations and deficiencies have to be fairly large
before it becomes worth the while of the local union to pursue legal
action. The other ramification, conflict with union officials, can be
much more serious in the short run. Specifically, it can lead to close
scrutiny from the union which may preclude or make much more difficult a subcontractor's attempts to bend or break work rules contained in the trade agreement. In this sense there is an accumulation of
disadvantage to the contractor who runs afoul of union officials who
are protecting the financial and on-site interests of their members.

13. The variable "foremanship" is operationalized in terms of the
frequency of holding the official management position. Respondents
scored the regularity with which they held an official appointment as
foreman from one project to the next on a five-point scale (never-
every job).

14. These regression coefficients appear in columns two and
four. Foremanship's coefficient with supervision is -.19 ($p < .05$) and
with self-direction is .49 ($p < .01$).

15. The coefficients for administrative consultation (-.21) and
(.25) are both statistically significant and in the expected directions.

16. The situation of one foreman I worked under illustrates this
nicely. "Bill" had worked for a large employer for a number of years.
During this time he had been assigned foreman's responsibilities in-
termittently. He had recently been informed that there was a chance of
becoming a regular foreman, with the possibility of eventually moving
up to a supervisorship. It was commonly felt among the men on the
job that that situation was partly to blame for Bill being so difficult to
deal with. His habit of daily reinforcing among the crew that he was
"in control" of the operation, was mostly an annoyance to the experienced members of the workforce. His tendency to offer encouragement while at the same time reminding you of how much
power he held (for example, "You do beautiful work. I mean it.
Because if it didn't look good you'd hear about it good and loud.
Nobody gets away with shitty work on my jobs.") was a bit more ir-
ritating. And intolerable is the only word to describe Bill's actions
toward the men just before, during, and just after a visit by one of his
supervisors to the site, or if the general contractor had one or two
minor complaints. It seemed as if the tension Bill experienced when

he was feeling supervised and evaluated was great enough to have an adverse impact on his ability to function effectively as a foreman.

17. In an early paper on power equalization that predates much of the recent interest in worker management, Strauss (1963) stressed the uses to which the distribution of power can be put by management. Creating the appearance of an equal distribution of decision-making influence can be used to placate workers' desires for greater involvement, while retaining control through indirect organizational channels. My own analysis of worker management (1981b) points out how complex organizational arrangements (for example, ESOPs; codetermination) are used to limit the amount of workers' direct power in decision making at the administrative levels.

18. Entering foremanship and the two consultation variables in separate steps in the regression analysis shows the spurious mentality-self-direction relationship to be controlled by the foremanship variable.

19. The basis for this analysis is role-set theory as developed by Robert K. Merton (1957; 1968). Chapter four will use this approach to develop issues of microlevel social alienation.

20. The Department of Labor's ratings of occupational complexity in the DOT have a narrow focus on task-related interactions. They thus miss this broader element of social relationships to people that occur in the labor process. In contrast, the degree of integration in the labor process is a core element of the alienation/division labor problematic which itself is central to Marx's analysis of production. The routinization and fragmentation of labor in which work becomes an isolated activity enhances the ease of managerial control. Correlatively, opportunities for social interactions on the job always threaten to undermine managerial hegemony by creating points of solidarity among workers. In his insightful and groundbreaking analysis of how game playing among workers tends to operate in the interests of capital, Burawoy (1980) tends to neglect the social alienation that characterizes the games workers engage in. In performing their jobs in isolation, workers' output becomes the mechanism of social exchange in the game. This reification, in which labor's product becomes the substitute for meaningful human contact among workers, explains game playing as acts of capitalist social reproduction within the Marxist framework, not as an exception to it.

21. Significantly, in this case mentality's impact on the depen-

dent variable is independent of managerial location. Again, this empirical finding bears on issues of workers' power on the job in relation to the division between mental and manual labor.

Chapter 3. Trade Unions, Contractors, and Employment

1. The following description represents a composite view of the local unions in 1979. The ten organizations varied in size from seventy members to approximately 2,000 when the study was conducted (although three of the local unions in the study merged between 1982 and 1983 to form a single local with a membership of about 1,000). While local union by-laws and national constitutions do specify somewhat different structural arrangements, procedures and use of slightly different nomenclature for various official positions and duties, the differences are relatively minor.

2. The academic study of the concept of power stems from the work of Marx and Weber. The literature on power is so vast that it would take us much too far afield to delve into it here. As an analytic strategy I distinguish between power—the ability to achieve desired outcomes even over the opposition of others (for example, see Weber 1978)—and source of power—social and material resources at the disposal of social actors which can be used to achieve desired ends.

3. Operational measures of militancy—strike militancy (recency of last official strike action, scored in years) and relations militancy (ratings of local union officials of the relative cooperation versus conflict defining their relationship to employers)—were combined into a single scale for statistical analyses. Unions with a more militant relationship with contractors were more apt to employ strike actions to resolve collective bargaining negotiations. They thus take place at discrete intervals. Relations militancy, on the other hand, reflects continuous associations within which opportunities for dispute, conflict or cooperation, and compromise arise. Nonetheless, they are related ($r = .49$) and form an acceptable scale (Cronbach's alpha = .63).

4. While the very small number of union organizations in the sample make it necessary to interpret the findings with extreme caution, the relationships are very suggestive. It is not within my scope to pursue fully the insights which may be provided by the comparison between monopoly and competitive sectors. If nothing else, there is the suggestion that differences in the processes and outcomes of labor

relations within industries may be as important as those which occur between them. As sociologists Baron and Bielby (1980) point out, the essential elements may be those pertaining to organizational level relationships. The same variables may in fact have different significance depending on the precise organizational context (Averitt 1968).

In the present case, I found intercorrelations among the locational variables to be strong and positive (table 3.1). Trades centrally located in the contruction process also tend to have larger memberships and larger employers; while less centrally located trades have smaller memberships and deal with smaller contractors. In line with a market segmentation perspective, militancy has statistically significant negative correlations with the locations variables. In general, locationally advataged unions are less prone to strike and more likely to view labor relations in cooperative dimensions than unions without structural sources of advantage. In addition, the complexity of work is also negatively correlated with militancy ($r = .48$). However, complexity is not statistically related to any of the other locational variables. This suggests that craft skill is a structural source of labor relations power, but not one which necessarily converges within location certrality or with size of union or contractor organization.

5. Contract bidding within the subcontracting structure makes it fairly common for projects to be partly union and partly nonunion. Such mixed projects are particularly troublesome for managers and agents of the various building trades. The Taft-Hartley Act (Section 8(b)(4)) makes many picketing actions at construction sites illegal secondary boycotts. Thus, the premier organizing weapon is turned against labor. The degree of trust that is required for informal (and illegal) cooperation between the trades creates a special problem of its own. According to one union official, it is under moderately poor economic conditions that mutual support comes about. When conditions are generally good (that is, low unemployment and future predictions of a continuation of the same) local officials having trouble with nonunion elements on projects also have difficulty eliciting cooperation from other officials intent on making the most of their run of good fortune. When the economic situation is very bad, officials themselves become too insecure and desperate to stick together against nonunion employers. According to this agent with many years experience, it is when nonunion problems seem to be distributed relatively evenly across the trades and all the trades are suffering from unemployment at a high, but not intolerable, level that mutual cooperation is most common.

6. Labor supply is operationalized for quantitative analyses as the mean number of weeks of unemployment for members of the craft union during the preceding twelve months. This variable should reflect the fairly stable pattern of unemployment among the membership, and thus the overall free availablity of labor within a given trade.

7. Robert Georgine, head of the Building and Construction Trades Division of the AFL-CIO, has expressed concern that the prevalence of project agreements are a serious and growing threat to the protections won over the years by local trade unions. The depth of the problem, according to Georgine, is such that, "if the trend continues, you won't need collective bargaining" (quoted in Burck 1979).

8. Two aspects of local union affiliation are particularly relevant to employment quality for individual craftspeople; regularity of attendance at membership meeting and the frequency of holding official appointment as a steward on the construction site. The first reflects the extent of active and visible involvement in craft union funtions. The regularity of attendance at local union meetings affects the opportunity to be heard by the leadership and other members on important issues. It also offers the chance to become acquainted with members of the current administration. Regular appointment to a union stewardship means a consistent union attachment. It indirectly taps a member's concern with knowing union rulcs and enforcing them on the job. Moreover, it has the inherent connotation of recognition by the current administration that makes stewardship appointments.

9. Local union leadership can also use their control over employment opportunities to coopt factions of active opposition. Such factions exist in almost all local unions, although they may pose differential degrees of threat. Local administrations are usually careful that their methods of distributing work do not lead to charges of discrimination against members of oppositional elements. Internal to the local itself, nondiscriminatory and fair distribution of work helps the administration hold on to an air of legitimacy in the eyes of the membership. Conversely, few actions tend to lower the esteem of an administration that resorting to punishing the opposition by threatening their opportunities for work. External to the local, discriminatory practices may undermine the administration's relationships with its international's administration if members of the opposition bring formal charges against its local's leaders. If nothing else, local union officials are expected to resolve their political conflicts internal to their local or district council . Inability to do so, often reflected by appeals to the higher authorities in the international, do not sit well with those

heading the organization. All this is not to say that discrimination and direct blacklisting do not occur. However, those in open opposition to local leadership usually try to protect themselves from the possibility of blacklisting by establishing employment opportunities independent of the administration's actions. For another, in the instances of blacklisting of which I have direct and personal knowledge, being the object of discrimination on the basis of political opposition tends to add an air of moral and emotional justification and immediacy to conflicts which otherwise appear to be differences of political or economic opinion. Therefore, it is more often the case that an administration will attempt to manipulate employment opportunities in order to avoid charges of discrimination while placing members of the opposition on jobs that isolate them as much as possible from the general membership.

10. Contractors use various methods to camouflage the true scale of their jobs. They can report the start of the job on a reduced scale, with only two or three workers. They then subsequently bring the job up to full scale at a later point. Alternatively, they can report the job when it starts with a full workforce and subsequently, under a convenient pretext, stop the job. They then fail to report to the local union offices when they restart the job. In both situations a contractor can claim that the job was duly reported and that the failure to report the change in status (an increase in the workforce or the restart of after a delay) was merely a matter of minor oversight or error on the part of somebody in the contractor's office.

11. From the contractor's side it may be a matter of getting a foreman to run two different jobs at one time, or performing estimating and supervising functions over and above normal foremanship duties. From the other, a foreman may be in a position to inflate his or her contributions to a job and thus put in for more hours than actually worked.

12. Lest this discussion here leave readers with the impression that the local trade union disappears from this process, I wish to point out some direct areas of union concern. First, most union dues are now collected through the check-off (payroll deduction made and submitted by the contractor to the union office along with fringe benefits). Thus unreported cash wages on which the check-off percentage is not taken deprives the union of funds for operating expenses. If cash wages become too prevalent, the loss of income can place the solvency of the local union in jeopardy. Second, there is the common speculation (and some proven instances) of collusion between con-

tractors and union officials by which union officials receive from the contractors some of the savings in exchange for looking the other way on such projects. Third, there are the reports of contractors making payments to third parties for organized protection against zealous union monitoring of projects on which deals have been struck.

13. The logic of this analysis follows that of path analysis. In the present case, unemployment and nonunion employment are taken to be endogeneous variables intermediary between the exogeneous variables (on-site organization, production location, management location, and union attachments) and job concessions. The regression shown in the table indicates the dependence of job concessions on all antecedent predictors.

14. When added to an equation containing all causally prior variables, the job concession variable has a significant regression coefficient with supervision ($B = .17$; $p < .01$).

15. For example, Taft-Hartley establishes guidelines for mandatory entrance to unions and unionized projects that preclude many effective uses of restrictive labor practices. Of course, there is always a gap between federal and state statutes and enforcement practices, especially in localized competitive markets. However, the legal standing of labor practices does indicate the difficulties associated with relying on them as the mainstay of a union's labor strategy.

16. The problem of transient members is particularly vexing for local unions struggling to establish or maintain a semblance of control over labor supply. Besides taking away employment opportunities, transient workers and contractors are difficult to monitor with respect to violations of trade agreement provisions. The chief means of restricting transients, who otherwise would join the union for one job and then drop out, is to establish high initiation fees and to require advance payment of three month dues. The hope is that it becomes discouragingly uneconomical for nonunion tradespeople and contractors to join for short-term employment opportunities (which actually may violate union working conditions and undermine wage scales).

17. I wish to emphasize that the following description may only be accurate for the particular northeastern geographical region in which I have done the research. Immigration and urbanization have made for a diversity of ethnic and racial groups that may not be characteristic of construction labor markets in other parts of the country.

Chapter 4. Alienation and the Labor Process

1. Non-Marxists have taken a rather cavalier approach, using alienation to refer to such varied subjective orientations as dissatisfaction and "disappointment with career and professional development" (Aiken and Hage 1966, 497), pessimism and anxiety about the future (Sheppard and Herrick 1972), and lack of interpersonal trust (Seeman 1967). Concern with empirical research and the increasing use of secondary analysis of survey data in which theoretical concepts are often adapted to operational variables rather than the reverse has contributed to the problem; facilitating the work of those seeking to "lay the ghost of Marx" (Etzioni 1975, 15).

2. I discuss these facets mostly as regards microlevel processes. However, I would like to offer the observation without a full elaboration that in principle they also operate at higher levels. The elements most central to a theory of alienation (estrangement, power, social resources, capacities for action) are informed by the analytic level at which such relations occur. Thus, the dialectic of alienatied relations assumes different forms, but not uniquely different processes at different levels of analysis.

3. Strictly psychological and subjective theories of alienation fall short of encompassing the multiform social facets of the alienation dialectic. In particular, they offer no explanatory mechanisms linking structurally determined conditions and action capacities for confronting them. Most resort to reductionist models such as frustration-aggression, discontent-rebellion, and rising expectations, psychodynamic contsructs, or philosophical notions of idealistic social transcendence ala Meszaros (1970). We thus come full circle. Psychologicalized theories of alienation having no fully articulated relationship to other social forms of alienation and bound by their original premises are forced to rely on psychological resolutions to social contradictions.

Strictly structuralist interpretations of alienation are similarly bound by their premises. Leaving no room for people to act as conscious and purposive agents in the broader dialectic of social transformations, such theories have difficulty explaining the motive force and political direction behind social actions intended to transcend societal arrangements. In consequence, such potentially useful concepts as "structural overdetermination" take on mystical qualitites that save the theory instead of furthering our understanding of the dialectic of social transformation.

4. This is one of the principal factors which, for Marx, makes the movement of class *in itself* to class *for itself* a problematic aspect of class relations. On the one hand, the objective revolutionary class must view itself as having the capacity to take action in its own behalf. On the other, the failure of the working class to come to such an awareness, related to structural characteristics of the processes of social production and reproduction, does not of necessity mean its objective absence. It is a two-fold problematic that defines the movement of the revolutionary class: workers' perceptions of themselves as individuals and as a class; and structural conditions that determine the likelihood of successfully confronting class antagonists. The convergence of these intertwined processes specifies whether a class will in fact come to act as a class for itself.

5. Ollman's analysis of character structure is a prime example of how a Marxist theorist, failing to treat alienation dialectically, by considering it only in its consequent forms, works himself into a theoretical corner. If people's character structures, product and cause of alienation notwithstanding, are as determinative as he assumes, then whence the revolutionary class?

Clearly, people with problem-solving capacities lagging seriously behind the social conditions with which they must contend stand little chance of success. In fact, Ollman himself attributes working-class authoritarianism and fears of freedom to the limiting influences of class-determined character structures. He is thus able to avoid denying to the working class social transcending capabilities only by adopting the untenable proposition that "the proletariat posses this ability whatever their degree of alienation" (1976, 245). The problem of how the alienated class transcends its own alienation has plagued Marxist theorists since Lenin proposed the vanguard party as a solution. Currently, structuralists following Althusser solve the problem by refusing to address it, while others seek the new class having the proper qualities.

6. Two points are worth interjecting here. First, the apparent contradiction between Lenin's position and my earlier comment that trade union awareness reflects an intellectually independent posture is resolved by considering the dialectic nature of the relationships. It is one of the internal contradictions of various states of consciousness (at individual and collective levels) that they reflect both subservience to, and liberation from, the dominant ideological mode. Secondly, the distinction between quantitative and qualitative demands does not mean that the former cannot engender unanticipated, qualitative consequences.

7. The idea that social positions have subjective or psychological impact is compatible with all structural analysis (including micro- and macrotheories), since it merely specifies a social significance that is not reducable to its constituent conditions. As a macrosociological phenomenon the reference can be made to the common culture shared by all those similarly situated in the social structure: for example, Gouldner's "culture of critical discourse," Habermas' "communicative competence," E. P. Thompson's "working class culture," and Rude's analysis of traditional ideologies. At the microlevel, the social location informs "social construction processes" (Berger and Luchman 1967) and processes of self-definition.

8. As shown in table 4.3, job satisfaction has significant inverse relation to class consciousness (B = -.13). In other words, those dissatisified in their working experiences are more likely to hold to a class conscious orientation, other things being equal. However, there also emerges from my analysis the indication that the effects of dissatisfaction on class consciousness are conditioned by workers' levels of alienation. Statistical tests for interactions between job satisfaction and other dimensions of alienation (not shown) suggest that the association between job satisfaction and consciousness is *less* strong for the more alienated tradespeople. A significant coefficient was obtained for the interaction between satisfaction and intellectual dependence. Marginal nonsignificant coefficients emerged for the interactions between satisfaction with powerlessness and self-estrangement.

9. From a methodological standpoint I could not adequately address such issues within the context of my present research. I have reported on my attempts to introduce nonlinear and simultaneous reciprocal-effects models elsewhere (Silver 1981a, 1982). However, data more reflective of the overall occupational structure and a longitudinal research design are obviously required for a more fruitful pursuit of these intricate and subtle relationships. The efforts of Melvin Kohn and his colleagues (Kohn and Schooler 1983) offer a good example of work of this kind.

Chapter 5. Crisis in Construction

1. The structural basis for cooperative efforts is clear. The balance in the equation is supplied by economic profit for developers, builders, and subcontractors on the one side and the promise of jobs for building tradespeople on the other. This generally leads local

union leadership to actively cooperate with employers and developers trying to win political approval of their development schemes.

2. For analyses of the interrelationships between construction labor market characteristics and the organizational and labor relations practices in the industry see Jackson (1984) and Silver (1982).

3. The elements of compatibility, both explicit and implicit, between craft production and workers control of the labor process can be seen fairly clearly in the analyses of Lipset (1956), Jackson (1984), and Gunn (1984). The economic and organizational requisites of the worker self-managed system are outlined in Gunn (1984) and Vanek (1977).

4. As much of the literature on worker-managed systems make clear, the relationships between worker management and worker's attitudes and motivations are far from simple. They are often conditioned by specific histories and extant conditions. For example, see Hammer, Stern and Furdon (1982), as well as the reports of Whyte and his colleagues on Jamestown (Whyte et al. 1983).

5. Suffice it to mention the use of employee pension money to help in the bail-out of Chrysler, as well as the use of pension funds by the Grumman Corporation's management to prevent an unwanted stock buyout.

BIBLIOGRAPHY_____

Achtenberg, Emily Paradise, and Peter Marcuse.
1983 "Towards the decommodification of housing: a political analysis and a progressive program." In Chester Hartman (ed.). *America's housing crisis.* Boston: Routledge and Kegan Paul.

Aiken, Michael, and Jerald Hage.
1966 "Organizational alienation: a comparative analysis." *American Sociological Review.* 31:497–507.

Aldrich, Howard E.
1972 "Technology and organizational structure: a re-examination of the findings of the Aston Group." *Administrative Science Quarterly.* 17:26–43.

Althusser, Louis.
1978 *For Marx.* London: NLB.

Andrews, Francis.
1974 *The medieval builder and his methods.* London: Rowman and Littlefield.

Applebaum, Herbert A.
1981 *Royal blue: the culture of construction workers.* NY: Holt, Rinehart and Winston.

Archibald, W. Peter.
1978 "Using Marx's theory of alienation empirically." *Theory and Society.* 6:119–132.

Argyris, Chris.
1954 *Human behavior in organizations.* New York: Harper Row.
1964 *Integrating the organization and the individual.* New York: Wiley.
1976 "Single-loop and double-loop models in research on decision making." *Administrative Science Quarterly.* 21:363–375.

Aronowitz, Stanley.
1973 *False promises.* New York: McGraw Hill.
1983 *Working class hero.* New York: Pilgrim.

Averitt, Robert T.
1968 *The dual economy.* New York: Norton.

Bacharach, Samuel, and Edward J. Lawler.
1980 *Power and politics in organizations.* San Francisco: Jossey-Bass.

Baron, James N., and William T. Bielby.
1980 "Bringing the firms back in: stratification, segmentation and the organization of work." *American Sociological Review.* 45:737-765.

Bell, Daniel.
1960 *The end of ideology: on the exhaustion of political ideas in the Fifties.* New York: Free Press.
1973 *The coming of post-industrial society.* New York: Basic.

Benson, J. Kenneth.
1977 "Organizations: a dialectical view." *Administrative Science Quarterly.* 22:1-21.

Berger, Peter L., and Thomas Luckmann.
1967 *The social construction of reality.* Garden City, NY: Doubleday.

Bernstein, Basil.
1971 *Class, codes, and control.* London: Routledge, Keegan Paul.

Blau, Peter M.
1955 "Cooperation and competition in a bureaucracy." *American Journal of Sociology.* 61:530-535.
1964 *Exchange and power in social life.* New York: John Wiley & Sons, Inc.
1972 "Interdependence and hierarchy in organizations," *Social Science Research.* 1 (April):1-24.
1977 *Inequality and heterogenity.* New York: Free Press.

Blau, Judith.
1979 "Expertise and power in professional organizations." *Sociology of Work and Occupations.* 6:103-123.

Blauner, Robert.
1960 "Work satisfaction and industrial trends." In W. Galenson and

S. M. Lipset (eds.). *Labor and trade unionism.* New York: Wiley.

1964 *Alienation and freedom.* Chicago: University of Chicago Press.

Blumberg, Paul.
1968 *Industrial democracy: the sociology of participation.* New York: Schacken.

Bourdon, Clinton C., and Raymond E. Levitt.
1980 *Union and open-shop construction.* Lexington, Ma.: D. C. Heath.

Braverman, Harry.
1974 *Labor and monopoly capital.* New York: Monthly Review Press.

Brecher, Jeremy.
1972 *Strike.* Boston, Ma.: South End Press.

Burawoy, Michael.
1980 *Manufacturing consent.* Chicago, Ill.: University of Chicago Press.

Burck, Gilbert.
1979 "A time of reckoning for the building trades." *Fortune.* 99:82.

Chandler, Alfred D., Jr.
1963 *Strategy and structure.* Cambridge, Ma.: The MIT Press.

Cherry, Mike.
1974 *On high steel.* New York: Quandrangle.

Clawson, Dan.
1980 *Bureaucracy and the labor process.* New York: Monthly Review Press.

Coser, Rose Laub.
1975 "The complexity of roles as a seedbed of individual autonomy." In Lewis Coser (ed.). *The idea of social structure.* New York: Harcourt Brace Javanovich.

Croxier, Michael.
1964 *The bureaucratic phenomenon.* Chicago, Ill.: University of Chicago Press.

Djilas, Milovan.
1957 *The new class.* New York: Holt, Rinehart and Winston.

Doeringer, Peter B., and Michael J. Piore.
1971 *The division of labor in society.* New York: Macmillan.

Durkheim, Emile.
1933 *The division of labor in society.* New York: Macmillan.

Eccles, Robert G..
1981 "Bureaucratic versus craft administration: the relationship of market structure to the construction firm." *Administration Science Quarterly.* 26:449–469.

Edwards, Richard C.
1975 "The social relations of production in the firm and labor market structure." in Richard C. Edwards, Michael Reich, and David M. Gordon, (eds.). Labor Market Segmentation, Lexington, Ma.: D. C. Heath, pp. 3–26.
1979 *Contested terrain.* New York: Basic.

Ehrenreich, Barbara, and John Ehrenreich.
1976 "Work and Consciousness." In *Technology. the labor process and the working class.* N.Y.: Monthly Review Press.
1979 "The professional-managerial class." In Pat Walker (ed.). *Between labor and capital.* Boston: South End Press.

Ellul, Jacques.
1964 *The technological society.* New York: Vintage.

Emerson, Richard M..
1962 "Power-dependence relations." *American Sociological Review.* 27 (February):31–41.

Etzioni, Amitai.
1975 *The comparative analysis of complex organizations.* New York: Free Press.

Fanon, Frantz.
1965 *The wretched of the earth.* New York: Grove.
1968 *Black skins, white masks.* New York: Grove.

Feldacker, Bruce.
1980 *Labor guide to labor law.* Reston, Va.: Reston.

Freidson, Eliot.
1982 "Occupational autonomy and labor market shelters." In Phyllis Stewart and Muriel Cantor (eds.). *The varieties of work.* Beverly Hills, CA: Sage, 39–54.

French, R. P., and B. Raven.
1968 "The bases of social power." In D. Cartwight and A. Zander. *Group dynamics.* New York: Harper & Row.

Fromm, Erich.
1942 *Fear of freedom.* New York: Holt, Rinehart & Winston.
1961 *Marx's concept of man.* New York: Frederick Ungar.

Galbraith, John K.
1967 *The new industrial state.* New York: Houghton Mifflin.

Gamson, William.
1968 *Power and discontent.* Homewood, Ill.: Dorsey.
1975 *The strategy of social protest.* Homewood, Ill.: Dorsey Press.

Geschwender, James.
1971 "Explorations in the Theory of Social Movements and Revolutions." In J. Greschwender (ed.). *The Black Revolt.* Englewood Cliffs, N.J.: Prentice-Hall.
1977 *Class, race and worker insurgency.* Cambridge: Cambridge University Press.

Giddens, Anthony.
1976 *New rules of sociological method.* New York: Basic.
1979 *Central problems in social theory.* Berkeley, Ca.: University of California Press.

Goldman, Paul, and Donald R. Van Houten.
1980 "Uncertainty, conflict and labor relations in the modern firm I: productivity and capitalism's 'human face.' " *Economic and Industrial Democracy.* 1:63–98.

Goldthorpe, John H., David Lockwood, Frank Bechhofer, and Jennifer Platt.
1969 *The affluent worker.* London: Cambridge University Press.

Gordon, Gerald, and Selwin Becker.
1966 "An entrepreneurial theory of formal organization." *Administrative Science Quarterly.* 11:313–344.

Gorz, Andre.
1967 *Strategy for labor.* Boston: Beacon.
1980 *Farewell to the working class.* Boston: South End Press.

Gouldner, Alvin W.
1954a *Patterns of industrial bureaucracy.* New York: The Free Press.

1954b *Wildcat strike*. New York: Harper Torchbook.
1976   *The dialectic of ideology and technology*. New York: Seabury.
1978a "The new class project, I." *Theory and Society*. 6:153–204.
1978b "The new class project, II." *Theory and Society*. 6:343–392.

Gunn, Christopher Eaton.
1984   *Workers' self-management in the United States.* Ithaca, N.Y.: Cornell University Press.

Gurr, Ted R.
1970   *Why men rebel*. Princeton, N.J.: Princeton University Press.

Gutman, Herbert G.
1966   *Work, culture and society*. New York: Vingage.

Haas, Jack.
1974   "The stages of the high steel ironworker apprentice career." *Sociological Quarterly*. 15 93–108.
1977   "Learning real feelings." *Sociology of work and occupations*. 4 147–170.

Haber, William.
1930   *Industrial relations in the building industry*. Cambridge, Ma.: Harvard University Press.

Habermas, Jurgen.
1970   *Toward a rational society*. Boston, Beacon.
1971   *Knowledge and human interest*. Boston: Beacon.
1973   *Legitimation crisis*. Boston: Beacon.

Hall, Richard H.
1975   *Occupations and the social structure*. Englewood Cliffs, N.J.: Prentice-Hall.

Hammer, Tove Helland, Robert N. Stern, and Michael A. Gurdon.
1982   "Workers' ownership and attitudes towards participation." In Frank Lindenfeld and Joyce Rothschild-Whitt (eds.). *Workplace democracy and social change*. Pages 87–108. Boston: Porter Sargent.

Jackson, Robert Max.
1984   *The formation of craft labor markets*. New York: Academic Press.

Johnson, Ana Gutierez, and William Foote Whyte.
1977   "The mondragon system of worker production cooperatives." *Industrial and Labor Relations Review*. 31;1.

Kalleberg, Arne L.
1977 "Work values and job rewards: a theory of job satisfaction." *American Sociological Review.* 42:124–143.

Kallenberg, Arne L., and Larry J. Griffen.
1978 "Position sources of inequality in job satisfaction." *Sociology of Work and Occupations.* 5:371–401.

Karasek, Robert A.
1979 "Job demands, job decision latitude, and mental strain: implications for job design." *Administrative Science Quarterly.* 24:285–308.

Kimberly, John R.
1976 "Organizational size and the structuralist perspective: a review critique, and proposal." *Administrative Science Quarterly.* 21:571–97.

Kohn, Melvin.
1969 *Class and conformity.* Illinois: Dorsey.
1976 "Occupational structure and alienation." *American Journal of Sociology.* 82:111–30.

1985 "Unresolved interpretive issues in the relationship between work and personality." Paper presented at annual meetings of the American Sociological Association, Washington, D.C.

Kohn, Melvin, and Carmi Schooler.
1973 "Occupational experience and psychological functioning: an assessment of reciprocal effects." *American Sociological Review.* 38:97–118.
1978 "Reciprocal effects of the substantive complexity of work and intellectual flexibility." *American Journal of Sociology.* 84:24–52.
1983 *Work and personality: an inquiry into the impact of social stratification.* Norwood, N.J.: Ablex.

Kornblum, William.
1974 *Blue collar community.* Chicago: University at Chicago Press.

Kusterer, Ken.
1978 *Workplace know-how: the improtant working knowledge of "unskilled" workers.* Boulder, Co.: Westview.

Landsberger, Harry.
1958 *Hawthorne revisited.* New York: New York State School of Industrial and Labor Relations.

Lenin, V.I.
1969 *What is to be done?* New York: International Publishers.

Lipsett, Seymour Martin Trowe, and James Coleman.
1956 *Union Democracy.* New York: Free Press.

Lukas, Georg.
1971 *History and class consciousness.* Cambridge, Ma.: MIT Press.

Marglin, Stephen.
1974 "What do boses do? the origins and functions of hierarchy in capitalist production." *Review of Radical Political Economics.* 6:33–60.

McDermott, John.
1981 *Crisis in the working class.* Boston: South End Press.

McGregor, Douglas.
1960 *The human side of enterprise.* New York: McGraw Hill.

Mallet, Serge.
1975 *Essays on the new working class.* St. Louis: Telos Press.

Mann, Michael.
1973 *Consciousness and action among the western working class.* London: Macmillan.

Marcuse, Herberrt.
1964 *One-dimensional man.* Boston: Beacon.
1972 *Counter-revolution and revolt.* Boston: Beacon.

Marshall, Ray, and Robert W. Glover.
1975 "Training and entry into union construction." *U.S. Department of Labor Manpower Research and Development.* Monograph 39.

Marx, Karl.
1956 *Selected writings in sociology and social philosophy.* New York: McGraw-Hill.
1963a *Early writings.* New York: McGraw-Hill.
1963b *The eighteenth brumaire of Louis Bonaparte.* New York: International Publishers.
1973 *Grundrisse: Foundations of the critique of political economy.* trans. *Martin Nicolas* London: New Left Review and Penguin Press.

Marx, Karl, and Frederick Engels.
1970 *The German ideology.* New York: International Publishers.

Mayer, Martin.
1978 *The builders.* New York: Norton.

Memmi, Albert.
1965 *The colonizer and the colonized.* Boston: Beacon.
1968 *Dominated man.* Boston: Beacon.

Merton, Robert K.
1957 "The role-set: problems in sociological theory." *British Journal of Sociology* 8:106–120.
1968 *Social theory and social structure.* N.Y.: Free Press.
1975 "Structural analysis in sociology." In Peter M. Blau (ed.). *Approaches to the study of social structure.* New York: Free Press.

Meszaros, Istvan.
1970 *Marx's theory of alienation.* London: Merlin Press.

Michels, Robert.
1962 *Political parties.* New York: Free Press.

Mills, Daniel Q.
1972 *Industrial relations and manpower in construction.* Cambridge, Ma.: MIT Press.

Montgomery, David.
1979 *Workers' control in America.* New York: Cambridge University Press.

Meyers, Richard R.
1946 "Interpersonal relations in the building industry." *Human Organization.* 5:1–7.

Noble, Daniel.
1977 *American by design.* Oxford: Oxford University Press.

Northrup, Herbert, and Howard G. Foster.
1975 *Open shop construction.* Philadelphia: The Wharton School.

O'Connor, James.
1973 *The fiscal crisis of the state.* New York: St. Martins Press.

Ollman, Bertell.
1976 *Alienation: Marx's conception of man in capitalist society.* London: University of Cambridge Press.

O'Toole, James et al. (HEW Task Force)
1973 *Work in America.* Cambirdge, Ma.: MIT Press.

Ouchi, William.
1977 "The relationship between organizational structure and organi-

zational control." *Administrative Science Quarterly*. 22:95–133.

Ouchi, William, and Jerry B. Johnson.
1978 "Types of organizational control and their relationship to emotional wellbeing." *Administrative Science Quarterly*. 23:293–317.

Pappenheim, Fritz.
1959 *The alienation of modern man.* New York: Monthly Review Press.

Perrow, Charles.
1970 "Departmental power and perspective in industrial firms." In Mayer N. Zald (ed.). *Power in organizations.* Nashville, Tenn.: Vanderbilt.

Pfeffer, Jeffrey.
1981 *Power in organizations.* Boston: Pitman.

Poole, Michael.
1981 *Theories of trade unionism.* London: Routledge and Kegan Paul.
1975 *Workers' participation in industry.* London: Routledge and Kegan Paul.

Quinn, Robert P., and Graham L. Staines.
1979 "The 1977 quality of employment survey." Institute for Social Research. University of Michigan.

Reckman, Bob.
1979 "Carpentry: the craft and trade." In Andrew Zimbalist (ed.). *Case studies on the labor process.* New York: Monthly Review Press.

Riemer, Jeffery.
1979 *Hard hats.* Beverly Hills, Ca.: Sage.
1982 "Work autonomy in the skilled building trades." In Phyllis Stewart and Muriel Cantor (eds.). *The varieties of work.* Pages 225–234. Beverly Hills, Ca.: Sage.

Rifkin, Jeremy, and Randy Barber.
1978 *The north will rise again: pensions, politics and power in the 1980's.* Boston: Beacon.

Roethlisberger, R. J., and W. J. Dickson.
1939 *Management and the worker.* Cambridge, Ma.: Harvard University Press.

Roos, Leslie L., and Roger I. Hall.
1980 "Influence diagrams and organizational power." *Administrative Science Quarterly.* 25:57–73.

Rude, George.
1980 *Ideology and popular protest,* New York: Pantheon.

Russell, Raymond.
1982 "The rewards of participation in the worker-owned firm." In Frank Linderfeld and Joyce Rothschild-Whitt (eds.). *Workplace Democracy and Social Change.* Pages 51–81. Boston Porter Sargent.
1985 *Sharing ownership in the workplace.* Albany, N.Y.: SUNY Press.

Salzman, Louis Francis.
1952 *Building in England down to 1540: a documentary history.* Toronto: Oxford.

Schooler, Carmi.
1976 "Serfdom's Legacy: an ethnic continuum" *American Journal of Sociology* 81:1265-1286.

Schur, Robert, and Marilyn Phelan.
1981 *The housing crisis: a strategy for public pension funds.* Washington D.C.: Conference on Alternative State and Local Policies.

Seeman, Melvin.
1959 "On the meanings of alienation." *American Sociological Review. 24:783–791.*
1967 "On the personal consequences of alienation in work." *American Sociological Review.* 32:273–285.
1975 "Alienation studies." *Annual Review of Sociology.*

Sennet, Richard.
1980 *Authority.* New York: Knopf.

Sennet, Richard, and Jonathan Cobb.
1972 *The hidden injuries of class.* New York: Vintage.

Serrin, William.
1971 *The company and the union.* New York: Vintage.

Shaiken, Hurley.
1979 "Numerical control of work: workers and automation in the computer age." *Radical America.* 13:25–40.

Sheppard, Harold L., and Neal Q. Herrick.
1972 *Where have all the robots gone?* New York: Free Press.

Silver, Marc L.
1981a "Craft production: work and alienation in the construction industry." Ph.D. Diss. Columbia University.
1981b "Worker management: a power-dialectic framework." *Work and Occupations.* 8 145–164.
1982 "The structure of craft work: the construction industry." In Phyliss Stewart and Muriel Cantor (eds.). *The varieties of work.* Pages 235–252.

Simmel, Georg.
1950 *The sociololgy of Georg Simmel.* New York: Free Press.
1955 *Conflict and web of group affiliations.* New York: Free Press.

Simmons, John, and William Mare.
1983 *Working together.* N.Y.: Knopf.

Smelser, Neil.
1976 *The sociology of economic life.* Englewood Cliffs, N.J.: Prentice-Hall.

Spenner, Kenneth.
1979 "Temporal changes in work content." *American Sociological Review.* 44:968–974.

Stark, David.
1980 "Class struggle and the transformation of the labor process: a relational approach." *Theory and Society.* 9:89–130.

Stinchcombe, Arthur L.
1959 "Bureaucratic and craft administration of production." *Administrative Science Quarterly.* 4:168–187.
1965 "Social structure and organizations." In J. G. March (ed.). *Handbook of Organizations.* Chicago: Rand McNally.
1974 *Creating efficient industrial administration.* New York: Academic Press.

Stone, Katherine.
1974 "The origins of job structures in the steel industry." *Review of Radical Political Economics.* 6:61–91.

Stone, Michael.
1983 "Housing and the economic crisis: an analysis and emergency progrem." In Chester Hartman (ed.). *America's housing crisis.* Boston: Routledge and Kegan Paul.

Strauss, George.
1963 "Some notes on power equalization." In H. Leavitt (ed.?. *The social science of organizations*. Englewood Cliffs, N.J.: Prentice-Hall 39–84.

Tannenbaum, Arnold.
1965 "Unions." In J. March (ed.). *Handbook of organizations*. Chicago: Rand McNally.

Thompson, E. P.
1963 *The making of the English working class*. New York: Vintage.

Thompson, James.
1967 *Organizations in action*. New York: McGraw Hill.

Touraine, Alaine.
1971 *The post-industrial society*. New York: Random House.

United States Department of Labor.
1977 *Dictionary of occupational titles*. Washington, D.C.: Government Printing Office.
1979 *Employment and training report of the President*. Washington, D.C.: Government Printing Office.

Vanek, Jaroslav.
1977 *The labor-managed economy*. Ithaca, N.Y.: Cornell University Press.

Von Beyme, Klaus.
1980 *Challenge to power*. London: Sage.

Weber, Max.
1978 *Economy and society*. Berkeley: University of California Press.

Whyte, William H..
1959 *The organization man*. Garden City, N.Y.: Doubleday.

Whyte, William Foote, Tove Helland Hammer, Christopher Meek, Reed Nelson, and Robert Stern.
1983 *Worker participation and ownership: cooperative strategies for strengthening local economies*. Ithaca, N.Y.: ILR Press.

Woodward, Hoan.
1965 *Industrial organization: theory and practice*. London: Oxford University Press.

Wright, Erik Olin.
1976 "Class boundaries in advanced capitalist societies." *New Left Review*. 98.

1978 "Race, class and income equality." *American Journal of Sociology.* 83:1368–97.

1979 *Class structure and income determination.* New York: Academic Press.

1980 "Class and occupation." *Theory and Society.* 9:177–214.

Yellen, Samuel.

1936 *American labor struggles.* New York: Monad Press.

Index of Proper Names

Subject Index _____